CREATING THE JEWISH FUTURE

CREATING THE JEWISH FUTURE

EDITED BY

MICHAEL BROWN
AND
BERNARD LIGHTMAN

ALTAMIRA
PRESS

A Division of Sage Publications, Inc.
Walnut Creek • London • New Delhi

For information address:

AltaMira Press
A Division of Sage Publications, Inc.
1630 North Main Street, Suite 367
Walnut Creek, California 94596
www.altamirapress.com

SAGE Publications, Ltd.   SAGE Publications India Pvt. Ltd.
6 Bonhill Street   M-32 Market
London EC2A 4PU   Greater Kailash 1
United Kingdom   New Delhi 110 048   India

PRINTED IN THE UNITED STATES OF AMERICA

99 00 01 02 03 04 05 06 07   8 7 6 5 4 3 2 1

Library of Congress Cataloging in Publication Data

Creating the Jewish future/ edited by Michael Brown, Bernard Lightman
    p. cm.
Includes bibliographical references and index.
ISBN 0-7619-9032-1 (acid-free paper).—ISBN 0-7619-9033-X
(pbk. acid-free paper)
1. Judaism—20th Century—Congresses. 2. Judaism—Forecasting—Congresses.
3. Jews—Intellectual Life—Congresses. I. Brown, Michael. II. Lightman,
Bernard V., 1950-

BM30.C74 1998
296/.0112 21   98-025340
                                                          CIP

Production and Editorial Services: Pattie Rechtman
Cover Design: Joanna Ebenstein

*Dedicated to Bernard I. Ghert,
a Jewish community leader of vision and conviction,
a man who makes things happen*

CONTENTS

PREFACE

This volume of essays grew out of a conference titled "Creating the Jewish Future," which took place at the Centre for Jewish Studies at York University in October, 1996. For the conference we brought together Jewish Studies scholars from Israel, the United States, England, and Canada with American and Canadian rabbis, students, and Jewish civil servants as well as leaders and rank-and-file members of the Jewish community. Our collective task was to grapple with a series of crucial questions: How can Jewishness and Judaism thrive in a period of unprecedented change? What will the Jewish future be in the twenty-first century? What is to be done at this most crucial moment in Jewish history? A dynamic group of international scholars in the same room for several days with passionately committed members of the Jewish community tackling this set of controversial questions proved to be an explosive combination. When the conference ended, we felt drained by the intensity of the discussions, but we were intellectually energized by their vitality and richness.

My co-editor, Michael Brown, and I are indebted to those who contributed to the success of the conference and who helped in the preparation of this volume. We wish to express our gratitude here. The conference would never have taken place without the vision and generosity of our sponsor, Bernard Ghert. The committee of brave souls who took on the daunting job of organizing the conference included Irving Abella (who provided inspirational leadership as chair), Sydney Eisen (who wisely pushed us to avoid the usual scholarly conference), Rachel Schlesinger (who set up the workshops), Michael Brown and myself. It was a very congenial group to work with.

Elisabeth Friedman did a superb job as conference coordinator. Alan Reitzes, Executive Director of the UJA/Federation of Greater Toronto, and Sandra Brown, President of the UJA/Federation of Greater Toronto, gave invaluable advice on how to draw in members of the community. York University faculty and Jewish community leaders served with enthusiasm as workshop co-chairs. The York Jewish Student Federation, headed by Pearl Gropper, ensured that students were well represented at the conference. Merle Lightman, Administrative Assistant at the Centre for Jewish Studies, checked and rechecked the local arrangements for the conference, and made sure that everything came off without a hitch. The manuscript for the book was put together by word processing expert Anna Foshay. Special thanks are due to Erik Hanson and Pattie Rechtman at AltaMira Press, who have ably overseen the publication with patience and good humor. Finally, the thoughtful, stimulating papers of our contributors challenged the conference participants to think in new ways about creating the Jewish future.

Bernard Lightman

Contributors

Irving Abella holds the J. Richard Shiff Chair for the Study of Canadian Jewry at York University and is president of the Canadian Historical Association. His works include *None Is Too Many: Canada and the Jews of Europe, 1933–1948* (1983 and 1991), which he co-authored with Harold Troper. That book received both the National Jewish Book Award (Holocaust) and the Sir John A. Macdonald Prize in Canadian History. Abella is past national president of the Canadian Jewish Congress and the present chair of the Commission on Jewish Leadership and Continuity of the Council of Jewish Federations of Canada.

Michael Brown is professor of Humanities and Hebrew and director of the Centre for Jewish Studies at York University. His most recent books are *The Israeli-American Connection, Its Roots in the Yishuv, 1914–1945* (1996) and *A Guide to the Study of Jewish Civilization in Canadian Universities* (1998). A staff member of Camp Ramah for more than twenty years, Brown directed the Ramah National Leadership Training Institute (Mador) for five years. He has been active as a volunteer with Toronto schools, serving as chair of the Associated Hebrew Schools Education Committee, and is a founding member of the Minyan Congregation.

Robert Eisen is associate professor of Religion and Judaic Studies at George Washington University and the author of *Gersonides on Providence, Covenant, and the Chosen People* (1995). He serves on the board of directors for the Foundation for Jewish Studies, the major adult Jewish education organization in the Washington, D.C. area, and lectures widely in the community.

Sydney Eisen is University Professor Emeritus at York University, where he served as dean of the Faculty of Arts and as the founding director of the Centre for Jewish Studies. His special field of interest is Victorian science and religion. Eisen has been both president and chairman of the board of the National Humanities Faculty. A life member of the boards of two Jewish day schools which he served as president, he holds the Toronto Jewish community's Ben Sadowski Award for Outstanding Community Service.

Jane S. Gerber is professor of Jewish History and director of the Institute for Sephardic Studies at the Graduate Center of the City University of New York. Author of *The Jews of Spain: A History of the Sephardic Experience* (1992) and, with Michel Abitbol, *Sephardic Studies in the University* (1995), she is past president of the Association for Jewish Studies and vice-president of the American Society for Sephardic Studies. She serves on the editorial boards of both the Jewish Publication Society and the Royal Institute for Interfaith Studies in Amman. She is also a member of the boards of the Westchester Jewish Conference, the Board of Jewish Education of Greater New York, and of Sephardic House.

Hillel Halkin is a noted author, critic, and translator whose works include the provocative and much praised *Letters to an American Friend* (1977). Born in the United States, he realized his Zionist convictions by making *aliyah* to Israel. He has been actively involved in the municipal affairs of Zichron Yaakov where he lives.

Susan Handelman is professor of English at the University of Maryland, College Park, where she has received a number of awards for outstanding teaching. Her books include *Fragments of Redemption: Jewish Thought and Literary Theory in Benjamin, Scholem, and Levinas* (1991) and *The Slayers of Moses: The Emergence of Rabbinic Interpretation in Modern Literary Theory* (1982). She is active in adult Jewish education through the Wexner Heritage Foundation and the Washington Jewish community and is at present a participant in the Jerusalem Fellows Program.

Paula Hyman is professor of Jewish History at Yale University. Among her recent works are *Gender and Assimilation in Modern Jewish History: Roles and Representations of Women* (1995) and *Jewish Women in America: An Historical Encyclopedia* (1997), which she edited with Deborah Dash Moore. A founding member of Ezrat Nashim, one of the first Jewish feminist groups, she serves as advisor to the Jewish Women's Archive. She has served as a member of the Wexner Foundation's Institutional Grants Committee, attended two UJA Young Leadership Division international conferences as a delegate, and chaired the Education Committee of Ezra Academy day school. She is a board member of the Jewish Foundation, the Jewish Federation Department of Education, and Congregation Beth El-Kesser Israel, all in New Haven.

Norma Joseph is associate professor of Religion at Concordia University where she is also convenor of the Chair in Canadian Jewish Studies and director of the Graduate MA Program in Judaic Studies. She was awarded the Leo Wasserman Prize by the American Jewish Historical Society for the best article of 1995. Since the early 1970s, she has promoted women's participation in Jewish religious and communal life as a founding member of the Canadian Coalition of Jewish Women for the Get, as founder and president of the International Coalition for Agunah Rights, as a founder of the Montreal Women's Tefillah and Tsedaka group, and as a director of the International Committee for the Women of the Wall.

Barry Kosmin is director of research at the Institute for Jewish Policy Research in London, a faculty member at the Graduate Center of the City University of New York, and a senior associate of the Oxford Centre for Hebrew and Jewish Studies. He has published widely and was the director of the 1990 National Jewish Population Study in the United States. Kosmin is a trustee of the New London Synagogue and of Congregation B'nai Israel in Millburn, New Jersey, a council member of the Jewish Historical Society of England, and a member of the Strategic Planning Group of the United Israel Appeal.

Bernard Lightman is professor of Humanities at York University where he has served as coordinator of the Science, Technology, Culture and Society Programme and as associate dean of the Faculty of Arts. He recently edited two books: *Victorian Science in Context* (1997) and *Science and Religion in Modern Western Thought* (1996, with Bernard Zelechow). He is an active member of Temple Har Zion in Toronto.

Martin Lockshin is associate professor of Humanities and Hebrew at York University and coordinator of the Programme in Religious Studies. He is the author of *Rabbi Samuel Ben Meir's Commentary on Genesis: An Annotated Translation* (1989) and *Rashbam's Commentary on Exodus: An Annotated Translation* (1997). Lockshin is a frequent adult education lecturer and a member of the Toronto Board of Jewish Education and chair of its Board of Licence and Review. He has served as a volunteer with several Jewish schools in Toronto and is now on the board and the Education Committee of the Bnai Akiva Schools.

Seymour Mayne is professor of English at the University of Ottawa, a poet, and the author, editor, or translator of some 35 books and monographs including *Children of Abel* (1986) and *The Song of Moses* (1995). He was co-editor with Glen Rotchin of *Jerusalem: An Anthology of Jewish Canadian Poetry* which received the Louis L. Lockshin Memorial Award. He is a founding editor of *Parchment*, the Canadian Jewish literary annual, and an active member of the Ottawa Jewish community.

W. Gunther Plaut is adjunct professor at the York University Centre for Refugee Studies and senior scholar at Holy Blossom Temple in Toronto where he served for many years as rabbi. A widely published author, his most recent books are *Haftarah Commentary* (1996), *Teshuvot for the Nineties* (1997), and *More Unfinished Business* (1997). He has served as president of the Minnesota Art Museum, the Canadian Jewish Congress, the Central Conference of American Rabbis, and the World Federalists of Canada. He chaired the Minnesota Governor's Commission on Ethics in Government and the Toronto UJA, served as vice-chair of the Ontario Human Rights Commission, and was co-founder of the Urban Alliance for Race Relations.

Alex Pomson is assistant professor of Jewish Education and Humanities and coordinator of the Programme in Jewish Teacher Education at York University. He has taught at the University of London (England) and served as vice-principal of a Jewish high school in London. Pomson is a member of the committees on Family Education and Children with Special Talents of the Toronto Board of Jewish Education and a member of the board and the Education Committee at Netivot HaTorah day school in Toronto. He serves as adult education lecturer and consultant to Jewish schools.

Aviezer Ravitzky is professor of Jewish Philosophy at the Hebrew University of Jerusalem. A prolific and widely translated scholar, his most recent works in English are *Messianism, Zionism, and Jewish Religious Radicalism* (1996) and *History and Faith: Studies in Jewish Philosophy* (1997). His communal activities include service as head of the Department of Humanities and Jewish Studies in the School for Educational Leadership in Jerusalem, as a fellow of the Israel Institute for Democracy, and as a director of Meimad.

Michael Rosenak is Mandel Professor of Jewish Education at the Melton Center for Jewish Education of the Hebrew University of Jerusalem. His books include *Roads to the Palace* (1995), *Commandments and Concerns: Jewish Religious Education in Secular Society* (1987), which won the National Jewish Book Award, and the forthcoming *"Tzarich Iyyun": Prakim BeMahshevet HaHinuch HaYehudi* [Hebrew]. He serves on the boards of HaMelitz, the Institute for Zionist-Jewish Education, and the Pardes Institute and on the steering committees of Yad Vashem (Educational Activities) and the David Yellin Teachers Seminary (Education on Jewish-Arab Relations).

Alvin I. Schiff is Irving I. Stone Distinguished Professor of Education at the Azrieli Graduate School of Yeshiva University and the author of six books and over 150 articles. He is a fellow of the Jewish Academy of Arts and Sciences and a holder of the Hebrew University's Rothberg Prize, of the Brandeis University Hornstein Award for Distinguished Communal Leadership, and the first UJA Educators Award for Outstanding Leadership and Service to the Jewish Community. He is chair of the American Advisory Council, Department of Jewish-Zionist Education of the Jewish Agency for Israel and the founding chair of the National Center for the Hebrew Language. He consults widely for Jewish schools.

Rachel Schlesinger is associate professor of Social Science and acting master of Vanier College at York University. Her recent books include *Canadian Families in Transition: A Workbook* (1992), *Canadian Families: A Resource Guide* (1989), and *Abuse of the Elderly: Issues and Annotated Bibliography* (1988), all written with Benjamin Schlesinger. She was a teacher at the United Synagogue Day School in Toronto and is currently on the advisory board of that school. She is a member of the Toronto Federation/UJA Continuity Commission, of the National Executive of Canadian Hadassah/WIZO, and of Toronto ORT and acts as a volunteer and consultant at the Baycrest Centre for Geriatric Care and the Betel Centre for Creative Living.

Michael Stanislawski is the Nathan J. Miller Professor of History and associate director of the Center for Israel and Jewish Studies at Columbia University. His works include *Tsar Nicholas I and the Jews: The Transformation of Jewish Society in Russia, 1825-1855* (1983) and *For Whom Do I Toil? Judah Leib Gordon and the Crisis of Russian Jewry* (1988), and he is a member of the editorial boards of the *YIVO Annual* and *Shvut*. Stanislawski serves on the academic committees of the Rothberg School for Overseas Students at the Hebrew University and of Project Judaica at the Russian State University of the Humanities. He teaches adult education for the Wexner Heritage Foundation and the JCC of the Upper West Side and is on the curriculum committee of the Rodeph Sholem Day School in New York.

Morton Weinfeld is professor of Sociology and holder of the Chair in Canadian Ethnic Studies at McGill University. A prolific author, his recent works include *Old Wounds: Jews, Ukrainians, and the Hunt for Nazi War Criminals in Canada* (1988, with Harold Troper) and *Trauma and Rebirth: Intergenerational Effects of the Holocaust* (1989, with John J. Sigal). Weinfeld is active formally and informally as a consultant to Jewish communal organizations nationally and in Montreal, where he co-chairs the Council on Jewish Identity and Continuity. A member of Congregation Doreshei Emet, he has been involved with the Jewish day schools attended by his children.

INTRODUCTION
Michael Brown

"Continuity" has become the buzzword of North American Jews in the 1990s. The word reflects the *fin-de-siècle* angst regarding health and future viability that has gripped the Jewish community at the approach of the new millennium. Some years ago Simon Rawidowicz noted that Jews were "the ever-dying people," throughout their long history living on the brink of extinction and in fear of it.[1] But, in fact, the present concern about survival represents a sudden and rather surprising reversal of attitude. It is especially surprising in North America, where forward-looking optimism has long been a hallmark both of the Jewish community and of society in general.

Only a few years ago none but the professional doomsayers doubted that North American Jewry would endure, and analysts such as Charles Silberman were predicting that the best of times was yet to come.[2] Since the end of World War II, the community had enjoyed unprecedented well-being. Abroad, the Jewish people, having suffered the loss of one-third of its numbers during the Holocaust, underwent a national renaissance in the new state of Israel. This rebirth in the national center seemed to energize Jewish life everywhere, including Canada and the United States. At the same time, for reasons largely unrelated to Israel, Jews at home in North America entered what seemed like a golden age. The signs were unmistakable: the decline of antisemitism and Jews' consequent full integration into the political, social, and economic life of the United States and Canada; the flowering of Jewish institutions now housed in grand new buildings; the emergence of North America as a major center of Jewish learning and theology with world-class scholars and thinkers to be found not only in seminaries and yeshivot, but also in public and private universities across the continent; and finally, the superior level of academic achievement, the high social status, and the personal affluence of most members of the community. The good fortune of North American Jews and Judaism paralleled the postwar prosperity of Canada and the United States.

By the 1990s, however, the winds of change were blowing across the continent. Despite the end of the Cold War and the collapse of communism, Canadians and, more acutely, Americans became afflicted with an unusual measure of self-doubt and concern for the future. This uneasiness was sparked, at least in part, by the unsuccessful Viet-Nam War abroad. It grew along with the violence and the seemingly intractable social and economic problems in the cities of the United States in particular. It was accompanied by shifts in the economy which threatened the present livelihood of many in the middle class and the future of their children. And it was marked by the eclipse of many of the values by which North Americans had long defined themselves.

As one might expect, Jews have shared in the general fear that the salad days of North America were beginning to wilt. But in addition to the collective unease, Jews have a number of newfound causes for anxiety particular to their own group. Considerable anecdotal information now confirmed by scholarly research has revealed an unexpectedly large number of defections from the community—largely through intermarriage—since the 1970s. Attrition has been accentuated by an exceptionally low birth rate. The worry over numbers is natural for a small people, and it has been heightened by the realization that a downsized community will be less able to provide the range of services to which Jews have become accustomed. A smaller community will be more vulnerable politically with regard to both domestic and foreign (chiefly Israeli) issues about which it is concerned.[3]

More serious even than the problems resulting from demographic shifts has been the loss of intellectual and spiritual vigor which the community has been experiencing, despite an unforeseen revival of traditionalism and an increasing number of people engaged in the study of Judaism. Perhaps masked earlier by enthusiasm for Israel and the activities required to ensure its viability, the erosion of many beliefs and practices that had long sustained Jewish life now began to manifest itself. Aggravating these difficulties has been the perception that Jewish social, religious, and educational institutions are inadequate to the new and difficult challenges posed by North American society at the end of the twentieth century. Particularly forceful criticism has come from feminists, some of whom question commitment to what they perceive to be a patriarchal, sexist tradition.

That success, to a degree, underlies the community's concerns presents no small irony but offers no great comfort. The decline of antisemitism in North America and Jews' acceptance by their neighbors have made assimilation a possibility for the many, not just the wealthy few. At the same time, one of the most important hedges against assimilation in the post-World War II era—Diaspora Jewry's involvement with the state of Israel—has been weakened. Israel's growing military security and economic prosperity, as well as its emerging cultural independence, have distanced its citizens from Diaspora Jews and diminished the role of the latter as defenders of the state.

Together these developments have contributed to the rapid mood swing of the North American Jewish community from almost unbridled optimism to gloomy pessimism. Collectively and individually, Jews have begun to question seriously their long-term future in North America and elsewhere in the Diaspora—their "continuity." A new phenomenon, which we might call "continuity anxiety," has now replaced the heady confidence of previous decades.

Jewish leaders have responded by putting continuity at the top of the communal agenda. There remain, however, considerable confusion and disagreement not only about the appropriate responses to the crisis, but even about its dimensions and nature. There is disagreement, for example, about whether the intense focus of Diaspora Jewry on Israel contributes to the weakness of the North American community or offers a potential solution to its problems.[4] And while there seems to be near unanimity regarding the vital role of education in guaranteeing continuity, many Jewish communities across the continent have actually decreased their annual educational expenditures since 1989.[5]

In pursuit of both definitions and responses, Bernard Ghert, one of Toronto's most experienced and thoughtful Jewish leaders, himself a former university teacher, decided to sponsor a conference on continuity in which academics, lay and professional communal and religious activists, and interested individuals from the community would attempt to outline the problems clearly and begin to think constructively about solving them. Echoing the words of Barry Shrage, a Boston Jewish community leader, Ghert asserted his desire to transform what seemed like an increasingly "fruitless debate about 'Jewish continuity' into a discussion concerning the shape of [the] . . . Jewish future and the purpose of Jewish existence."[6]

It was thought that a conference held in Toronto might have a special contribution to make to the continuity issue. The reason has to do with the differences between Canada and the United States. To a considerable extent the two Jewries are part of the same continental community, as Barry Kosmin points out in his chapter in this volume. Canada, however, has a Jewish population of about 350,000, while that of the United States is between five and six million. Because of its size, the Canadian community is more manageable and more cohesive than the American. Canada's Jewry is "closer to the boat" with a much higher percentage of first- and second-generation members. It has more Yiddish speakers, proportionately more Orthodox Jews, many more children in Jewish all-day schools, a lower intermarriage rate, and a stronger Zionist movement. Many of these differences can be attributed to the particular history and political and social dynamics of the country at large, to its binational make-up and its rather conservative character, and, more recently, to its multicultural ethos. For Jews (and other "ethnics"), these characteristics have resulted in much more gradual and hesitant acculturation and integration into the life of the country than has occurred south of the border and much greater communal solidarity.[7] Some of the Canadian "lessons" regarding assimilation are clearly not applicable to other countries. But some of Canadian Jews' successful experiences can be instructive for others; and Canadians can learn from the more rapid and radical developments in the United States.

There were also good reasons for choosing the Centre for Jewish Studies at York University as conference host. Like many of its sister institutions, York is dedicated to the pursuit of academic excellence. What is less usual about the university is the intensity of its commitment to community service. York is well known for its outreach programs to Toronto's ethnic communities, and many of our faculty members are eager participants in the life of the Jewish community. For nearly two decades York's Faculties of Education and Arts have offered a program to prepare teachers of Hebrew and Jewish Studies for Jewish schools, and faculty members have been closely involved with the city's Jewish schools and with other Jewish institutions. Almost no one at York would accept the recent suggestion of a leading American scholar of Judaica, "that the history of intense involvement of Judaic scholars . . . in the affairs of the Jewish community is over," that the scholars "have enough to do sitting at . . . [their] desks and conducting . . . classes."[8]

In part, York's orientation is a result of its youth. Ours is a new university, a child of the sixties, the era of relevance and responsiveness. The commitment reflects the shared belief of faculty, students, and administration in the importance of being receptive to the vibrant urban community to which we belong. Toronto is now one of the most ethnically diverse cities in the world, and many of York's students are immigrants or the children of immigrants, the first members of their families to receive a university education. The university has attempted in many ways to participate actively in the life of this multicultural society.

For many years, Professor Sydney Eisen, the founding director of the Centre for Jewish Studies at York University, has worked closely in community endeavors with Bernard Ghert who came to appreciate the unusual orientation of York and of the Centre. As a result, Ghert, the sponsor and initiator of the "Creating the Jewish Future" conference, felt comfortable in withdrawing from hands-on involvement in its planning and execution. He had, however, given us a clear mandate with which we were in agreement. Neither he nor we at the Centre wanted yet another conference in which scholars would set out problems *ex cathedra* and then retire to their lofty perches. Nor did we want a conference in which practitioners with a wealth of experience in making things happen would conceive policies in haste without the benefit of the long-range thinking typical of the academician. Our goal was to mount a conference which would bring together theoreticians and practitioners, academics and community activists, who would share their concerns and learn from each other by adjusting theory to reality and suggesting how analysis might inform policy.

The conference itself was to have two parts: scholarly lectures on critical areas of Jewish life; and workshop discussions designed to elicit model community programs blending the insights of the lecturers and the experience of the activists. To ensure that the lectures would be directed towards immediate and actual issues we decided to invite as presenters only academics whom we knew to be not only ranking scholars, among the most highly regarded in their disciplines, but also involved participants in Jewish life. (The biographies of the contributors to this volume should be of more than usual interest to its readers.) We sought out veteran and younger scholars who have devoted themselves to studying the Jewish experience and who at the same time have played a role in Jewish community affairs. We believed that such people would have a better grasp of the needs and concerns of the community and be better able to judge the workability of particular policies that might emerge from the discussions. To facilitate constructive workshop sessions, we invited seasoned professionals and lay leaders to act as discussion facilitators in each workshop group.

One of the early decisions of the planning committee and the conference chair, Professor Irving Abella, one of Canada's most prominent historians and a leader of the Canadian Jewish community, was to avoid the word, "continuity." As noted at the outset, it has negative connotations; it is backward-looking and implies chronic worry and doubt. We hoped to inspire the conference participants—and through them members of Jewish communities across North America—to think positively about meeting the challenges on the horizon. After some deliberation, we decided to call the conference: "Creating the Jewish Future." The title is pretentious; it promises much more than any one conference or volume can expect to achieve; it appears to ignore the powerful, homogenizing societal forces that militate against Jewish continuity or that of other small religious or ethnic groups in North America and elsewhere in the global village. But if North American Jewry wishes to survive into the next millennium, it cannot allow blind forces to determine its destiny. It must create its own future out of the legacy of the past and the realities of the present. As Morton Weinfeld notes in chapter 19 of this volume, the future is not determined; it need not be accepted passively; it can be shaped and created. But if the community is to take its fate into its own hands, then present reality and future goals must be clearly defined and squarely faced.

The specific issues to be addressed appeared to fall into two broad interrelated categories: the philosophical questions relating to the meaning of Judaism; and the "technical" questions relating to the organizational frameworks for the transmission of meaning. The first category encompassed three areas: faith, Israel, and secular culture in the Diaspora. The second category included the areas of education and gender roles, in which the overlap of philosophy and organizational framework is quite prominent, and the areas of demographics, political organization, and economics. The topics appear here in that order, although the last three are discussed together.

The planning committee had wrongly supposed that in Toronto, an intensely Zionist community, there would be more public interest in the sessions devoted to Israel than in any other, and these sessions were selected to open the conference. In fact, however, despite their being scheduled for early on a Sunday morning, the sessions and workshops devoted to religion aroused the greatest excitement and engagement and the largest public audiences. Questions of faith and religion disconcert some Jews, as is evident in Irving Abella's afterword to this book. Clearly, though, they are uppermost in the minds of Jews concerned about the future. As a result, it is those essays which begin this volume. We have, however, given equal weight herein, as we did in the conference, to questions of meaning and purpose and to those of organization and tactics. We did so out of a conviction that creating the Jewish future requires serious attention to issues of both kinds.

The closing section of the book presents some of the suggestions that emerged from the workshops and discussions. As the conference chair notes in his summary, the workshop discussions were highly animated. There was little apathy in evidence, although, of course, the group was self-selecting. In the end, few concrete program proposals were presented in these sessions. On the other hand, the strength of feeling and commitment and the eagerness for change and innovation in the areas of education and religion, in particular, are evidence of a firm foundation on which to build a better, more secure Jewish future.

The reader will be the judge of the extent to which our conference and volume have contributed to the shaping of that future. It is worthy of note at the outset, however, that all the conference participants—academics, community activists, and general public, whether Americans, Europeans, Israelis, or Canadians—appear to take continuity as a given. They assume that the "ever-dying people" will survive in the twenty-first century and beyond, although they fully appreciate the causes of the current anxiety and acknowledge that conscious effort will be needed in order to ensure survival. There seems to be little certainty among them regarding the contours of the future except that it will not duplicate the past or the present. On the other hand, there is virtual consensus that the real gains of the post-World War II era will not be reversed. Interestingly, although North American Jews in general continue to be quite concerned about antisemitism, none of our presenters seems to believe it will be a serious threat to the community in the foreseeable future.[9]

As is evident in the following essays, trenchant analysis and promising policy proposals to guide future leaders exist in abundance. Danger may be waiting in ambush for North American Jewry, but the academics and community activists who participated in our conference and volume appear guardedly confident about the ultimate purposes and worth of Jewish existence and their own ability to influence the fate of the community. We believe that their commitment and enthusiasm justify the title of the conference and of this volume.

Notes

[1] Simon Rawidowicz, "Israel: The Ever-dying People," in his *Studies in Jewish Thought*, ed. Nahum N. Glatzer (Philadelphia: Jewish Publication Society, 1974), pp. 210–24. The essay was first published in Hebrew as "Am ha-Holekh va-Met" [Hebrew], *Metsudah* 5–6 (1948): 134–48.

[2] See his *A Certain People: American Jews and Their Lives Today* (New York: Summit Books, 1985).

[3] Compare Jonathan D. Sarna, "The American Jewish Community's Crisis of Confidence" [Hebrew], *Hadoar* 76 (9 May 1997): 8–10.

[4] For an early formulation of the ambiguities inherent in North American Jews' intense attachment to Israel, often to the extent of excluding other dimensions of their Jewishness, see Jacob Neusner, *Stranger at Home* (Chicago and London: The University of Chicago Press, 1981), pp. 99–128 and elsewhere.

[5] See "Education Funding Dips, Study Shows" *Forward* (2 August 1996).

[6] Barry Shrage, president, Combined Jewish Philanthropies of Greater Boston, "Jewish Studies, Jewish Community and Jewish Literacy: Creating a Revolution in Jewish Life," in *Association for Jewish Studies Newsletter* 46 (Fall 1996): 4.

7   On Canadian "differences," see among other works, *Multiculturalism, Jews and Identities in Canada*, eds. Howard Adelman and John H. Simpson (Jerusalem: Magnes Press, 1996), and the bibliography cited there; Harold Troper and Morton Weinfeld, *Old Wounds: Jews, Ukrainians and the Hunt for Nazi War Criminals in Canada* (Chapel Hill and London: University of North Carolina Press, 1989); and Michael Brown, "The Americanization of Canadian Zionism, 1917–1982," in *Contemporary Jewry: Studies in Honor of Moshe Davis*, ed. Geoffrey Wigoder (Jerusalem: The Institute of Contemporary Jewry and the Hebrew University, 1984), pp. 129–58.

8   Robert M. Seltzer, president, Association for Jewish Studies, "Jewish Studies in the Jewish Community," Association for Jewish Studies *Newsletter* 46 (Fall 1996): 1. Seltzer and Shrage, along with Samuel Heilman and Paula Hyman, participated in a *Newsletter* symposium entitled, "Jewish Studies in the Jewish Community." The actual topic of the symposium was the role of university scholars of Jewish Studies in community continuity campaigns.

9   The widespread fears of contemporary American Jews regarding antisemitism are reflected in *1997 Annual Survey of American Jewish Opinion* (New York: The American Jewish Committee, 1997), pp. 20–24.

PART
1

FAITH AND RELIGION
IN A
"SECULAR" AGE

1

FAITH AND RELIGION IN A "SECULAR" AGE: AN INTRODUCTION

Martin Lockshin

We who are concerned about creating a Jewish future must surely consider the question of the relevance of religion in contemporary society, but we should not expect to find much agreement about it. Many contemporary Jews feel that religious identification is not crucial for the Jewish people today, and that in the future, it will be even more peripheral. Most Jews in the future (the logic goes) who choose to identify Jewishly will be attracted to other forms of Jewish identification—cultural, national, or ethnic. The argument can be made that even today the largest and "most Jewish" Jewish community is that of the State of Israel. There, fewer than 30 percent of the Jews define themselves as "religious." Some may think, then, that religion is passé, the outdated way that Jews used to identify themselves, that Jewish communities ought to concentrate their resources on cultivating other forms of identity more meaningful to modern Jews.

Others, however, claim that religion has, historically, always been at the center of Judaism. They may also believe that it will always be that way, that the core of the Jewish community will continue to consist of those who define their identity as religious. In fact, according to the common sociological definitions of a "Jew" today, religion still plays a crucial role—even when those defining Jewishness are avowedly non-religious. Almost all Jews today pay lip service to Rashi's classic determination that according to *halakhah* (Jewish law), there is nothing that a Jew can do to avoid being considered Jewish. There is virtually no ethical position, no cultural position, no political position that, when adopted by a born Jew, would cause people to say, "That person is no longer Jewish." But when a Jew adopts another religion—particularly Christianity—almost every contemporary Jew (and the organized Jewish community) relates to him or her as a non-Jew. Even the most secular of Israel's Jews considers Messianic Judaism to be a distasteful perversion and thinks of Jewish-Christianity as a contradiction in terms. (One writer, in the August 1996 *Commentary* symposium on Jewish belief, said that Jews today seem to define themselves as "un-Christians," just as Seven-Up promotes itself as "Uncola."[1]) If Judaism were *not* defined as a religion, then Jewish identity would not exclude the possibility of being Christian. Even the most avowedly secular Jews, then, still on some level, relate to Judaism as a religion.

Will this continue to be the case in the future? Are we or are we not today living in a secular age in which religion is out of place and perhaps irrelevant? Ought religion to become less central or more central to our definition of ourselves as a community and as individuals in the twentieth century and beyond? And if religion should remain a significant factor, what precisely do we mean by religion? The essays in this section all approach these issues from different perspectives.

Rabbi Gunther Plaut argues that our age is a truly secular one in which science has displaced religion and has become the system in which people put their trust. He considers it a major problem of our age that society is convinced of the certainty of scientific and secular knowledge. Promoting religion in such an environment is, he feels, very difficult.

Our other two writers are not so certain. Professor Robert Eisen sees signs that science today does not speak to many people and that large numbers of Jews are attracted to forms of understanding that seem almost santithetical to the scientific. And Professor Susan Handelman describes our age as a post-modern one, filled with uncertainties, an age in which even the certainty required to deny a religious truth claim is lacking. Perhaps we really do not live in a secular age, only in a profane one.

The terms "religion" and "faith" are also interpreted differently in the three papers. Rabbi Plaut discusses organized institutional religion and the ways in which it may fall short of fulfilling real, present needs. Professor Eisen concentrates on the increasing popularity of the ancient, esoteric form of Jewish faith, kabbalah. Professor Handelman looks at religion and faith as phenomena that are neither institutional nor kabbalistic (at least not in the traditional sense of that term).

What the papers have in common is an assumption that we are living in a unique age. They are agreed that Judaism should adapt itself to the new realities. And they seem to feel that it can.

Notes

[1] Michael Medved, "What Do American Jews Believe," *Commentary* 102, No. 2 (August, 1996): 71.

2

THE REVIVAL OF JEWISH MYSTICISM
AND ITS IMPLICATIONS FOR THE FUTURE
OF JEWISH FAITH

Robert Eisen

One of the more intriguing developments in Jewish religious life in recent years has been the resurgence of popular interest in Jewish mysticism or kabbalah.[1] Kabbalah has been a source of fascination particularly among young Jews since the sixties, and this interest shows no signs of waning. Courses in kabbalah are now common in Jewish Studies programs in the universities and in adult education programs in North America, Europe, and Israel. Books and materials touching on kabbalah are selling briskly in Jewish bookstores. I myself have taught kabbalah at the university level and in Jewish adult education programs in the Washington, D.C. area, and I am always struck by the level of interest in this subject.

What is perhaps most remarkable about the revival of kabbalah is the variety of young people it seems to attract. I have encountered young Jews drawn to kabbalah from the entire religious spectrum—Orthodox, Conservative, and Reform. They include those who have been brought up as Jews, as well as those who have "returned" to their Jewish roots later in life. Most interesting is that kabbalah seems also to appeal to the unaffiliated. Young Jews who have little or no connection with the institutional life of the Jewish community will often relate exclusively to this aspect of Judaism.

To be sure, kabbalah does not appeal to everyone. My perception is that the interest in it is in great part generational, that it speaks primarily to the middle-aged or younger. I have also encountered a good many Jews, including rabbis and educators, who are perplexed, even alarmed, by the current attraction to kabbalah. I often hear expressions of derision and hostility, assertions that interest in kabbalah is nothing more than a passing fad or an interest of those on the fringe.

I speak not just as an observer. I myself was drawn to kabbalah in my teens and early twenties, although I should hasten to add that I was never at any point a true mystic. Moreover, since my early twenties, my religious interests have moved in a rather different direction. My scholarship has actually focused on the school of thought considered to be the rival of mysticism: the rational philosophy of such thinkers as Maimonides. Yet I have never stopped studying kabbalah or being intrigued by it.

It is my purpose here to discuss the revival of kabbalah. How is interest in it manifested? What are the causes of this interest? To whom precisely does it appeal? And most important, what implications, if any, does its revival have for the future of Judaism?

I must confess my limitations here. Many of my observations are based primarily on personal impressions, as well as conversations that I have had with friends, colleagues, and students over the years. When I speak about attitudes towards kabbalah, I have not conducted exhaustive surveys, nor do I have statistics to back up my points. In fact, to my knowledge, no formal studies of such attitudes have ever been done. Moreover, I am neither an intellectual historian nor a sociologist either of whom may be better equipped to deal with some of the questions raised here. What I offer is a series of observations that I hope will provide the basis for research and further discussion.[2]

Let me begin with some basic definitions and history. First, the term "mysticism." While there has been much debate among scholars as to how one defines mysticism, I think I can satisfy most viewpoints by saying that mysticism is an attempt to have a direct and intimate relationship with the divine. Now the division between mysticism and normal religion is not necessarily a sharp one. After all, ordinary religious people strive to have a close relationship with the divine. The point is that mystics are much more focused on this type of experience and attempt to achieve it in an unusually intense form.

The term "kabbalah," which means "tradition," refers to schools of Jewish mysticism that date back to the 1100s in western Europe and which developed throughout the medieval and modern periods. Contrary to common belief, kabbalah was never a monolithic phenomenon. It encompasses a variety of mysticisms that are often quite different from one another. In recent years, scholars have tended to classify these schools into two groups.[3] One is ecstatic or prophetic kabbalah, which emphasizes meditation as a means to achieving a close relationship with the divine. Its founding father was Abraham Abulafia, a thirteenth-century Spanish Jew, who devised techniques of meditation on the letters of the Hebrew alphabet.

By far the more popular brand of kabbalah is somewhat more intellectual in character.[4] Known in academic circles as theosophic kabbalah, it produced a complete and elaborate theological system focused on the ten *sefirot*—a practically untranslatable term—which are attributes of God that explain all of God's characteristics and activities. While God's essence is entirely unknowable, the *sefirot* allow us to comprehend what we can know about God within the bounds of limited human understanding. Over time, the *sefirot* were given standard names: Crown, Wisdom, Understanding, Lovingkindness—to name the first four. The kabbalists conceived of the *sefirot* as having a standard arrangement and order, and never tired of explaining their qualities and characteristics. Each was considered a limitless world in itself reflecting some aspect of God's infinite being. Each was seen as having a unique role to play in God's activities.

What makes this form of kabbalah such a powerful theological system is that by understanding the *sefirot* one not only penetrates the inner life of God, one also unlocks the secrets of the entire universe. This is because the kabbalists believed that everything in the world below was a reflection of the divine world above. Therefore the *sefirot* were more than divine attributes; they were the building-blocks for the world below. The world was created and continues to be sustained through them. The kabbalists therefore expended great effort in describing how the *sefirot* and their interaction with each other could explain events in the world. They linked all natural phenomena with the *sefirot*. For instance, each of the four basic elements according to medieval science—fire, air, earth, and water—was seen as corresponding to and having its source in one of the *sefirot*. Human psychology could also be explained in a similar fashion, since the human soul was understood to be constructed on the paradigm of the *sefirot*. Our qualities of love, anger, or mercy were all viewed as manifestations of one or another of the *sefirot*. Most important from a Jewish perspective is that the kabbalists explained the divine commandments in light of the *sefirot*. Each commandment was seen as interacting in its own special way with the world of the *sefirot*. The goal of observing the commandments was to bring harmony to the *sefirot* and thereby aid in the process of redeeming the world.

The kabbalists generally conceived of this theological system as nothing less than a body of wisdom directly revealed by God to Moses on Mount Sinai along with the Torah. It was then secretly passed on from generation to generation to the select few worthy of such wisdom. In the medieval period, this type of kabbalah found its most sophisticated expression in the *Zohar*, a text which appeared in thirteenth-century Spain and in the school of Rabbi Isaac Luria in sixteenth-century Palestine.

It should be pointed out that both types of kabbalah were often treated as wisdom for the elite. Attempts were made to restrict access to kabbalah because it was believed to be potentially dangerous if studied by the uninitiated. The fear was that the unqualified student might easily misinterpret its doctrines and be led into heresy, or he might incur divine punishment for delving into mystical secrets without having first mastered the more basic teachings of Judaism. Eventually, the public dissemination of kabbalistic teaching was perceived to be dangerous for the Jewish community as a whole, especially in the wake of the messianic movement of Shabbetai Zvi in the seventeenth century, which drew much of its inspiration from kabbalah and wreaked havoc on Jewish communities throughout the world.

A school of kabbalah that should be mentioned is Hasidism. Popularly associated with ultra-Orthodox Judaism, heroic stories about rabbis, and fervent singing and dancing, at its core Hasidism is actually an outgrowth of medieval kabbalah, though their exact relationship is the subject of much debate among scholars. Hasidism began in eastern Europe in the 1700s at the inspiration of Rabbi Israel ben Eliezer, known popularly as the Ba'al Shem Tov. It molded the themes of earlier kabbalah into a form that has given it wide appeal and popularity—even outside ultra-Orthodox circles.

Kabbalah encountered substantial opposition from Jewish scholars at the beginning of the last century when Judaic Studies first entered the universities. They saw it as a corruption of the Jewish spirit, a repository of outdated magic and superstition. Their motives were unabashedly apologetic; they believed that kabbalah had no place in an enlightened era in which Jews were attempting to find common ground with the European society to which they had recently been admitted. The negative view of kabbalah among Jewish intellectuals was successfully countered by the efforts of one man: Gershom Scholem. Scholem, a German-born scholar based in Israel for most of his academic career until his death in 1981, almost single-handedly created the modern academic study of kabbalah and ensured respect for it among intellectuals and laymen alike.

With this background in mind, we are now in a position to appreciate the various forms which the modern interest in kabbalah assumes. As a general observation, it may be noted that kabbalah now reaches a wider and more varied audience than at any time in its history. Most Jews who take an interest in it do not accept the taboos about studying kabbalah at too young an age.

With respect to the type of kabbalah being studied, my impression is that most people focus on theosophic kabbalah, although some go further in their explorations by incorporating ecstatic kabbalah into their studies and taking courses and workshops in meditation.[5] This latter trend appears to be growing in popularity in recent years. In the adult education programs in Washington in which I am involved, both types of mysticism are taught. Many who take an interest in kabbalah do not differentiate between the two and assume that both are part of a common system, an approach that has its antecedents in medieval kabbalah.[6]

Contemporary kabbalah students vary widely not just with respect to the content of the material they choose to study—or experience—but also in terms of their whole orientation toward the subject. Many study kabbalah simply out of curiosity and make no personal investment in it; others are true believers, who understand kabbalah as the exclusive means for comprehending metaphysical reality. They study as a means of unlocking the secrets of the universe. For the most part, the exponents of this group identify themselves as Orthodox. They include the various branches of Hasidism, perhaps the best known of which is Habad, or Lubavitch. Some, however, who espouse this view are not formally connected to a Hasidic sect. Rabbi Philip Berg, for instance, is an Orthodox teacher based in Israel who has founded centers for the study of kabbalah in a number of cities in Israel and throughout the world.[7]

Others are believers in a far different sense. Liberal in their political and social orientation and not necessarily identified with any specific denomination of Judaism, they study kabbalah as part of a more general search for spirituality. Representative of this approach is Zalman Schachter-Shalomi, the popular but controversial rabbi, who until recently was the spiritual leader of the left-wing Philadelphia-based organization, ALEPH: Alliance for Jewish Renewal.[8]

A characteristic of this last approach is a tendency towards syncretism with other mystical traditions. In fact, a number of books have appeared recently exploring comparisons between kabbalah and Eastern forms of mysticism—those found in Hinduism and Buddhism, in particular. Some, though not all, of these books are sophisticated in method and content; perhaps the best is Roger Kamenetz's *The Jew in the Lotus: A Poet's Rediscovery of Jewish Identity in Buddhist India* published in 1994.[9] Kamenetz, himself an academic, provides a detailed and often fascinating account of a series of meetings that took place in India in the fall of 1990 between the Dalai Lama, the spiritual leader of Tibetan Buddhists, and a group of rabbis and Jewish academics. Over a number of days, the discussions covered a whole series of issues in Judaism and Buddhism with much attention being paid to mysticism. The Jewish leaders who took part in this dialogue included figures as different in their orientation towards Judaism as Irving Greenberg, a modern Orthodox rabbi, and the aforementioned Rabbi Zalman Schachter-Shalomi.

What are the causes for the resurgence of interest in kabbalah? Undoubt-edly, impetus for its rediscovery is rooted in the ferment of the late sixties and early seventies. That was an era in which a significant portion of Ameri-can youth rebelled against societal norms, a rebellion that in part manifested itself in a search for meaning in various forms of spirituality. The effects of that era are still very much with us. In a recent book, Wade Clark Roof has examined the religious beliefs and affiliations of the aging generation of baby boomers who were at the forefront of the sixties revolution. He discovered that many of these people have settled into middle age and family life but are still engaged in a quest for spirituality that often leads them to find religious expression outside the established institutions. Many pursue mysticism. As some of Roof's examples indicate, Jewish baby boomers exhibit much the same behavior, seeking religious fulfillment outside the synagogues. The phenomenon of *havurot* (informal groups for prayer and study) is perhaps most indicative of this trend. Thus it would appear that interest in kabbalah among young Jews—an issue which Roof does not deal with explicitly—is connected with this larger pattern of behavior.[10]

But perhaps, more significantly, for many young Jews the study of kabbalah is emblematic of a rebellion against Judaism itself. Many young people reared in affluent Jewish communities in America in the last two or three decades perceive the Judaism of their elders to be dry and lifeless. For them, the syna-gogues are too large and impersonal, more like social clubs than holy places for cultivating a heartfelt relationship with God. Jewish education, moreover, is in a troubled state. Most young Jews get their knowledge of the tradition in after-school Hebrew schools filled with unruly students. Perhaps, most impor-tantly, religion in the typical suburban Jewish home is lacking both in content and inspiration. It is a common complaint of people in my generation that one is encouraged by parents to get a good education and choose a high earning profession, while the development of religious and spiritual interests is never set out as an important life-goal. Thus what kabbalah has done is to provide young Jews with a form of religion that they see as vibrant and spiritual in sharp contrast to the religion of their elders.[11]

A key word here seems to be "spirituality," a term I have already used a number of times in this essay and to which I must give some attention. It is this element that so many young Jews identify as the crucial ingredient miss-ing from the Judaism of their parents and as the focus of their own quest for religious meaning. In the last two or three years, popular journals, maga-zines, and newspapers that report on Jewish issues have been filled with articles about the explosion of interest in spirituality among young Jews.[12]

The problem is that "spirituality" is hard to define, because it is used in popular discourse for a variety of religious phenomena, though its meaning is rarely delineated. It seems to share much in common with mysticism in that it too refers to a quest for an intense, personal, and inward relationship with the divine. Yet it appears to denote a much broader search for a connection with the divine than that identified with mysticism. While mysticism is highly focused and disciplined—at least in Judaism—spirituality involves a much more general orientation towards experiencing the divine, and is achieved through a wide range of expressions, from prayer and ritual to music, dance, meditation—even the exploration of psychic phenomena and alternative medicine. Spiritual expression can also take the form of social action. It is assumed that spirituality is highly individualized; all are expected to find their path to the divine in their own unique and creative way. This kind of quest, with its emphasis on individuality, is in tension with, though not always outside of, standard religious denominations and institutions.[13] A full examination of the new spirituality and its connection to kabbalah is beyond the scope of this paper. But if am I correct in my perception, the latest revival in kabbalah should be viewed as part of a much broader resurgence of interest in spirituality among young Jews.

Another factor in the revival of kabbalah is that in recent times there has been a general loss of confidence in the ability of human reason and science to answer ultimate questions or even to solve mundane problems. The causes of this phenomenon are many. It is, at the very least, the product of a period that has witnessed two world wars and barbarism aided and abetted by technology. Among philosophers, this skepticism has found expression in a rebellion against rational philosophical systems, first with Existentialism, and more recently in such schools of thought as deconstruction and postmodernism. The turn to mysticism might, therefore, be viewed as an attempt to find a viable theological framework in Judaism in response to disenchantment with science, technology, and philosophical rationalism.

We should add here that Jewish youth may be particularly prone to a loss of confidence in rational philosophy because of the Holocaust, the event which epitomizes this century's horrors. This unparalleled manifestation of evil has forever altered the Jewish people in every dimension of its physical and spiritual existence. It constitutes what seems to be an insurmountable challenge for young Jews interested in a rational understanding of the world from a Jewish perspective.

So far, we have emphasized only the negative in looking at the interest in kabbalah as a product of either rebellion or disenchantment. But there is undoubtedly much that is also positive in kabbalah that explains its appeal. Kabbalah, after all, is not a new phenomenon; it has been studied by

Jews for centuries. In fact, since its beginnings in twelfth-century Europe, it has been one of the most enduring dimensions of Judaism. In practically every century for some eight hundred years, it has claimed adherents from among the greatest of Israel's sages. Its rediscovery, therefore, reflects a longstanding attraction.

What is it then about kabbalah itself that makes it so attractive to young people today? Perhaps the most obvious reason—both today and in past centuries—is that it is a highly provocative and exotic dimension of Jewish thought that makes far-reaching claims. Ecstatic kabbalah in its most extreme form promises that through meditation one can make direct contact with God. Theosophic kabbalah teaches that by studying the *sefirot* one potentially has access to all the secrets of the universe. There is perhaps no need to explain why these things are attractive. Kabbalah appeals to some of the deepest curiosities that we have not only as Jews but also as human beings.

But these generalities do not tell the whole story. Gershom Scholem argued that kabbalah—in particular, the more popular theosophic variety— has had great attraction throughout the ages because of its mythical character. Scholem is, of course, using the term "myth" here in its technical sense. Myth refers to a genre of literature or oral tradition by which cultures attempt to grapple with questions of ultimate meaning. Myths take the form of stories about supernatural beings often set in a distant, primordial epoch. Kabbalah is very much myth in this sense. The *sefirot*, which define the world of God and all of reality, are not merely abstract symbols; they take on the character of vivid images and supernatural personalities that interact with each other. Thus, for instance, the *sefirot* are divided into male and female potencies that unite with each other in erotic union—an idea that may be shocking to Jews unaccustomed to kabbalistic speculation. A common refrain in the *Zohar* is that the last of the *sefirot*, depicted as a queen, unites with the sixth of the *sefirot*, depicted as a king.[14] To cite another example of this mythical orientation, evil, according to one strain of kabbalistic thought, asserts itself in the world because there is a demonic realm, the *sitra ahra*, literally "the other side," outside of the realm of the *sefirot*. This realm, which is populated by all sorts of evil angels and demons, occasionally invades the *sefirot*, gains dominion over the above-mentioned queen, and takes her captive.[15] Thus, kabbalah, like all mythologies, attempts to answer the ultimate questions which human beings ask by telling stories about supernatural beings, which in the case of kabbalah can even reside in the inner being of God himself.

Scholem argued that by using mythical images to describe God and His activities, kabbalah made God accessible. God is no longer the abstract deity of classical Judaism who cannot be imagined or seen, but a series of vital and active qualities given the shape of vivid personalities and images which human beings can easily picture. Such anthropomorphism may appear to border on idolatry. The kabbalists, however, have managed to convince Jews throughout history that not only was such imagery acceptable, it was, in fact, Judaism's most exalted way of understanding God and the universe.[16]

Undoubtedly, Scholem's observations are very much relevant today. The mythical description of God provides a conception of the divine that stimulates even the modern imagination by transforming the God of the Bible, and the universe as a whole, into an exotic amalgam of personified attributes and qualities. We might add to Scholem's observation that the mythical element not only makes God more accessible, it gives kabbalah an enduring quality that has allowed it to transcend the kind of radical shifts in intellectual perspective witnessed in the modern period. The mythical images in kabbalah—as with many mythologies—tend to draw on the most basic of human themes. Erotic motifs, such as the image of a king uniting with a queen, tend not to go out of style; they have appeal across the generations. A motif in kabbalah that is particularly significant in this regard is that of the *sefirot* as family members—mother, father, daughter, son.[17] This imagery speaks to one of the most central and time-honored features of Jewish culture: its emphasis on family life. Thus, kabbalah manages to speak past contemporary philosophical and scientific skepticism by depicting God and the universe in terms of imagery that strikes a chord with the most basic instincts that we have as Jews and human beings.[18]

Another appealing feature of kabbalistic myth is that it attempts to deal with the most intractable of philosophical problems by means of motifs that do not require absolute rational consistency. To cite an example mentioned earlier, kabbalists explained the existence of evil—one of the most difficult of philosophical problems—through mythical images: evil is caused by a demonic realm outside the *sefirot* nurtured by the power of Judgment in God Himself that has proliferated beyond its proper bounds. As Scholem points out, this theory of evil is striking in its boldness in making God the source of evil.[19] Rational philosophers resisted this type of explanation, since God who is entirely good, cannot be the source of evil.[20] But rational problems of this sort did not have the urgency for the kabbalists that they did for the philosophers. Kabbalists assumed that human reason has limited value for answering such questions, and that kabbalistic symbols reflect a deeper and truer reality than that which human logic can penetrate.[21] Given the current climate of skepticism towards rational thought-systems, it is understandable that this mythical way of answering ultimate questions is appealing to young people today. Kabbalah is no less concerned than other thought-systems with the basic philosophical questions that plague humanity in general and Jews in particular. Yet kabbalah allows one to have an authentic Jewish response to these questions without having to solve all issues within a perfectly consistent rational framework.

Yet another reason for the appeal of kabbalah today is the perception that it is an ancient body of wisdom, and therefore authentic and authoritative. I call this a "perception," because kabbalah has had a long history; it has undergone many stages of evolution and has manifested itself in a multitude of variations. Also, it betrays influences from the non-Jewish world—Neoplatonism and Gnosticism, in particular—as academic scholars have shown. Yet kabbalists throughout the ages have expended great effort to paint kabbalah as a wholly Jewish, unified, and consistent—in a word, monolithic—body of thought, as required by the traditional claims of divine origins. Innovations or borrowings from non-Jewish sources have been labeled faithful renditions of traditional doctrines.[22] And, interestingly, kabbalah is often taught this way in popular circles today, even to those who do not accept the claim of its divine revelation at Mount Sinai. A perusal of popular kabbalah literature confirms this impression.

We should also add that the conception of kabbalah as ancient wisdom gives it an advantage over the thought-systems of other modern Jewish philosophers and theologians. The latter are almost always self-consciously defined by current, but ephemeral, intellectual trends in the non-Jewish world, a characteristic that has led to a bewildering variety of approaches in modern Jewish thought. Thus, for instance, the modern era has produced thinkers as divergent in their orientations as the neo-Kantian Hermann Cohen and the pragmatist Mordecai Kaplan. One may consider the restless quality of modern Jewish philosophy and theology a virtue in that it allows for the constant re-evaluation of Judaism in light of contemporary wisdom. But in my experience that is not necessarily the perception. Young Jews often want clear guidance in their religious lives and have little patience for a discourse so divided and beholden to outside influences. Kabbalah offers an alternative as a body of thought believed to be an ancient bedrock of wisdom, Jewish through and through, and not subject to the vagaries of current intellectual tastes.

Kabbalah has appeal in the modern period because it also has much to say about human psychology. This is an aspect of kabbalah that has only begun to be explored.[23] The psychological insights which kabbalah provides are predicated on the notion that the *sefirot* not only explain the inner life of God but also the inner mental life of human beings. This is the kabbalistic interpretation of man being created in God's image; the human soul is constructed on the model of the *sefirot*. To give a simple example of how this notion can be utilized for psychological purposes, I will cite a recent essay by Edward Hoffman, a psychologist and student of kabbalah. Hoffman explains that kabbalah offers a healthy view of human psychology by encouraging balance between various character traits. In an ideal world the *sefirot* are supposed to be in perfect harmony. This principle of harmony is not only applicable to God but to human beings as well, given that they are modelled on the paradigm of the *sefirot*. What kabbalah therefore tells us, Hoffman argues, is that a healthy psychology involves balancing such conflicting characteristics as Love and Judgment, two of the central *sefirot*, or balancing intellectual attributes represented in the first triad of *sefirot* (Crown, Wisdom, Understanding), with the emotional ones represented in the second (Lovingkindness, Judgment, Beauty or Mercy).[24] Since the advent of Freud, we have become acutely aware of—some might say obsessed with—psychological issues, and the fact that kabbalah speaks to this aspect of our lives is surely a factor in its popularity.

One reason that kabbalah is particularly alluring to Jews of a liberal orientation is its considerable potential for illuminating comparisons with other mystical traditions, especially those of Eastern origin. We have already noted that syncretism often accompanies the study of kabbalah among Jews searching for a broadly defined spirituality. Popular literature on kabbalah offers ample illustrations of this tendency with some of the most striking examples to be found in the realm of ecstatic kabbalah.[25] In *The Jew in the Lotus*, for example, Roger Kamentez recounts an extensive discussion between the Dalai Lama and members of the Jewish delegation visiting him comparing kabbalistic and Buddhist meditation practices.[26] Interesting comparisons can also be made between theosophic kabbalah and other mystical traditions. Medieval kabbalah, for example, developed an elaborate doctrine of reincarnation that is remarkably similar in some ways to that found in Buddhism and Hinduism.[27] This parallel, according to Kamenetz's account, was also a source of lively discussion between the Dalai Lama and his Jewish visitors.[28]

For obvious reasons the discovery of such parallels is deeply appealing to liberal Jews in search of spirituality. It allows them to relate to authentically Jewish doctrines that at the same time have potentially universal meaning. A common assumption in the popular literature on kabbalah that reflects this direction in thinking is that there exists a universal mystical consciousness of which kabbalah is only one expression.

With all that I have said, it should be no surprise that the revival of kabbalah has begun to have an effect on Jewish theology. The reasons that make it appealing to lay people also suggest interesting possibilities for the theologian: that kabbalistic symbols are vivid and multi-faceted images; that their timeless quality makes them an ideal springboard for theological speculation.

A handful of theological works has appeared in the last decade or so in which kabbalistic and Hasidic doctrines are used to give a comprehensive interpretation of Judaism. Some of these works combine kabbalistic symbols and metaphors with a sophisticated knowledge of Western learning, a development which I find most intriguing. This approach is by no means a revolution: Jewish theologians in this century, such as Martin Buber and Abraham Joshua Heschel, incorporated kabbalistic and Hasidic ideas into their thinking. But what seems to be different about the more recent thinkers is the degree to which kabbalistic ideas define their thought-systems. The recent authors make kabbalistic and Hasidic concepts their starting-point and the very framework for their thinking.

Two books in particular are noteworthy. The more important is Arthur Green's recently published *Seek My Face, Speak My Name: A Contemporary Jewish Theology*, which attempts to deal with the three major issues of Jewish thought—creation, revelation, and redemption—by drawing heavily on kabbalistic thinking, in particular Hasidic conceptions of God.[29] Green focuses chiefly on the Hasidic notion of divine immanence, the idea that God is close at hand in the world and manifest in our very being. The second book is by Daniel Matt, *God and the Big Bang: Discovering Harmony Between Science and Spirituality*.[30] Matt's basic premise is that there is much affinity between the world as conceived in kabbalah and that of modern physics. He suggests that the Big Bang Theory and the kabbalistic understanding of creation, for instance, have much in common. Matt also argues that the notion that energy and matter are interchangeable has a counterpart in the Lurianic idea that matter was created from the sparks of God's light falling into the primordial abyss as the *sefirot* were being created. God's light here is equated with energy. Matt's whole approach points to a new and interesting direction for modern Jewish theology. There is great potential for modern theologians to explore the parallels between kabbalah and modern science.[31] In this century, modern physics in particular has revealed a revolutionary understanding of the universe that at times does sound remarkably similar to that of kabbalah.

Yet, with all that I have said, I do not want to appear overly enthusiastic about the revival of kabbalah. There is much that disturbs me about this phenomenon. For one, kabbalah has its unpleasant side, something about which young people who study it are often unaware. For instance, feminists are sometimes impressed with the possibilities that kabbalah presents for bolstering the image of women. They note that God is perceived as both male and female, in that there are male and female *sefirot*. Yet one does not have to delve very deeply into kabbalah to see that its image of the feminine is not all that positive. For instance, the female powers in God, particularly the last of the *sefirot*, are often accorded close association with the realm of evil and the demonic. Thus the stereotypes that Jewish feminists are fighting against are in many ways reinforced in kabbalah. Similar observations can be made about the view of non-Jews who are also identified with the domain of evil.[32]

But my difficulty with the modern interest in kabbalah goes beyond the subject-matter itself. I am also disturbed by the pedagogic format within which it is frequently studied. Most of the students who explore Jewish mysticism—not to mention a good number of the teachers who teach it—are unequipped to deal with it properly. Except in rare instances, the texts are not studied in the original. Instead, there is reliance on translations, when available, and summaries and expositions in secondary literature. Most students, moreover, do not have the proper background in biblical and rabbinic literature to appreciate kabbalah. It is important to keep in mind that the kabbalists formulated their speculations and wrote their treatises with the assumption that their audience had full command of biblical and rabbinic texts upon which they themselves drew. This was a discipline for the elite. Furthermore, their whole mode of thinking and interpretation was largely an outgrowth of earlier material, rabbinic midrash in particular. Thus the absence of an adequate background in Jewish learning almost guarantees an incomplete or distorted understanding of kabbalah.

Perhaps what most disturbs me about the revival of interest in kabbalah is that I question whether many of the young Jews who have gravitated towards it have a solid commitment to Jewish religious practice and to participation in Jewish communal life. I have encountered many young people who seem to view kabbalah almost as a way of escaping such responsibilities. They see it as an opportunity to experience Jewish spirituality in an exotic way without Judaism making any concrete demands on them. More than one person has told me that he or she is drawn to kabbalah because it allows them to be Jewish in a spiritual sense without the "empty ritual" and "dry legalism" of rabbinic Judaism.

One is certainly entitled to see rabbinic Judaism as dry and empty. Sophisticated Jewish thinkers, especially in the modern period, have rendered that same judgment. But what is ironic and troubling about this approach is that historically much of the Jewish mystical tradition actually saw itself as a justification for the norms of rabbinic Judaism. In the theosophic kabbalah in particular, one studied the *sefirot* not only to understand the inner life of God and the universe, but to be able to perform the commandments better. As mentioned earlier, the purpose of observing the commandments was to have a positive effect on the *sefirot* which were believed to be out of harmony since creation.[33]

When kabbalah is used as a pretext to escape the imperatives of a Jewish way of life oriented toward action it becomes a significant distortion of Judaism. That bodes ill for the future of the Jewish community. We are, after all, living in an age when Jews face a series of unprecedented practical challenges, challenges that cannot be addressed by airy spirituality alone. We are being torn apart by inter-denominational strife; we are struggling with assimilation; we have yet to resolve how to relate to the non-Jewish world while maintaining our identity, and the role of the State of Israel for Judaism is still far from clear. This is not to say that the cultivation of spirituality is unrelated to these problems. One does not want to draw too sharp a distinction between the spiritual and the practical. In fact, I should hope that our struggle with practical concerns will be informed by a Jewishly-defined spirituality. But I am concerned when spirituality is a means to escape rather than confront responsibilities, especially in an age when the practical problems facing the Jewish people are so formidable.[34]

As for the future, I certainly have some deep concerns about the revival of kabbalah. Young Jews are being caught up in an aspect of Judaism that they often do not understand well, and that is not necessarily making them into better Jews. But I think we must acknowledge that the interest in kabbalah will be with us for years to come. Not everyone will or should be interested in kabbalah. But if history is any indicator, there will always be a sector of the Jewish community that will find this dimension of Judaism deeply appealing. I also believe that the revival of kabbalah can be a healthy return to an important and enduring dimension of the Jewish heritage. There *is* a need for a revitalization of much of Jewish life and practice, and kabbalah, which has been a source for such vitality in the past, can serve in this role again. Theology also stands to benefit from the revival, as thinkers like Arthur Green, who blend kabbalistic notions with Western learning and philosophical thought, have shown.

There are practical implications to these observations. On the one hand, I believe that the educators and rabbis must take note of the resurgence of interest in kabbalah and attempt to channel its energy in positive directions, setting aside any prejudices they may have about kabbalah. Young people who are interested in it are not necessarily on the fringe. Hebrew schools in particular should find ways to include the study of kabbalah and Hasidism in their curriculums, as some have already done. On the other hand, effort should be made to ensure that kabbalah is studied in its proper context. It should not be taught in isolation from classical Judaism out of which it grew. It should not be allowed to become a form of escapism from the practical demands of Judaism and Jewish communal life.

I should like to conclude by emphasizing that there could be serious consequences if we entirely ignore the spiritual needs of young Jews. Young people who look for an appealing form of Judaism and do not find it may be lost or even find their way to other religions. In fact, there is ample evidence that this is already happening. As we look to the future, we must meet the challenges that confront us. Therefore, a significant challenge that confronts us as we look to the future is to accommodate the mystical dimension of Judaism, to provide healthy outlets for it, and to find a place for it in the ever-evolving mosaic of Jewish religious experience.

Notes

[1] I will be using these two terms interchangeably, since the type of Jewish mysticism studied on the popular level nowadays is almost always kabbalah. As I note below, kabbalah is a form of Jewish mysticism that emerged in western Europe around the twelfth century and evolved into a variety of schools in the medieval and modern periods. There were other schools of Jewish mysticism both before and contemporaneous with the development of kabbalah. For instance, there was a pre-kabbalistic rabbinic school of Jewish mysticism, known as *merkavah* mysticism. We also have a school of mysticism in medieval Germany (*hasidei ashkenaz*) which developed around the time that kabbalah was emerging. Since, however, these schools are generally not studied today except by scholars, our concern will be exclusively with kabbalah.

[2] I would like to thank the following friends and colleagues who reviewed earlier drafts of this paper and provided me with valuable insights and suggestions: Susan Handelman, Marc Gopin, Joel Hecker, Yehudah Mirsky, and Max Ticktin.

[3] Here I follow Moshe Idel's introductory discussion in kabbalah: *New Perspectives* (New Haven: Yale University Press, 1988), pp. ix–xx.

[4] The distinction between ecstatic and theosophic kabbalah has been questioned in the most recent scholarship. Elliot Wolfson, in a recent book, *Through A Speculum that Shines: Vision and Imagination in Medieval Jewish Mysticism* (Princeton, N.J.: Princeton University Press, 1994), has shown that much of what is known as theosophic kabbalah was focused on the experiential dimension of mysticism much the same way that ecstatic kabbalah was. Theosophic kabbalah, therefore, may

not have been as "intellectual" as Gershom Scholem and Moshe Idel have claimed. Nonetheless, the distinction between the two is, I believe, still operative in the contemporary popular study of kabbalah that is the subject of this chapter.

5   This phenomenon has drawn much inspiration from Aryeh Kaplan's works on Jewish meditation, which, to my knowledge, were the first popular treatments of this issue; see *Jewish Meditation: A Practical Guide* (New York: Schocken Books, 1985); and *Meditation and Kabbalah* (York Beach, Me.: Samuel Weiser, 1989).

6   See Idel, *Kabbalah*, pp. xvi–xvii, who argues that from Lurianic kabbalah onward, there was a tendency to conflate the two approaches.

7   There are other Orthodox thinkers who fall into this category. R. Aryeh Kaplan, mentioned in n. 5 above, was a popular Orthodox author who wrote about Jewish thought. Before his death in 1982, Kaplan published a number of works many of which deal with kabbalistic themes. I should also mention R. Adin Steinsaltz, who, I am told, is affiliated with Habad Hasidism. Among his many other accomplishments is the popular *Thirteen Petalled Rose*, trans. Yehudah Hanegbi (New York: Basic Books, 1980), which attempts to give a poetic exposition of a number of kabbalistic concepts.

8   Reb Zalman, as he is popularly known, has published a number of books. See, for instance, *Fragments of a Future Scroll* (Germantown, Pa.: Leaves of Grass Press, 1975), and more recently, *Paradigm Shift: From the Jewish Renewal Teachings of Zalman Schachter-Shalomi*, ed. Ellen Singer (Northvale, N.J.: Jason Aronson Press, 1993). In this group we should also include Lawrence Kushner, a Reform rabbi who has published numerous books dealing with mystical matters of one sort or another, including *Honey From the Rock: Visions of Jewish Mystical Renewal* (San Francisco: Harper and Row, 1983), and *The River of Light: Spirituality, Judaism, Consciousness* (San Francisco: Harper and Row, 1981).

9   Roger Kamenetz, *The Jew in the Lotus: A Poet's Rediscovery of Jewish Identity in Buddhist India* (San Francisco: HarperCollins, 1994).

10   Wade Clark Roof, *A Generation of Seekers: The Spiritual Journey of the Baby Boom Generation* (San Francisco: HarperCollins, 1993).

11   One issue that needs to be examined is to what extent this rebellion is specifically a Jewish phenomenon. In many respects, the rebellion against what young Jews perceive as the dry institutional religion of their elders is symptomatic of a more general pattern of religious behavior among baby boomers, Jews and non-Jews alike, as described in detail in Wade Clark Roof's book.

12   See, for instance, *Hadassah Magazine* 78:3 (November 1996) and *Sh'ma* 27/522 (November 1996), two Jewish journals which in the same month devoted an entire issue to this phenomenon.

13   For a discussion of the term "spirituality" in a Jewish context, cf. Arthur Green, "Restoring the Aleph: Judaism for the Contemporary Seeker," an essay prepared for the Council for Initiatives in Jewish Education, 1 November 1995, pp. 7f.

[14] For further details about these sexual motifs, see Gershom Scholem, *Major Trends in Jewish Mysticism* (New York: Schocken Books, 1961), pp. 225–28; idem, *On the Kabbalah and its Symbolism*, trans. Ralph Manheim (New York: Schocken Books, 1989), pp. 104f., 154f.; Fischel Lachower and Isaiah Tishby, *The Wisdom of the Zohar: An Anthology of Texts*, trans. David Goldstein (Oxford: Oxford University Press, 1991), vol. 1, pp. 298–302, 371–73. Elliot Wolfson has done extensive work on this issue; see his *Circle in the Square: Studies in the Use of Gender in Kabbalistic Symbolism* (Albany: State University of New York Press, 1995).

[15] For theories of evil in medieval kabbalah, see Scholem, *Major Trends*, pp. 235–39; idem, *On the Kabbalah,* pp. 122–28; idem, *On the Mystical Shape of the Godhead,* trans. Jonathan Chipman (New York: Schocken Books, 1991), pp. 56–87; Lachower and Tishby, *Wisdon of the Zohar,* vol. 1, pp. 371f., 447f.

[16] Scholem discusses the mythical character of kabbalah throughout his writings. See *Major Trends,* pp. 7f., *On the Kabbalah,* pp. 87–117; and the excellent analysis of Scholem's views by David Biale, *Gershom Scholem: Kabbalah and Counter-History* (Cambridge, Ma.: Harvard University Press, 1978), pp. 92–103, 121–47.

[17] Gershom Scholem, *Kabbalah* (New York and Scarborough: Meridian, 1974), p. 110.

[18] This insight is in some sense implied by Scholem in that he consistently describes kabbalah as attempting to recapture the "primitive" element in religion that is lost once institutionalization sets in; see for example, *Major Trends,* pp. 7–8. Scholem also explicitly argues that the kabbalistic views of evil were superior to those of the philosophers because they attempt to grapple with the everyday fears of the common man; see Biale, *Gersholm Scholem,* p. 125.

[19] Scholem, *Major Trends,* pp. 35–36.

[20] Ibid.

[21] Here I follow Scholem's views on kabbalistic symbolism spelled out in *Major Trends,* pp. 25–28.

[22] The most striking example of the first of these features is, of course, the composition of the *Zohar,* which Moshe de Leon claimed was an ancient *midrash* composed by R. Shimon bar Yohai. Scholem's thesis that Moshe de Leon was the sole author has been questioned recently; yet scholars are in general agreement with Scholem's assessment that the *Zohar* is a late medieval text.

[23] For a popular treatment of this topic see Edward Hoffman, *The Way of Splendor: Jewish Mysticism and Modern Psychology* (Boulder/London: Shambhala Publications, 1981), and the essays edited by him in *Opening the Inner Gates: New Paths in kabbalah and Psychology* (Boston: Shambhala Publications, 1995). For the first scholarly treatment of this topic, see Mortimer Ostow's *Ultimate Intimacy: The Psychodynamics of Jewish Mysticism* (Madison, Ct.: International Universities Press, 1995). Here prominent scholars of kabbalah and professional psychoanalysts share insights about the kabbalah in a dialogical format.

[24] Edward Hoffman, "The Tree of Life and the 'City of the Just': Kabbalistic Exercises in Inner Growth," in *Opening the Inner Gates*, pp. 5–19.

[25] Edward Hoffman's *The Way of Splendor* provides a particularly good example of this tendency. Scholars of kabbalah, such as Gershom Scholem and Moshe Idel, have also noted intriguing parallels between kabbalah and other mystical traditions. In some instances, there is even speculation that kabbalah was directly influenced by these traditions.

[26] See Kamenetz, *Jew in the Lotus*, pp. 191–210. The similarity may have a historical explanation. Both Scholem and Idel point out that the major medieval exponents of ecstatic kabbalah, Abraham Abulafia and his disciples, developed techniques for meditation that exhibit parallels with, and were likely influenced by, Islamic Sufism and Indian Yoga. See Scholem, *On the Kabbalah*, p. 180; Moshe Idel, *The Mystical Experience in Abraham Abulafia* (Albany: State University of New York Press, 1988), pp. 14, 24; idem, *Studies in Ecstatic Kabbalah* (Albany: State University of New York Press, 1988), pp. 74–76, and chapters 6 and 7.

[27] Scholem makes note of this similarity between kabbalah and Buddhism with respect to reincarnation in his essay on reincarnation in kabbalah in *On the Mystical Shape*, p. 212. Scholem entertains a possible connection between the kabbalistic view of reincarnation and "Indian religion" in general in kabbalah, p. 344.

[28] Kamenetz, *Jew in the Lotus*, pp. 84–90.

[29] Arthur Green, *Seek My Face, Speak My Name: A Contemporary Jewish Theology* (Northvale, N.J.: Jason Aronson Press, 1992).

[30] Daniel Matt. *God and the Big Bang: Discovering Harmony Between Science and Spirituality* (Woodstock, Vt.: Jewish Light Publishing, 1996).

[31] In fact, there is ample precedent for this approach stretching back several centuries, as David Ruderman's scholarship has shown. See most recently *Jewish Thought and Scientific Discovery in Early Modern Europe* (New Haven and London: Yale University Press, 1995), pp. 118–52, 213–28, 264, 369.

[32] See Scholem, *On the Mystical Shape*, pp. 140–96; Lachower and Tishby, *Wisdom of Zohar*, vol. 1., pp. 371–88; vol. 2, pp. 447–545. For attitudes of kabbalah towards non-Jews, see Moshe Hallamish, "Some Aspects of the Attitudes of the kabbalah Towards Gentiles" [Hebrew], in *Philosophia Yisra'elit*, eds. Asa Kasher and Moshe Hallamish (Tel Aviv: Papyrus, 1983), pp. 49–71.

[33] The exact relationship between halakhic Judaism and kabbalah has been a subject of debate between Scholem and Idel. Scholem tends to see the relationship between the two as one of tension, while Idel stresses their harmony. For Scholem's views on this issue, see Biale, *Gersholm Scholem*, p. 121, and Idel's programmatic critique in kabbalah, pp. 28–29, as well as his extensive discussion of this issue in chapters 7 and 8.

[34] Arthur Green's insistence that praxis accompany a life of spirituality permeates the second section of his book, *Seek My Face, Speak My Name;* see especially pp. 132–34.

3

CROSSING THE VOID:
A POSTMODERN JEWISH THEOLOGY

Susan Handelman

When I received the original invitation to address a conference on the subject, "How to create the Jewish future at this crucial moment in Jewish
history," I was very honored, but also reluctant to accept. I felt a bit like
Moses, when God suddenly called him in the wilderness and told him to go
and tell the Pharaoh to let the people out of Egypt. Moses responded: "Who
am I to go to Pharaoh and to bring this people out of Egypt?" (Ex. 2:10–11),
and there followed a protracted argument.

Of course, I was asked, not because I am in any way a prophet or on the
level of Moses, but because I am an academic who has written books about
postmodernism and Jewish thought. We academics do a kind of very abstract work which is "about Judaism," but not necessarily "lived Torah."
Jewish community leaders and teachers, I think, have as much to tell us as
we do them. For they are more in touch with the people, "laboring under
their burdens," if I may continue the Exodus motif. Although I will discourse academically here, it may be more in my role as a teacher of college
students and adults, and as one of the "perplexed who also seeks a guide,"
that I have something to say. Nevertheless I also feel like Moses, when he
described himself in that reluctant interchange with God as, "slow of mouth
and heavy of speech" (Ex. 4:10) .

The official title of this section is "Faith and Religion in a 'Secular Age.'"
I am glad "secular" was put in quotes because one of my main points is that
we are not in a secular age, but a post-secular age, and this is, in part, what
defines the postmodern condition. At its best, I would say, postmodernism
can be a way for Jews who have passed through the fragmentation and secularization wrought by modernity to renew themselves Jewishly—a way to
reconnect to a "pre-modern" faith but also to reconfigure it so that it does
not deny or suppress all that we have learned and experienced in modernity.

I want to sketch here what a postmodern faith might be like, and how it would relate to the lived situation of our students, friends, congregants, and colleagues, both "academics and *amcha*." First I will attempt to characterize this "post-secular generation," then give a brief definition of what I mean by "modern" and "post-modern," then move to commentary on some texts from the Bible, Talmud and Hasidism, and then finally to some personal conclusions.

THE POST-SECULAR GENERATION

To describe this "post-secularism," let me relate an incident that happened this past spring. I often teach in adult Jewish education programs. One was a series for a group of young Jewish adult leaders. During one of my classes on the biblical story of Adam and Eve, I was using an approach that had always worked well. A very sharp woman attorney about age forty-five, who in previous classes had expressed a strong feminist point of view and a very cynical attitude toward traditional forms of Judaism and rabbinic authority, burst out: "I am tired of analyzing all this from a literary and historical and feminist point of view. I want to know what I can personally believe, and how it helps me relate to God, and what I can teach my kids, and how it affects me spiritually. . . . They are always teaching us about 'What Jews believe.' But I need to know what *I* believe."

This remark keeps ringing in my ears, and we all need to attend to it, for she is very characteristic of the times. I was struck by an article in a Jewish Studies program newsletter from the University of Massachusetts written by Professor Julius Lester describing a course he teaches on "Religion in Western Literature." The students who take the course, he says, are searching for something, but "they are at the age when the word 'God' reminds them too much of the parents, priests, rabbis, and ministers they want to leave behind. Yet the need for transcendent meaning is as present in their lives as an open sore."[1] These are the children of those who came to adulthood in the 1960s. Again, Lester:

> Few shared childhood with both biological parents. Many of them have parents who are alcoholic. Some students have been institutionalized because of their problems with alcohol or drugs. Many are trying to piece themselves together after experiences of sexual abuse, physical abuse, or the death of a parent. They are so young to have suffered so much. They bristle with a keenly-honed cynicism, believing in nothing and trusting no one. How could it be otherwise? They have been betrayed in fundamental ways.[2]

I recognize this description in my students and even in many of the adults I teach. And yet I recognize what Lester sees, that "they want to believe. They simply do not know how." I also am amazed at the hidden spirituality all around me in my daily life in America. There is hardly a week that goes by without my having some utterly surprising encounter with an average person—a taxi driver, a stock boy, a hairdresser, a saleswoman, a secretary—in which in the course of conversation, a seemingly typical secular American suddenly expresses some deep yearning for, or faith in, God.[3] Flying to Toronto for the conference, I sat next to a Canadian-Jewish woman, late middle-aged, prominent in Jewish communal life, who confessed to me that though she spends so much of her time working for Israel and is involved in many Jewish activities, she feels a painful "void inside" to use her phrase, searching and yet not knowing how to believe.

In sum, people today are looking desperately for God and for a communal expression of that connection. We jostle against one another in this postmodern, multicultural world, but it is secular only on the surface. This is what "religious fundamentalists" do not understand; they are still fighting a "modernity" that has already exhausted itself.

MODERNISM AND POSTMODERNISM

Now at this point, I face the unenviable task of defining postmodernism "on one foot." I must first express my discomfort with large categorical statements about what postmodernism "is." There are many kinds: from the philosophical intricacies of deconstruction, to complex global political developments, to certain artistic practices. But I must proceed and make some simplistic generalizations nevertheless. The prefix "post," of course, means "after." Postmodernism means that we come "after" the era of modernism. "Post" also implies a "critique" of modernism.

But modernism is not solely a twentieth-century phenomenon (the word was first used in the fifth century). In academia we now call the period of the Renaissance in the fifteenth and sixteenth centuries "Early Modern Europe," because there we find the origins of modern scientific thought, of rationalism, of notions of history as linear and progressive. There the idea of the individual, autonomous self begins to flourish. In the eighteenth century Enlightenment, of course, these ideas fully develop, along with democracy, the quest for objective scientific and historical truth, ideas of universal morality, and the revolutionary overturning of traditional authority. Modernism is the imperative to "make it new," as the poet Ezra Pound put it.

Postmodernism, as a critique of modernism, develops especially in the late twentieth century when, after a century of barbarous slaughter, we have lost our faith in human reason, technology, the university, progress, revolution, and universal truth. (Postmodernism can also be said to be the fissures and cracks within modernism that accompany its entire historical development.) Much postmodern discourse in the humanities today is a "hermeneutics of suspicion" devoted to showing how what has purported to be universal, rational, and autonomous is not so, but rather a mask for hidden ideologies. In academia, postmodern interpretations often attempt to "overcome oppression" by unmasking these hidden ideologies, unconscious desires, and unjust power relations.

The postmodern sensibility is skeptical of Grand Ideologies. And we have seen in our time, how all the great "totalizing" systems of the nineteenth century (systems that purport to explain *all* of reality) have broken apart: communism, socialism, even Zionism. (I am amused to read that in China today, the weekly *Computer News* sells more copies than the *People's Daily*, the mouthpiece of the Communist Party.) But we also witness everyday in the newspapers how the void created by the end of Grand Ideologies also generates a severe backlash, a regression to the most primitive forms of ethnic and nationalist self-assertion. Needless to say, this is something one feels so painfully in the Middle East.

Philosophically, postmodernism is a critique of what has been called the "Dogma of Immaculate Perception": the idea that there is a neutral, detached observer who sees things objectively, as they are "in themselves." Postmodern science, for example, recognizes that science is not a description of nature as it is in itself. As Niels Bohr, the famous physicist, said, "Physics is not about the way nature is, but about what we can say about the way nature is." In other words, we are always interpreters who make meanings rather than find facts.

Now if that is the case, postmodernism allows us to return to the language of theology and religious texts with a new seriousness—to see how they construct meaning. For it was only modernism that was so corrosive of traditional faith in religion. The modernist scholarly tools and values applied to Jewish texts since the Enlightenment emphasized "empirical fact," "critical-scientific approaches," and the "accurate historical reconstruction" of religious texts. These approaches often undermined traditional beliefs in divine revelation from Sinai and a historical transcendent truth. At the same time, those "modernist" approaches themselves reflected a kind of "literalist" mentality which, I think, sparked a flip or shadow side—an equally literalist, fundamentalist, defensive response.

As the brilliant rhetorical theorist, Chaim Perelman, observed in his masterwork, *The New Rhetoric*, the skeptic and fanatic are flip sides of the same coin; they both maintain that the only criteria for truth are those which are "absolute and indubitable."[4] The skeptic thinks that no one can fulfill the criteria, whereas the fanatic thinks he or she indeed has done so. When truth is defined differently--postmoderns might say "contextually" or "rhetorically," or as a function of the dynamic between community, text, and interpreter, or kabbalistically as beyond all ontologies of presence and absence—then one can come to new affirmations. In this sense, postmodernism has become "skeptical of skepticism." This is the path taken by some of the most interesting twentieth-century Jewish thinkers, especially two who have inspired me: Emmanuel Levinas, the French-Jewish philosopher who died in 1995; and Franz Rosenzweig, the great German-Jewish philosopher who died from Lou Gehrig's disease in 1929.

However we may define the postmodern, it is the period of "post-assimilation." Postmodern Jewish philosophers, such as Levinas and Rosenzweig, all follow that path of return to Judaism from a prior engagement with "universal Western philosophy." That, too, is my personal path. We are all engaged in a kind of *teshuva* (return.) Yet, let me pause here and ask: "Aren't renewal and return, *teshuva*, the eternal task of the Jewish people?" *Teshuva*, as the ancient rabbis said, preceded even the creation of the world. And we are, as Simon Rawidowicz so well characterized us, " the ever-dying people." We are constantly confronting disasters, catastrophes, the undermining of our foundations—and then reconstructing foundations and renewing ourselves. So I think we need to overcome a certain hubris about our generation and its challenges.

"HERE I AM": FREEDOM, OBEDIENCE, AND FAITH

At this point, I want to attempt a more concrete definition of a postmodern Jewish self and faith by resorting to a more traditional Jewish mode: commentary on a text. That is simultaneously a more traditional, and a more postmodern move—for one of the major tenets of postmodernism is that we are inevitably situated in our speech and text-traditions, and we must give up the arrogance of claims to knowledge outside of them (there is no Immaculate Perception). And so, postmodernism is a critique of the notion of a free, coherent, autonomous, individual, isolated self, of a Cartesian mind meditating in solitude in order to deduce pure, logical, clear, universal truths.

The pressing concern of the contemporary North American Jewish community is often formulated as the preservation of "Jewish identity." But how do we define this term? What is the content of the Jewish "I"? To

begin with, identity and selfhood in Levinas and Rosenzweig are not constructed through the Cartesian ("I think, therefore I am") but through the
biblical cry of "*Hineni*" (הנני) "Here I am." These are the famous words
with which Abraham responds to God before the *akedah*, the sacrifice of
Isaac (Gen. 22:1), and which Moses uses at the burning bush. Before he
protests that he cannot accomplish the mission, Moses, too, says "*Hineni*"
(Exodus 2:4). And this is the phrase which the prophets use when they are
called by God.

Fortuitously, our conference was held in the week of the Jewish calendar when the Torah portion of the yearly cycle was "*Lech lekha*" (Go you
forth) (Gen. 12-17). This section begins with God's call to Abraham, "*Lech
lekha*" (לך לך),

> Go you forth from your land, and your birthplace, and the house of your
> father to the land that I will show you. I will make you a great nation and I
> will bless you and I will make your name great, and you will be a
> blessing . . . and in you, all the families of the earth will be blessed.
> (Gen. 12:1-4).

Interestingly, those are precisely the verses that begin the "creation of the
Jewish future"—as distinct from the creation of the world and the universal
human future represented by Adam and Noah in the previous narratives of
Genesis. God calls to Abraham, the first Jew, to go forth, but it is to a very
undefined future. And the subsequent events in this Torah portion of "*Lech
Lekha*" are seemingly the opposite of those promises and blessings: there is a
famine in the land; Abraham has to descend to Egypt; Sarah is endangered
when she is taken into the house of Pharaoh; Abraham has an inter-family
conflict with his nephew Lot; Sarah is barren and Abraham without progeny;
there is a war of the regional kings and the capture of Lot; there is a prophecy
of four hundred years of slavery for Abraham's descendants; and Sarah and
Hagar are in conflict. In sum, it is not easy to "create the Jewish future."

When, in the next *parsha* (weekly Torah portion), a son is finally born to
Sarah, God asks Abraham to sacrifice the beloved child. Of the *akedah*,
Rosenzweig writes the following in *The Star of Redemption*: when God calls
out to Abraham in direct address, in all his particularity (Gen. 22:1)
"Abraham," then Abraham answers

> all unlocked, all spread-apart, all ready, all-soul, "Here I am." Here is the I,
> the individual human I, as yet wholly receptive, as yet only unlocked,
> only empty, without content, without nature, pure readiness, pure
> obedience, all ears.[5]

What is so postmodern about this? First, the self is here defined as "empty."

It comes to be only in relation to the direct address of another, and that address is a call that claims the self and to which it is obligated—the self is compelled in a kind of non-freedom prior to any freedom. Emptiness turns into ethics.

A Hasidic interpretation notes that the letters that compose the Hebrew word for "I" *'ani* (אני), *'aleph, nun, yud*, when re-arranged, spell "nothingness" (אין) *'ayin*. If modernism gazes into the self and sees an abyss that terrifies, postmodernism accepts with equanimity that lack and seeks to cross and recross it. Without the voice of God, though, that emptied self can become the cynical laugh of a character from a Samuel Beckett play, or a self trying to fill itself through games of power and sexuality as unmasked in the philosophy of Michel Foucault. In his essay, "Compassionate Postmodernism," Peter Ochs has characterized postmodernism as "redemptive" of modernity—and that is a distinctively Jewish perspective without which secular postmodernism often degenerates into another form of nihilism.[6]

But what does the word "obedience" have to do with the word "postmodern"—which in much secular academic thought is instead connected with the values of transgression, subversion, interrogation. We often recoil when we hear the word "obedience". We think of a dangerous docility, of abdication of intellectual thought, of mindless fundamentalism. But there is another kind of obedience, as Peter Pitzele notes in his book on the Bible, *Our Fathers Wells*:

> The word *obey* comes from the Latin word meaning "to listen, to hear."
> Abraham *listens* to the call to leave his native land. . . . He experiences the
> call as something coming from a God who is felt to be Other and outside
> him. But this God is also inside him. Deep speaks to deep. . . . Abraham is
> not being obedient to some external dictate, to some chain of command.
> On the contrary, he breaks with customary conventions. . . . What Abraham
> obeys flashes upon him like a beacon, points a way, then disappears. . . . On
> each step of his journey he must renew his commitment to his task, for his
> obedience is voluntary, not compelled.[7]

The Talmud also deals with this issue of obedience and truth. In the famous passage in *Shabbat* 88a, it, too, voices concern about an external compulsion which would invalidate the revelation at Sinai. The biblical text (Ex. 19:17) tells us that the Israelites stood *b'tahit ha har* (בתחתית ההר)—translated idiomatically "at the foot of the mountain," but having a more literal sense of "at the underside" or "nether side." Here the Talmud comments:

> Rav 'Avdimi bar Hama bar Hasa said: "This teaches us that the Holy One
> Blessed be He turned the mountain over on them like a cask and said, 'If you

accept the Torah, all is well; if not, here will be your grave.'" Rav 'Aha bar
Jacob said: "Based on this, a major complaint can be lodged against the Torah."
Rava said. "Nevertheless they reaccepted it willingly in the days of Ahasuerus,
for it is written [Esther 9:27]: 'The Jews (קימו וקיבלו) *kimu ve-kiblu*, confirmed
and accepted.' They confirmed what they had accepted previously."

The original context of the verse from the Book of Esther is Mordecai's
sending of a letter to the Jews instructing them henceforth to celebrate annually
the victory over their enemies on the fourteenth and fifteenth of the Hebrew
month of Adar. And so they "confirmed and accepted upon themselves and
their descendants" to celebrate these two days. This verse is reinterpreted by
the Talmud in our passage to mean that the Jews confirmed what they had
accepted *previously* at Mt. Sinai. On this verse, the classic medieval commentator,
Rashi, explains: "For if they were brought to judgment about why they had
not fulfilled what they had accepted upon themselves, they could answer that
they were compelled by force to accept it." It was not of their own free will.
Nevertheless, they re-accepted it freely a thousand years later in their exile in
the Persian Kingdom of 'Ahasuerus—as a result, says Rashi, "of the love of the
miracle that was done for them" on Purim.

Purim is, in its own way, a holiday made for a postmodern sensibility: a
holiday of masks, inversions, comic mockery, and concealment of God whose
name is never mentioned in the Book of Esther. For the rabbis to make out
of this a second Sinai is an act of hermeneutical genius and profound theology.

In Levinas' commentary on this passage, he understands the relation of
Sinai and Purim to signify a certain "non-freedom" prior to freedom, one
which makes freedom possible—a prior saying of (נעשה ונשמע) *Na'aseh Ve-
Nishma'* (Ex. 24:7) "We will do and we will hear/obey/understand," a prior
calling to responsibility.[8] And that constructs the self; the self is defined by
saying "*Hineni*, Here I am for you."

The contemporary Quaker educational theorist, Parker Palmer, has some
eloquent things to say about the ways knowing, freedom, and obeying relate
to one another—about defining postmodern truth. Noting also that the
English word, "obedience," does not mean slavish adherence but comes from
the Latin root *audire* which means "to listen," Palmer writes:

> At its root, the word "obedience" means not only "to listen" but "to listen
> from below." How fascinating that this is also the common sense meaning of
> the word "understand," which suggests that we know something by "standing
> under" it. Both obedience and understanding imply submitting ourselves to
> something larger than any one of us, something on which we all depend.
> Both imply subjecting us to the communal bonds of truth. The objectivist
> will doubtless argue that the personalist mode of knowing is dangerously

subjective. But the complex of word and images I am exploring here opens up a new sense of what "subjective" knowledge might mean—for that word also means "to place under." In that sense of the words, I am arguing for a subjective conception of truth, a truth to which we must subject our selves. Truth calls us to submit ourselves, to the community of which we are a part, to fidelity to those bonds of troth in which our truth resides.[9]

In other words, "truth is troth, " and Palmer uses the image of covenant to express this:

> The English word "truth" comes from a Germanic root that also gives rise to our word "troth," as in the ancient vow, "I pledge thee my troth." With this word, one person enters a covenant with another, a pledge to engage in a mutually accountable and transforming relationship, a relationship forged of trust and faith in the face of unknowable risks. To know something or someone in truth is to enter troth with the known, to rejoin the new knowing what our minds have put asunder. To know in truth is to become betrothed. . . .[10]

These words are a wonderful "Quaker" *drash* or homily on the rabbinic interpretation in *Shabbat* 88a of the Jews standing "at the underside of the mountain." They also characterize a postmodern notion of truth. They are words which should deeply resonate with Jews in relationship to our connection to the idea of Covenant, more specifically regarding the meaning of the Covenant that God made with Abraham at the moment the Jewish future was being created. They should also help to explicate the meaning of "continuity": how that future becomes an inheritance to the next generation.

Those same words beautifully illumine the tradition that the first words we teach a child when she or he learns how to speak are contained in the verse from the end of the book of Deuteronomy (33:4): "The Torah which Moses commanded us is the inheritance of the Congregation of Jacob." *Torah tziva lanu moshe, morasha Kehilat Yaakov* (תורה צוה לנו משה מורשה קהלת יעקב). The famous midrash on this verse says, "Do not read it *morasha* (מורשה— "inheritance") but *me'orasa* (מאורסה—"engaged, betrothed").

We do not stop here, however. As everyone knows, the romance of the initial engagement eventually wears off. There is then a lot of learning: how to live with the beloved through ups and downs, crises and difficulties, unexpected troubles. We move from Mt. Sinai to forty years of contentious desert wanderings and into the turbulence of a history bound by the Covenant. As Levinas also notes, when the Jews accepted the Torah on Purim, they did so in a different state of awareness, in full cognizance of its price; for the thousand years between Sinai and the Persian exile were filled with the difficult consequences resulting from that first acceptance.

Levinas also points out that at the end of the aggadic (legendary) discussion of the scene at Sinai and the overturned cask in *Shabbat* 88a, there is another scene of a *min*, a sectarian or heretic, observing the sage, Rava, buried in study. Rava is holding his fingers beneath his foot so tightly that blood is spurting from them. The sectarian mocks the sage for belonging to a people whose mouth was too quick to speak and accept the Torah. First, "he says to Rava, you should have listened to see if you could accept and fulfill, not the obverse." As Levinas interprets Rava's posture, study—the forceful exercise of intellect, so forceful that blood is spurting from his fingers in his intense concentration—comes after, and as result of, the *na'aseh*, the "we will do," the primary acceptance of obligation.[11]

I have been using the English word "faith." But I would prefer to use the Hebrew word for faith, "*emunah*." The root of this word is the three letters, *'aleph, mem, nun* (א.מ.ן) signifying confidence, trust, and in the verbal forms, meaning to train or educate, foster, nurse, bring up. In the noun forms, "*'omanut*" means "art"; "*'uman*" is a "craftsman." Thus philology teaches us that "*emunah*," faith, is not "blind obedience"; it is a craft, a skill, and it needs to be educated, trained, nursed through study and learning and teaching. Moses, after all, is not referred to as "Moses, our Prophet," but as "Moses, our Teacher."[12]

RABBI NACHMAN: CROSSING THE VOID

I began this essay with a reference to Moses' reluctance to go to Pharaoh, with Moses' description of himself as heavy tongued, unable to speak. I conclude it with a Hassidic interpretation of that text, which I hope will tie together all the things I have been trying to articulate. For is it only postmodernism that has talked to us about ruptures, radical reinterpretation, alternative epistemologies, and the need for revealing a new face to the Torah? Was that not also the project of kabbalah and Hasidism? All too often Hasidism is characterized as "pre-modern." But as Arthur Green has argued, we err greatly by restricting the study of Jewish responses to modernity to the thinkers who came from the heritage of German philosophy—figures such as Hermann Cohen, Buber, Rosenzweig, Levinas, and others.[13] Kabbalah and Hasidism played a key role in the modernist Jewish revival. We see this clearly in Buber's retellings of the Hasidic tales and in Scholem's academic investigations of kabbalah. But as Edith Wyschogrod and others have pointed out, this was a Hasidism formed in the image of the German romantic reaction to modernity. Now it is time for a "postmodern" reappropriation of Hasidic texts which understands their deep roots in kabbalistic ways of thinking about God's withdrawals and absences, about fragmentation, shattering of the vessels, exile and repair.[14]

In the kabbalah, the primal act of Divine creation involves the *tzimtzum*, the self-contraction or withdrawal of God in order to open up a space, a void, *halal panui* in which the finite universe could be created. (I find it interesting that the "Ari," Rabbi Isaac Luria, developed this notion in sixteenth century Safed coincident with the rise of early modern Europe. The modernist focus on the self seems already to have its postmodern counter-echo in Luria.) I am using "postmodernism" now not only in reference to a certain historical or cultural moment— but also to indicate a certain sensibility. The vacated space of kabbalah becomes for me another metaphor for modernity's shattering of the vessels, absence of God, and fragmentation. A Jewish postmodernism would come to help repair those vessels, while recognizing that this can only be done by first inhabiting the cracks and ruptures. Ultimate repair belongs to a horizon beyond all our conceptual systems.

One of the Hasidic masters who knew well how to inhabit the void, who felt keenly God's absences, was Rabbi Nachman of Bratslav. He has an extraordinary teaching in his *Likktuei Moharan*.[15] God tells Moses in Exodus 10:1-3, 24: "Come to Pharaoh, for I have hardened his heart...so that I may place these, my signs, in their midst . . . that you may know that I am God." Rabbi Nachman's exposition is quite complex, and I will give only a small piece of it. First, he interprets the word, "Pharaoh," to refer precisely to the vacated space, the *halal*, created by the *tzimtzum*, the primal act of the divine contraction and withdrawal to enable creation. The word *pharoah* (פרעה), he adds, comes from a root meaning "annihilation" and "removal" as in Exodus 5:4 where the Pharaoh says to Moses "You have removed (תפריעו) (*tafri'u*) the people from their work." It is also related to the root meaning "uncovering and revealing."

So, says Rabbi Nachman, it is precisely in the vacated space from which God has withdrawn, that there arise all the philosophical questions which have no answer, which pain and confuse us, and which hardened our hearts. But Rabbi Nachman then interprets the name "Hebrew" (עברי)—*'ivri*—in a reparative sense as coming from the root *'iver* (עבר). In this sense, it means "to cross over, or ford some space." This signifies that the Jews, the Hebrews—*'Ivrim*—have the task and power to cross the void created by the *tzimtzum*, the empty space where God is absent. That is why God is called in Exodus 5:3, "God of the Hebrews." The root also yields the word *'ever* (עבר) meaning the "sides" of a river. According to the Lurianic notion of *tzimztum*, the empty space is created by the image of God contracting his light to the "sides."

The notion of this vacated space, an absence where there is yet a presence of God is an epistemological and ontological paradox, unsolvable in terms of human intellect. Needless to say, a postmodern world, a post-Shoah world, is one in which we seem to be in an empty place from which God is withdrawn. Secular postmodernism (especially deconstuction) leads us right into this emptiness—this vision of flickering presence in absence. The key question is, "How do we find God there?"

Rabbi Nachman reminds us that somehow God is still "there" in the void; without some trace of the divine creative power to give it "life," even the Void could not exist. This is a paradox human reason cannot resolve. For Rabbi Nachman, only the great *tzaddikim*, the most holy ones, can fully enter that void and cross over without falling into confusion, doubt, and heresy. And that is precisely why Moses has to come to Pharaoh, to the place where God cannot be found, to ford the void and cross to the other side.

But inside the confusion of the vacated space there is silence—a level of thought that is beyond words. This silence is the deeper meaning of Moses' description of himself in Exodus 4:10, as *Kvad peh u-chvad lashon*, "slow of speech and slow of tongue," which I cited at the beginning of this essay. A level of silence beyond speech. It is a silence necessary for being able to "Come to Pharaoh," to come into the vacated space. Moses has to find in that space the traces, the signs, the letters, and the fragments that will enable creation. This is also the task and power of Israel, the *'Ivrim*, who through their *'emunah*, their faith, cross the void. On this level, beyond speech, Moses ultimately comes to song, for every form of wisdom according to Rabbi Nachman has its own song and melody. And the song of *'emunah* that crosses the vacated space is the meaning of the song Moses sings in Exodus 15 after the Jews crossed the Red Sea.

Here Rabbi Nachman returns us, like Levinas, to the give and take of intellectual debate. He gives an extraordinary interpretation of *mahloket*—dispute, argument, rabbinic debate—which, he says, enacts the same process of Creation. In the *tzimtzum*, God withdraws light to the sides and creates the Vacant space; only in this way can a finite creation occur without being absorbed and nullified by God's infinite light. Similarly, through dispute, the Sages separate and "go to the sides," forming a Vacated space. The words of their disputes then enter this space and become part of the act of Creation. Rabbi Nachman's "prooftext" is a creative re-reading of Isaiah 51:16: "I have placed my words in your mouth . . . that I may plant the heavens and lay the foundations of the earth, and say to Zion you are my people (*'ami* עַמִּי)." The *Zohar* (Introduction 5a) says: "Read the word not as *'ami*, my people, but *'imi*, 'with me' (עִמִּי), meaning to be a collaborator with Me; just as I can create heaven and earth through my words, so can you."

Now, for Rabbi Nachman, only those of the stature of Moses could safely enter the void. But I would say that each of us ordinary, postmodern Jews has already been thrust into it. Each of us, like Moses, is called to "come to Pharaoh"; and each of us is "slow of speech." We need to remember that we are 'Ivrim, that we must cross and recross that void. We do so not only with the complex words of our academic debates and disputes, but also with our silence and our emunah.

CONCLUSION

So, finally, I have now both given a lecture to, and written an essay for, an audience. But an audience is not the same thing as a community. Jewish faith, emunah, comes not out of lectures, but out of being Jewish together, and that means so many things. Among them are doing mitzvot together, and singing the davenning (prayer) together, eating Sabbath and holiday meals together, consoling friends in times of trouble, and exulting with them in times of joy. And good Jewish learning is not lectures, but hevrutah: arguing with your study partner about the meaning of a text and working on it together.

Universities call themselves "communities," but they are so only in a very limited sense. Academic discourse, as sophisticated as it is, lacks many dimensions of language. My colleague, Phillis Levin, an accomplished poet, once told my students in a poetry criticism class, that reading a poem out loud and hearing the rhythm are often what give you the understanding of the things you can't figure out. Perhaps this is what Rosenzweig meant in the second part of The Star of Redemption when he said that the Song of Songs is the focal book of revelation. The "meanings" of a song cannot be gotten just from reading the lyrics on the page; lyrics are often flat and senseless; one has to hear the song performed; meaning comes as much from the rhythms, the crying out of the singer, the kri'ah . . . which is also the Hebrew word for "reading" (קריאה).

The Talmud says that one should part from one's friend with a word of halakhah. So as I close, here is one on song and silence. The halakhot of writing shira ("song") as part of a sacred text, such as a Sefer Torah require that the shiroth be written with large spaces between the phrases. Every phrase is distanced from another by a certain kind of space, "a space on top of a brick," as the Talmud describes it. For every phrase written, one leaves a blank space parallel to it. These blanks take us back to the halal, the vacated space—the place where our philosophies and our "isms" fail us.

These are the blanks, the fissures we live with in a postmodern world. We bridge them only with a certain kind of *'emunah*, or at least we imagine what crossing and recrossing those spaces might be, if only in the sounds without words. So I come to the end of my discourse and into silence.

Two more brief remarks. When Rosh Hashana falls on Shabbat, according to *halakhah*, we do not blow the *shofar* until the second day of the holiday. Once in a Jerusalem synagogue on such a day, we were asked to spend five minutes in silence at the point in the prayers when we would have blown the *shofar*—to try to hear the voice of the *shofar* which that day was in the silence, the *kol demmama daka*.

This, perhaps, is a postmodern way of hearing the voice of God, which has been so muffled in our world. The story is told of a person who came to a master of prayer and asked him, "What does God say to you?" The other replied: "Nothing, He just listens." "But what do you say to God?" the man asked. "Nothing, I just listen."

Notes

1   Julius Lester, *Judaic Studies News* (Department of Judaic and Near Eastern Studies, University of Massachusetts) (Spring 1966): 2.

2   Ibid.

3   A few years ago, the *Library Journal* published an intriguing article by Barbara Hoffert ("Spiritual Guidance," *Library Journal* 115:19, [1 November 1990]: 58–63) on religious publishing in the 1990s, and how changes in religion in America have spurred religious publishers to find new kinds of books to meet people's changing needs. The article noted that secular readers are suddenly seeking spiritual guidance, and religious readers are moving beyond the standard sources:

"As the publishers themselves are beginning to discover, people want religion based less on theology and more on their own experiences . . . and to experience the holy not as an intellectual exercise but as something they can bring into their lives to provide healing and wholeness" (58).

Publishers have met these needs with books about the big issues of contemporary life in the U.S.: divorce, child abuse, addiction, co-dependecy, AIDS, abortion and ecology. Harper published a book by Gerald May entitled *Addiction and Grace: Love and Spirituality in the Healing of Addictions* (San Francisco: Harper San Francisco, 1991), which argues that to be alive is to be addicted. It was expected to appeal only to clergy but sold 50,000 copies.

We in the Jewish community might be tempted to think that this is a phenomenon more connected to the non-Jewish world—that our families are still intact, non-addicted, safe from AIDS. But that is not the case, as any of us who works with high school or college students knows.

4   Chaim Perelman and L. Olbrechts-Tyteca, *The New Rhetoric: A Treatise on Argumentation*, trans. J. Wilkinson and P. Weaver (South Bend: University of Notre Dame Press, 1969), p. 62.

5   Franz Rosenzweig, *The Star of Redemption*, 2nd ed., trans. William Hallo (New York: Holt Rinehart, 1970; Notre Dame: Notre Dame University Press, 1985), p. 176.

6   Peter Ochs, "Compassionate Postmodernism: An Introduction to Rabbinic Semiotics," *Soundings* 76:1 (1993): 139–52.

7   Peter Pitzele, *Our Father's Wells: A Personal Encounter with the Myths of Genesis* (New York: Harper San Francisco, 1995), pp. 90–91.

8   Emmanuel Levinas, "The Temptation of Temptation," in *Nine Talmudic Readings by Emmanuel Levinas*, trans. Annette Aronowicz (Bloomington: Indiana University Press, 1990), p. 40.

9   Parker Palmer, *To Know As We Are Known: Education as a Spiritual Journey* (San Francisco: Harper San Francisco, 1983), 67–68.

10   Ibid., p. 31.

11   Levinas, "Temptation of Temptation," pp. 46–48.

12   For further elaboration, see my essay "Emunah: the Craft of Faith," *Crosscurrents: Religion and Intellectual Life* 42:3 (1992): 293–313.

13   Arthur Green, "A Hasidic Master Reads the Bible: The Sefat Emet as a Radical Interpreter," Lecture for the Washington Foundation for Jewish Studies, (Washington, D.C., *Bible Heritage Series*, 15 February 1996).

14   Edith Wyschogrod, "Hasidism, Hellenism, Holocaust: A Postmodern View," in *Interpreting Judaism in a Postmodern Age*, ed. Steven Kepnes (New York: New York University Press, 1996), pp. 301, 318.

15   Nachman of Bratslav, *Likkutei Moharan* (Jerusalem: Agudat Meshek Ha-Nahal, 1959), no. 64 on "Bo 'El Par'oh."

4

LEARNING AS A ROAD TO FAITH

W. Gunther Plaut

Jews in the Diaspora have the same "faith" problems as other members of Western society, ranging from avowed secularism to religious fundamentalism. The majority of educated Jews say that they "believe in God," but they are de facto secularists and treat religion as a marginal enterprise. One of the reasons is that the Holocaust has cast doubt on the image of a just and compassionate God; another is the rise of a self-affirming religion of scientism,[1] which proclaims that science has the ultimate answers to everything. Yet, science and religion need not be at odds; the synagogue has never experienced the conflict that continues to harass Christian churches.

At this point in the late twentieth century, churches and synagogues are no longer the central institutions of the community they once were. Synagogues now serve a new and limited function. They are "service stations" one visits when life cycle occasions demand it or make it desirable.

And yet, Jewish continuity is not possible without faith in God. How can we recover such faith? With religion in significant cultural disfavor, there is—for Jews at least—another way to recover the treasures of Judaism. It lies in study as a gateway to faith. תלמוד תורה כנגד כולם "studying Torah is worth as much as anything," says a central Jewish tradition.[2] Faith and the performance of all other *mitzvot* (commandments) are considered to be the likely consequences of study, which is therefore at the head of the list of commandments. With Jews increasingly being raised in a secular mode, undirected learning may lead to disbelief rather than belief, an affirmation of scientism rather than Judaism. But it is a risk worth taking, and indications are that the odds are favorable. Will study ever lead to commitment? Perhaps not, or not always. But learned Jews are likely to assure us continuity and perhaps open the door to *mitzvot*. The interactive possibilities of the Internet will put the student in contact with others who search, and that itself is a promising scenario.

The title of this section speaks of "faith and religion." I take "faith" to be the personal and "religion" the communal, as well as the organized expression of faith. A community of individual believers may or may not have the same religion, but as Jews we belong to the same overall structure of expressing our convictions. The individual Jew, to use Hillel's warning, must not act alone, for himself/herself. The separation of too many Jews from the community was disastrous in Hillel's time and it still is—and I believe that those who envisaged this book have combined the two, personal faith and communal religion.

Both are to function in our "secular" age. Unlike others, such as Susan Handelman in the preceeding essay, I am not quite sure what, in the framework of this book, "secular" means when put in quotation marks, though I surmise that it aims to call our attention not to the strict dictionary use of the word, but rather to serve as a circumlocution for Western society and its values. Most people in the rest of the world, especially in Asia and Africa, make faith the guiding light of everyday life, and many pursue it with enormous vigor and an urge to share it with unbelievers. But such religious fervor is generally absent from Jewish society. There are notable exceptions, of course, particularly in the United States and Israel.

Therefore, I shall address myself to the subject as I understand it: What can we say about God and the conveyance of belief to our increasingly university-trained Jewish people? The old method of the *cheder melamed* (the teacher in traditional Jewish elementary schools) no longer works. We cannot simply say, "Don't ask questions!" People will question—or worse, will have already come to the conclusion that the answer is "no" and therefore find no need to question at all.

I begin with a discussion of "religion," leaving the more difficult matter of "faith" for the end. The word "religion" comes from two Latin parts: *re*, again, and *ligare*, to tie or bind. Though "religion" was an old term with the literati, it came into common use as a reaction to the French Revolution. The latter allowed people the free personal expression of opposition to the Church and culminated in the raising up of a goddess of reason, whose image was paraded through the streets of Paris as the herald of a new age. In contrast, religion was seen as binding people to divine authority and, by definition, preaching unreasonable limits and constraints.

The Hebrew term for religion is *"dat"* which traces its roots to the Persian and thence to an Indo-European term that means "making someone do something." In Hebrew, *dat* has come to mean both law and religion, leaving no room in the language for "religious" as a spiritual expression, a meaning current in Western culture. *Dat* is perceived as being an aspect of "law," and thus in Judaism, *halakhah* or Jewish law has stood alone at the centre of the religious enterprise.

Such notions present no problem to most Orthodox groups. But they present a formidable terminological barrier for others, who object to removing religion from the realm of the spiritual and locating it in cultic practice as a legal and communal anchor. Though the majority of Israelis are to a large extent non-observant or even avowedly atheistic and secular in the philosophic sense, the national environment bespeaks *halakhah* and binds them, if not to God, then to the rules of a state that marks out significant areas for public observance and rule.

Jewish living in the Diaspora is fundamentally different. While the traditional Jewish environment begins with community and ends with the individual, Western society and its Jewry begin with the individual and only then focus on the common weal. Most Westerners do not consider themselves subject to *dat* in the original sense, "to make someone do something." They subscribe to the principle that "you can't make me do anything," and whatever I do, I do out of personal desire, not because it is "law." Hence, Church and State are essentially separate realms, even in countries other than the United States, where the doctrine of separation has been ensconced by long practice and Supreme Court interpretations of the Constitution.

For Westerners, religion is thus not public but private and voluntary. To be sure, a majority of Jews and non-Jews alike will assert that they "believe in God," but just precisely what this means is quite unclear. For a Jew, it should not be enough to have merely a *framework of belief*—in fact, belief in God is nowhere defined or specifically required in the Hebrew Bible, which contains no articles of faith or dogmas in the sense that Christianity and Islam came to feature them. Judaism has essentially been a system of *mitzvot* that were to be observed, rather than a theological affirmation of faith, which came later, in medieval days.

That fact is worth some closer examination. The biblical word that approaches the sense of "belief" is להאמין (*leha'amin*), which is best rendered as "to trust." Torah expects us indeed to *trust* God, but *belief* as a theological/philosophical concept is absent. Belief is positing a mental perception, such as "I believe it is raining outside," or "I believe the earth is round," or "I believe that there is a God." Genesis begins the tale of creation not with an assertion that there is a Creator; it assumes that as a given. The Hebrew *leha'amin* simply posits the existence of God. It asks us to trust the Ineffable One to abide by the Covenant and to be just and merciful. The oft cited prophetic pronouncement, אם לא תאמינו כי לא תאמנו (*'im lo' ta'minu ki lo' te'amenu*)[3] does not mean (as is often claimed), "If you don't believe [in God] you will not be established," but "If you do not trust [God] you [too] will not be trusted." The Torah reports that at first the enslaved Israelites were inclined to trust God's promise,[4] but when Pharaoh oppressed them even more severely, they no longer listened to Moses, מקוצר רוח ומעבודה קשה (*miqotzer ruah ume 'avodah qashah*), "because of depression and hard work."[5]   Later, when freedom had come to the children of Israel and they displayed their lack of trust in God's steadfastness and wanted to turn back to Egypt rather than go forward to the Promised Land, they were condemned to die in the desert.   God is in fact called אל אמונה (*'el 'emunah*),[6] a God who can be trusted.

The Ten Commandments begin by stating "I am the Eternal your God, who brought you out of the land of Egypt, out of the house of bondage." We are not asked to *believe* that there is Someone who says, "I am." Rather, we are asked to *remember* what God has done for us, and that the rules subsequently laid down are part of the covenantal trust relationship and therefore eternally binding.   Thus, neither Torah nor tradition commands us to *believe* in the sense we use that term today but only to remember what God has done and who we are, and go on from there by pursuing discrete ways *to do or not to do*. This means that Judaism is not a philosophical system; rather, it is *halakhah*, a path of life based on *mitzvot*. Acceptance of this fundamental structure of the Divine/human relationship distinguishes religious Jews—of whatever shade or denomination—from secularists. The latter do not assent to Judaism's a priori assumption, namely the existence of a God who makes demands on us; theirs is indeed a matter of disbelief in Judaism's *conditio sine qua non*.

The society in which we live makes any belief a strictly private matter with which the state is not concerned.   Thereby religion has been relegated more and more to the margins of life.   Religious expressions and constraints are notable by their absence.   The family structure is deteriorating, and marriage has become an option rather than the rule.   Anyone familiar with the Internet is aware that unfettered behavioral patterns are common and, in turn, have spawned problematic attempts to introduce censorship.

What precisely has brought all this about?   Why has secularism moved to the center and driven religion from its stronghold to the periphery?   The answer is not difficult to find.   Western society has adopted a new *emunah*, and, going back to the days of the Goddess of Reason, has replaced the old God with the god of science.   It is not religion in the sense of binding us to anything, and certainly not *dat*. Rather, it is the religion of scientism—to be distinguished from science—that distorts our understanding of the word religion, which in this view becomes an oxymoron.

Science is the pursuit of understanding the external world and its functioning, from the stars that are billions of light years away from us to the subatomic particles at the center of material existence. It posits the uniformity of natural law and tests this law in a thousand ways. It is never satisfied with the results of its quests, for even when success crowns a particular search, the scientist knows that much more still needs to be explored and that a full understanding of the universe may, in fact, forever elude us. Still, scientific inquiry will press on, for the desire to know is built into the very psyche of the human species, a quest to which the metaphor of the Torah's Tree of Knowing Everything gives vivid testimony.[7] Adam and Eve were punished for not obeying God's prohibition, but the desire to know survived their expulsion from Eden. The Torah and Jewish tradition generally are not opposed to the pursuit of knowledge, and therefore science did not become the enemy that Christian churches considered it for a long time, especially when it tested the frontiers of accepted notions of cosmic functioning and human origins.

But when science denies the reality of the religious realm because the latter is not subject to verification by scientific tools, it arrogates to itself the definition of universal truth and becomes a substitute for religion. Scientism, as distinct from science, itself becomes a religion. The first Russian cosmonaut, when returning from his historic journey, was asked what he had seen out there. His answer included his famous observation that nowhere had he seen God. To him, the boldest experiment of the human race showed that God was a fiction and religion the pursuit of an illusion.

Much of Western society is distinguished by that very fact. When it comes to religion, it adopts a position that can be expressed by an oxymoron—it believes in non-belief, and the substance of non-belief is the human enterprise we call "science." Many, if not most, take it for granted that all problems have a solution and that science represents the key to it. While halakhah is founded on God and the practices of the Jewish people, scientism is founded solely on the capacity of the human species. God becomes at best the One who has endowed us with reason and given us the tools of science, but who thereafter retreated into the nebulous spheres of dusky, old-fashioned synagogues, churches, and mosques.

In sum, the society in which we live is secular at its roots, and to a significant degree that is true even for those who affiliate with religious institutions and claim belief in God. It is not an operative God in whom most people believe. For most people, God is little more than a concept to which one resorts in moments of crisis, but is not an integral part of one's way of life.

Jews have joined this parade. They have literally adopted the saying of the Psalmist, "The heavens are the heavens of the Eternal, while the earth has been given over to human beings."[8] The majority deny God, not by words they utter, but by what they believe deep down and by what they do and fail to do.

The picture I have painted is not exaggerated. Church steeples may rise high into the air and synagogues may be magnificent structures, but high-rise buildings dwarf and overshadow them. The religious enterprise was once visibly central, and in the Jewish community it commanded near-universal respect. Today, it has moved (or rather, been moved) to the margin of society and is so perceived by most people, including Jews. I have spent my life amongst ordinary Jews (and a few extraordinary ones). Because they consider rabbis as the representatives of the religion they profess but don't observe, they treat them as persons who are different, slightly mysterious, and essentially marginal to their lives. After all, they reason, rabbis don't know the real world. People believe, and not infrequently admit, that Judaism has little to do with their daily existence. Make no mistake, this belief is shared also by some who proclaim themselves to be Orthodox.

Only those who have grown up or live in a totally isolated environment away from universities, newspapers, radio, and television still believe in an operative God who governs every aspect of their lives by divine will and fiat and to whom Jews owe unswerving fealty. Most others who confess to some belief are vague about what it means. For the majority, science with its great promise has become the new god that will lead them out of insecurity, poverty, and war into the Promised Land of stability and affluence. The problem Jews in the Diaspora face is not primarily mixed marriage but the absence of a meaningful belief in a living God.

This leads me to emphasize that, before we can begin to think of Jewish continuity, we must acknowledge a fact of Jewish life. Since religion and modern society are out of sync, Jews who believe in God live at the margin of society—and therein lies a basic challenge: *We must be aware that we are at the margin and convert this knowledge into a springboard of significance.* What is required of us is not to endorse our current values but to criticize them. Religion must be counter-cultural and insist that its main goal is to shake our society's absolute belief in the validity of scientism and reintroduce to it the power of faith.

That task is difficult, for scientism is easily mistaken for science. It makes no specific claims, and—unlike most religious orthodoxies—does not even assert that it has possession of the truth. Rather, it takes for granted that it has the *capacity* to know everything. This is precisely what distinguishes it from science itself, yet that distinction is well hidden. Outside of positivist philosophical schools, humanistic congregations, and atheistic organizations, scientism has produced neither a hierarchy nor a statement of beliefs. It is a non-verbalized faith, an interpretation of the nature of science, its goals, and potential. Because science has accomplished so much, people believe that it has unlimited possibilities, and that belief accords divine powers to human capacity. It also suggests that, since religion and faith cannot be brought under the microscope of science, they lack ultimate substance.[9] In this view, if science and religion are in conflict, people are likely to choose science and neglect the possibilities of faith.[10]

Added thereto is the shadow that the remembrance of the Holocaust has cast across the arc of Jewish belief. The question of a good and merciful God who guides and protects the Chosen People has been shaken to its roots. Traditional Judaism taught regarding past disasters (like the destruction of the Temple) and some circles continue to aver regarding the Holocaust (and other contemporary murders), that these events happened because of Jewish sin? The great majority of our people either abandon God because of this notion or reject that conclusion.

Battling the erosion of faith is a formidable task for any religion and especially for us. The struggle requires the revival of convictions that have been relegated to the periphery of public and private consciousness.

The synagogue as we know it is, I am afraid, not ready to serve as the vehicle for this revival, a revival that will take one form in Israel and another in the Diaspora. Here in the Diaspora, the synagogue is increasingly becoming a life-cycle service station. You can use it when you need it or want it for special occasions, and you visit it on a few days during the year. You pay your dues, which amounts to little more than making sure that the service station is there when you drive in. The religious service to which people go on *yom tov* or when they attend a "bar mitzvah service" as invited guests, is endured as irrelevant, incomprehensible, and unconnected to what the visitors know or believe. On Shabbat after Shabbat in many, if not most, North American synagogues, one can observe a dreary phenomenon: young people who have been invited to the bar/bat mitzvah of a friend leave the shul the moment the star performer has done his or her bit. They came for a show, and when the show is over, there is no reason to stay. The performers are forced to remain behind, but the audience can do as it pleases.

Are those who are traditional and practice *mitzvot* really different? Do they point the way to our salvation? I do not know what is in their hearts and minds and how they really feel about their relationship to God. I *do* know that among those who go to traditional synagogues and are willing to talk frankly and openly, the habit of compliance with *halakhah* has not eradicated their deep-seated doubts about the way God impacts on our lives. The Holocaust remains a formidable question-mark, even if they have managed to overcome the spurious perceptions of scientism.

There is another obstacle to overcome. The decline of the traditional simple faith relates to what we know of the universe. That universe is vast beyond imagination—something which does not in itself conflict with belief in a Creator. It is so vast that the earth on which we live appears infinitesimally small, but our Jewish tradition holds that on this speck of cosmic dust, there exists one tiny group among billions of humans whom the Creator of the universe has chosen, one tiny portion to represent the Divine on earth. It *is* difficult to believe.

More than that, it is difficult today for most people to maintain an old-fashioned faith in a God whose will is expressed in the minutiae of the *halakhah*. It is hard for the average Jew to appreciate why, when it comes to food, any seal of *kashrut* is not sufficient, and some demand *glatt* kosher; and the latest expression of this super-religiosity is the claim that even *glatt* kosher cannot possibly satisfy the true believer. I listen to the language of those who have embraced such views and am disturbed when I hear such believers, young and old, declare with assurance that "Hashem wants it this way." Strict observance has taken the place of rational belief, and attention to all elements of *halakhah* is equated with elementary ethics. I do not doubt that those who subscribe to such beliefs and practices will be Jews tomorrow—and most likely their children as well—but whether this continuity will extend to their grandchildren is not at all assured. Certainty that permits no doubt and practice that is inflexible have in the course of human history always yielded to the onslaught of change.

There is an undeniable flight of many people into the arms of an unquestioning faith, whose fundamental principle is a certainty that keeps believers from evaluating any of its major assumptions. But Judaism, at its best, has never been fundamentalist. The very fact that belief in God is never detailed in the Torah should serve as a warning. Yet I find that today among fundamentalists, any disagreement with the putative past is impossible. Maimonides and Rashi would be shocked to learn that it is rarely or ever permissible to disagree with their remarks or rulings, since they are now considered to be unchangeable expressions of God's will.

What we thus confront are two Jewish factions that do not communicate with each other, nor do they know each other. The one forswears traditional belief and frequently, though not always, discards traditional practice; the other forswears the doubts of modernity and demands unquestioning adherence to the details of tradition. The result of this confrontation is increasing intolerance on both sides. On the religious front, it has resulted in the isolation of the fundamentalist element in our society, which, in turn, has altered the once participatory stance of mainstream Orthodoxy. Where formerly there was mutual acceptance, there is now a rejection of pluralism, a stance that, in Israel, is enforced by making religion an arm of the State.

What is at play here is the confrontation between ideology and pragmatism. When Orthodoxy was relatively weak, participation with non-Orthodox elements in communal affairs was advantageous and even necessary, and this participation extended to religious organizations like the (now defunct) Synagogue Council of America. In my earlier days in Chicago, the Twin Cities, and Toronto, I co-officiated with Orthodox colleagues at weddings or other life-cycle events. In smaller North American towns, this may still be possible; in the larger centers, Orthodox rabbis will now do what Australian, South African, and British rabbis have done all along: they will not share a public platform with non-Orthodox rabbis. They fear that such an appearance might give the impression that other religious expressions have some validity. They will sit with gentile clergy, but not with me; gentiles are no threat to their integrity, but I am.

Yet, having said all of this and having conveyed my unhappiness over the development of our religious life on the left, middle and right sides of the spectrum, I adhere to my conviction that Jewish continuity without faith has limited prospects. But I also believe that a closed, fundamentalist system of belief will not be able to assure the continuance of any but the small segment of our people who subscribe to it. It may work better in Israel, at least for a while, but it will not work in the Diaspora.

Jewish humanism is a reality, but it will only go so far. Jewish culture can be but a temporary framework for our survival and can serve as a short-term holding pen for certain types of practice. But it will not be able, in the long run, to resist the pressures of the majority culture. Humanism can function as one of the building blocks of regeneration, if it helps us to strive for the ethical life in an unethical age. Our youth will subscribe to this ideal. Young people are idealists—let's give them a good and noble goal for which to strive.

But the sustaining foundation of our continuity will be neither humanism nor fundamentalism. It will be the kind of faith that accepts science as a partner, yet sees scientism as the enemy. It acknowledges the importance of rationalism, yet understands that "knowledge" is not limited to scientific measurement or subject to experiment. Faith is of a different dimension; it posits the existence of a Divinity that has endowed human beings with special capacities, but also with certain inherent limitations. The road to God is strewn with obstacles of doubt, and the rational mind must wrestle with them.

For two-and-a-half years, I lived under Hitler, and as an American soldier I opened the first concentration camp that the Allies came upon. I confess freely that my faith, which was simple, though never unquestioning, was severely tested in the process.[11] Over the years, my certainties have weakened but not my will to find my way as a believing Jew. I have come to the conclusion that, for the searcher, there is but one way to capture the deeper reality of our being, and that is through learning and studying the past *and* present, what has been said before *and* what is being said today, and using that learning as a stepping stone to commitment. I have dedicated a good deal of my life to the study of our sources and to the discussion of the kinds of issues raised in this volume, and that effort has been made easier by the increasing level of education found among North American Jews. On this level, our people are ready to discuss the possibilities of faith and to contemplate the cohabitation of science and religion. But I fear for the synagogue in its traditional form, because of its use as a "drive-through" for life-cycle events without dealing with what really ails us.

This issue has occupied me for many years. In 1975, I sketched out the kind of synagogue that I believed would meet the requirements of a new age. It would be a synagogue radically different in its ability to foster search, no longer confined to the walls of an edifice, but a living community reaching out to its members, going into their homes, into their places of work, in an outreach program of great spiritual and physical proportions. My ideal synagogue would no longer be merely a service station where members come when they need us, but a place where people obtain both respite and spiritual nurture. And those of us whose holy task it is to teach will aim at moulding Jews into synagogue members who affirm the worth and importance of Diaspora, yet love the people and the land of Israel without apology or excuse.

They will be members: who are willing and eager to study and in time will commit themselves to doing *mitzvot*, who will not shrink from calling themselves partners in a holy enterprise, and who will not flinch when they are called to piety; who are not above believing in a God who demands and therefore come forward and say: "Since I want to be a Jew, I must live like one; I must, because I want to, and I want to because I must"; who will take the risk of shaping their environment to the social and physical visions of Judaism, and who will understand that to be religious Jews means to be often opposed to the policies of governments and the tendencies of the society in which they live. Last but not least, they will be members who will find for themselves teachers who make them part of a common search for ways to reach the holy God of the Covenant.[12]

These are goals I now harbor with greater hope than when I first contemplated them, for, despite all the set-backs and roadblocks of the secular society, today's communications and learning present new possibilities. As we enter the twenty-first century, we can explore the possibilities of Judaism in the new electronic universe. We can foresee a cyber-synagogue that speaks to all who are willing to see or hear what message our religion has. There we will find the young, rather than the middle-aged and the grey heads. There we will encounter people who are willing to experiment and, dare one say it, really take a chance on God. At this point, we know too little about the possibilities of this new virtual reality, but I am convinced that traditional methods of communication will be fantastically amplified through the electronic medium. Its great advantage is its very existence. It is a challenge to the imagination, unfettered by the restrictive adage, "My grandfather didn't know about it, therefore it can't be good or worthwhile."

Torah and Talmud are already being taught at numerous web sites, and they produce interactive participation that face-to-face encounters in an actual class room rarely achieve. Pupils ask questions about history and *halakhah*, and not only does the teacher attempt an answer, but other students do so as well. The virtual class room has a reality of its own, and we are only at the beginning of its development. In the not too distant future, we will see each other studying, without anyone leaving his/her accustomed place; we will hear each other if we want to hear and be heard; we will record the encounter and participate in ways we cannot yet fully envisage. I anticipate that the desire to learn will be realized in a much more welcoming environment. CD-ROMs will facilitate the asking of the right questions, and the questions will produce ready answers. The process will stimulate both curiosity and the desire to learn more and more.

When Moses brought the news of impending liberation to the Jewish slaves in Egypt, he faced the instability of their trust in God. They could not grasp the enormity of what lay ahead, and their work load did not allow them the constancy of vision.[13] In a manner of speaking, we are in a similar situation, with one important difference: we *know* that vast changes are upon us, though we cannot envisage their extent to the fullest.

Above all, I believe that there is an irrepressible desire in the human heart for grasping the mantle of spirituality. As Jews we can begin to meet this desire by making study the new center of the Jewish enterprise. Our tradition earlier made study, *talmud Torah*, the apex of Jewish doing, because it was seen as leading to everything: to faith, to God and to all *mitzvot*.

That notion is worth a closer look. The basic passage appears in the *Mishnah:*[14]

> These are things for which no precise measure is prescribed [by the Torah]: *pe'ah,*[15] first fruits,[16] the offering for the festivals,[17] deeds of loving kindness, and the study of Torah. These are the things whose fruits one enjoys in this world, while the capital is saved for the world-to-come:[18] honouring father and mother, deeds of loving kindness, making peace between people; but the study of Torah surpasses [or is equal to] all of these.

Talmud Torah is given its unique position by the Talmud, because it leads to action.[19] Knowing what Torah asks of us will move us to do God's will and perform the *mitzvot* of tradition.[20]

The *halakhah* has further amplified this order of priorities and draws the consequences. It places the house of study above the house of prayer and rules that one may run from the synagogue to the study house, but not vice versa, and that one may use the proceeds of the sale of a synagogue in order to build a *beit hamidrash,* a learning center, but not vice versa.[21] According to this traditional view, the *mitzvah* of learning is the gateway to all other *mitzvot.*

In the history of humanity, the religion of scientism is very new and but a moment in the course of time. It, too, advocates study, but it limits study to exploring natural phenomena, as if all truth were to be found in them. We have not, as yet, assimilated scientism's deforming role and the consequent disbelief in God. We must frankly recognize that fact. I do not know whether I am right, and whether what I am trying to say will have any relevance tomorrow. But I make bold to suggest that it has relevance today. Our young people are leaving us in droves, though many take refuge in the arms of fundamentalism. Some of that fundamentalism is inherently Jewish, but most of it stems from the mindset of contemporary society. It is well to realize that scientism itself is a form of fundamentalism. It posits, as an unspoken premise, the non-reality of any force outside of its purview. In its perception, religious people engage in inherited superstitions. In my opinion, embracing the philosophy of non-faith is the road to the dissolution of the Jewish people. If they are to have a meaningful, liberated and liberating future they have to be reassured about *the relevance of faith, the reality of God and the importance of maintaining the Jewish people.*

Knowing that the yearning is there and knowing also that Judaism does have the potential of responding to this yearning, universities, like synagogues, must open their doors to sustained Jewish study. York University, the host for the symposium reflected in this book, now has a Centre for Jewish Studies, and its success is essential to our community. The synagogue is in a state of radical transformation, and it is study, and study alone, that has a realistic chance of assuring Jewish existence tomorrow. Such study is the springboard to the possibility of disbelief but also to the likelihood of belief and commitment. We must invest in that likelihood, and I suggest that we can persuade our youth that learning is a gateway to spiritual success. What shape the future will have, I do not know, but its essence may be an awareness of God. In many ways, the search is part of the finding. This, I believe, is the meaning of the prophetic injunction: דרשו יהוה בהמצאו קראהו בהיותו קרוב (*Dirshu YHVH behimatz'o, qera'uhu biyhoto qarov*, "*Seek God wherever He is, call Him when He is near*").[22]

Adults of all ages are our target; the infantilization of Judaism has proved to be a dead end. We will know that we are on the right way when our communal leadership is given to knowledgeable Jews rather than to the financially potent. Learning is an uncertain way, because we do not know where it takes us. But to me, it is the only way. Faith without critical examination will ultimately lead to the black holes of disillusionment or fundamentalism. The kind of learning that the university exemplifies and with which the synagogue can ally itself will spark new hope and foster the future of our people.

Notes

[1] The use of this term is entirely unrelated to either the Christian Science Church or the Church of Scientology. It describes the way many people think about the goal and potential of science.

[2] On the implications of this saying, see below. "Torah," literally "teaching," is here used in its wider sense of "Jewish learning"; its narrower meaning is "Pentateuch."

[3] Isaiah 7:9. The Hebrew root means to take care or support (in the Qal form); to be firm and reliable (in the Niphal); and to trust (in the Hiphil). The word *amen* represents usually an affirmation of what has been said; in many Psalms, the Vulgate translates it therefore as *fiat*. The Eternal is once called "God of Amen," which the King James version rendered as "God of Truth" (Isaiah 65:16) and the JPS translation as "true God," because the word *emet* (truth) is related to the same root. See also Israel Abrahams, "Belief," in *Encyclopedia Judaica* (Jerusalem: The Macmillan Company, 1971), vol. 4, cols. 429ff.

[4] Ex. 4:31.

[5] Ex. 6:9. "Depression" is the meaning of a similar Ugaritic idiom.

[6] Deut. 32:4.

7   Genesis 2:17 and thereafter in ch. 3. In the Hebrew it is literally called "The Tree of Knowing Good and Bad," a merism that means "everything." For comments see W. G. Plaut, ed. *The Torah: A Modern Commentary* (New York: UAHC Press, 1981), p. 30.

8   Psalms 115:16.

9   In this respect, it mirrors the assertions of positivism that conclusions must be supported by verifiable observations or they have no objective validity. Therefore, statements about God have no meaning. See K. R. Popper, *Conjectures and Refutations: the Growth of Scientific Knowledge* (New York: Basic Books, 1965), p. 39. This view, however, has been shaken by the present understanding that *all* knowledge is uncertain, and that the presumed conflict between science and religion can no longer be sustained as a given. See K. Wilber, *Eye to Eye: the Quest for a New Paradigm* (Boston: Shambhala, 1990), p. 44. See also E. Zerin, "Methods of Human Knowing," *Transactional Analysis Journal* 25:2 (1995): 150–55.

10 I have devoted a small book to the discussion of this presumed conflict: *Judaism and the Scientific Spirit*. New York: Union of American Hebrew Congregations, 1962. See especially pp. 66 ff.

11 I have written repeatedly about personal faith and its testing. See e.g., *The Case for the Chosen People* (Garden City, N.Y.: Doubleday, 1965); *Unfinished Business* (Toronto: Lester & Orpen Dennys, 1981); *More Unfinished Business* (Toronto: University of Toronto Press, 1997).

12 The lecture in which these thoughts were first developed in broad outline was published in the *Yearbook of the Central Conference of American Rabbis* 75 (1975): 172.

13 See above, note 5.

14 *Pe'ah* 1:1.

15 "Corner," referring to the four corners of the field that the farmer was not to cut, because they were to be left to the poor (Lev. 19:9 and 23:22). The Torah does not prescribe how large the corner is to be, but the Rabbis (in the following mishnah) ruled that the farmer had to determine the size of the *pe'ah* in accordance with the size of the field, the number of poor people in the community, and the yield of the harvest.

16 They are dedicated to God (Deut. 26:1 and following).

17 When the prescribed pilgrimages for Pesach, Shavuot and Sukkot were to be brought (Deut. 16:16–17).

18 Even though we enjoy the fruits of doing good in this world, that enjoyment does not diminish our reward in the world-to-come.

19 *Kiddushin* 40b.

20 The Talmud enumerates other examples that fit the description of the mishnaic passage. Thus, *Kiddushin* 39b adds hospitality to wayfarers; and *Shabbat* 127a further adds visiting the sick, intense prayer, maximum attendance at the house of

study, and judging one's neighbor fairly. The daily prayer book includes a combined list taken from various sources, to be recited every morning.

21 See *Megillah* 26b. See also *Shulhan 'Arukh, Yoreh De'ah* 246 and commentaries.

22 Isaiah 55:6 is traditionally rendered as "Seek the Eternal while [or where] He can be found; call upon Him while He is near." Rashi understands it as a challenge to seek God before judgment is rendered; *Metzudat David* interprets it as "while you are still in the land of Israel." My reading would understand it as "Seek the Eternal, [for] therein is the finding; call upon God as you come close."

PART
2

THE CENTRALITY OF
ISRAEL
IN THE JEWISH WORLD

5

ISRAEL AND THE DIASPORA: AN INTRODUCTION

Michael Brown

According to an ancient rabbinic tradition, the land of Israel—especially Jerusalem—is טבור הארץ, the center of the earth. Although this seems at first glance to be a strange notion, an observer of the contemporary media might think that it has gained wide currency. What the rabbis meant, of course, is not the newsworthiness of the Middle East but that the land of Israel has been central to Jewish identity from time immemorial. The book of Genesis relates that Abraham, the ancestor of the Jewish people, was commanded by God: "Leave your birthplace and set out for the land that I shall show you." And he and his family "set out for the land of Canaan" (Gen. 12:1, 12:5). From that point in hoary antiquity until Roman times—with a few interruptions—the land of Israel was the country of the people of Israel.

In the millennium following the loss of all vestiges of Jewish autonomy in the year 70 C.E., the land was gradually emptied of most of its Jewish inhabitants. Yet until modern times, it was universally regarded by Jews and non-Jews as the Jewish homeland, the place to which that landless people would return in God's good time. Beginning in the late eighteenth century, some Jews came to believe that the connection with the antique mother country had outlived its days, that Jews would never again wish to return there. And some non-Jews, especially in western Europe, charged that the connection to the Holy Land called into question Jews' loyalty to the states in which they then resided. At the same time, other Jews and non-Jews found an inspirational example in the new national movements and looked forward to the similar renewal of the land of Israel.

With the birth of Zionism in the late nineteenth century, the longstanding connection of the Jews to the Holy Land assumed a variety of new guises. One of these was exemplified by the essayist Asher Ginsberg, better known by his pen name, 'Ahad Ha'Am. 'Ahad Ha'Am looked forward to the spiritual, cultural, and linguistic renaissance of the Jewish people and to the creation of its new spiritual center in the land of Israel. That center, he believed, would become the heart of the nation, most of whose citizens would continue to live in the Diaspora. Theodor Herzl, the founder of the World Zionist Organization, had a different vision. Although he also foresaw a Jewish cultural revival in the old homeland, he expected the land to become once again the demographic and political center of the Jewish world. Herzl was convinced that Zionism would enable the masses of Jews who lived in countries where they were unwanted—especially eastern Europe—to return to the birthplace of their people, to rebuild their lives, and to renew the Jewish polity.

Over time and in the light of events that altered the Jewish world dramatically—the emergence of Diaspora communities in the New World, the Bolshevik Revolution, the Holocaust, the rise of Arab nationalism—opposition to Zionism was relegated to the lunatic fringe of most Jewish communities. And in the Western world, at least, most non-Jews came to believe in the right of the Jews to their own state. At the same time, the advocates of the competing visions of 'Ahad Ha'Am and Herzl learned to live together. Zionism assimilated both approaches to the Jewish future; the state-in-the-making took on the twin tasks of ingathering the exiles and reinvigorating the cultural and spiritual life of the nation.

In the post-1948 years, the centrality of the land of Israel and the state in Jewish life became the most widely accepted article of faith both in Israel and in the Diaspora. According to some observers, it was now the only value common to Jews of differing shades of belief and political opinion. Increasingly in these years, assimilating Diaspora Jews came to see Israel as a surrogate for their own Jewishness. For many, giving money to Israeli institutions and offering political support became substitutes for personal involvement in Jewish communal or religious life at home. Visits to Israel took on the aspect of pilgrimages promising instant conversion or at least a booster shot of faith and ethnicity. Israelis—at least Israeli officialdom—have been loath to reject proxy Jewishness. It reflected their own belief that they were creating a new Jewish life and society for the entire people; it provided a sense of purpose to sustain them in the face of physical danger and economic hardship; and it served the purpose of securing the needed support of Diaspora Jewry for the embattled, fragile state.

Over time, acting as the secular and religious "priests" of the whole people of Israel, to paraphrase the Bible's term, has, however, proved to be an increasingly difficult and often burdensome task for a nation most of whose citizens are dedicated, as might be expected, to the everyday, "normal" pursuits that occupy the people of other societies. And as they become a "normal" people, many Israelis find themselves alienated from Jewish tradition and theology, the very things which they have in common with Diaspora Jews. Most members of the Israeli cultural elite now respond chiefly to the needs of the society in which they live; many of their concerns tend to appear irrelevant to Jews abroad. At the same time, Jews in most Diaspora countries now feel secure in their places of residence and no longer look towards Israel as a potential haven of safety. They are intermarrying and assimilating in unprecedented numbers and also becoming alienated from Jewish tradition and theology. These developments seem to many observers to herald the post-Zionist phase of Jewish history, when the visions of both 'Ahad Ha'Am and Theodor Herzl will be outdated and inapplicable.

In the two essays that follow, Hillel Halkin and Aviezer Ravitzky explore aspects of these trends. Halkin is concerned chiefly with the rift between Diaspora and Israeli Jews over the question of the centrality of Israel in Jewish life. It is, he suggests in his controversial remarks, an inevitable and not altogether regrettable rift. Ravitzky looks at the other side of the coin. He discusses the debate in Israel over the centrality of Judaism and Jewishness in Israeli life, perhaps the central question if the country is ever to become the spiritual and cultural center of the Jewish people.

6

RELIGIOUS AND SECULAR JEWS IN ISRAEL: A CULTURAL WAR?

Aviezer Ravitzky

In recent years, Israeli society has been driven by the tensions in the relationship between religion and state, between the sacred and the profane, between halakhic ruling and individual liberty, and between particularism and universalism. According to widely held public opinion, these tensions reflect a definite tendency toward cultural fragmentation and may undermine the nation's collective identity. That tendency, it is said, threatens to rip apart the foundation of the classic Zionist synthesis and the Israeli ethos derived from it. Have the basic values and consensus that once provided the foundation for Israeli society given way to a postmodern, post-Zionist disintegration? In this essay, I shall outline a somewhat different way of looking at these very same developments and attempt to show that the current confrontation between religious and secular Israelis does not necessarily represent a process of alienation and disintegration. Rather, it can be seen as an expression of social liberation and cultural plurality.

The political and social status quo that has governed relations between the secular and religious communities, I shall argue, was the product of a mistaken assumption—shared on both sides of the aisle—that its rival was bound to shrivel and maybe even disappear. The current confrontation is in part a function of a new recognition by the contending groups that their rival represents an enduring and vital reality which will continue to reproduce and flourish. Second, the current struggle reflects dissatisfaction with the dominant and monolithic model, long considered to represent the "authentic" Israeli. And it is thanks to this challenge that previously marginalized groups (Sephardim, the religious, Revisionists) have been able to gravitate towards the center of society. Third, the many controversies swirling around the question of religion and state stem from the fact that Zionism's historical foes—the Ultra-Orthodox on one side and the Reform on the other—have been integrated into the fold. They, too, are deeply involved in the debate regarding the image of the Zionist state and argue bitterly for the state to endorse their respective conceptions of Jewish identity. As a result, the State of Israel no longer reflects the victory of a particular (nationalist) Jewish faction, but has become a broad and decisive forum, where the struggle for the Jewish future is played out. And that struggle has consequences, not only for the Jews of Israel, but for Jews everywhere.

All this is not to deny that amidst all the rumblings there lurks a real danger of disintegration. In fact, it is my intention to depict the roots of this social conflict in all their fierceness. Nevertheless, it is my belief that these developments are creating new focal points of collective identity and are granting a substantive "home" to formerly neglected groups. They contain within them the potential seeds of a multi-faceted society, which represents more accurately the complexities of the contemporary Jewish experience.

CONTENDING PREDICTIONS

In 1949, about a year after the State of Israel was established, Arthur Koestler published *Promise and Fulfillment: Palestine 1917–1949*. There Koestler analyzed the historical developments that had led to the creation of the state, depicted Israeli ways of life and experiences, and attempted to predict what the future held in store for the new society taking shape in the Jewish state. While conceding that it was difficult to foresee at such an early juncture the direction of the new Hebrew civilization, he believed that one thing was "fairly clear: within a generation or two Israel will have become an essentially 'un-Jewish' country."[1] Koestler thought that, already, youths born in Israel showed definite signs of becoming a breed apart from their cousins in the Diaspora, "and with each generation this contrast was bound to increase." In due time, Koestler was convinced, a Hebrew identity and culture would emerge that would be altogether foreign to the Jewish experience.[2]

But what of the prediction uttered some thirty years earlier by the famed American sociologist, Thorstein Veblen, regarding the likely destiny of the hypothetical Jewish community that the Zionists proposed to establish in Palestine? In the event that the Zionists managed somehow to realize their hopes of returning the Jews to their ancient homeland, it was Veblen's contention that the ingathered people would withdraw into themselves and concentrate exclusively on their own particular heritage—on "studies of a Talmudic nature." Integration with modern European culture would cease, and the special circumstances which had enabled the leading lights among the Jewish nation to turn outwards, and to make seminal contributions to Western science and culture would no longer exist.[3]

The subject of these conflicting predictions is, of course, Jews living in modern-day Israel. In Koestler's opinion, they were not supposed to be Jews at all. In contrast, Veblen believed that they would be "too" Jewish—Jews untouched by world culture. Koestler imagined them interested only in the present and future, whereas Veblen presumed they would be preoccupied with things past.

Which of the two, if either, had it right? How we answer that question depends on which Israeli social circle, cultural group, or ideological camp we examine. At one end of the social spectrum, several segments of the population seem to be rapidly approaching the fulfillment of Koestler's prophecy, that is, complete alienation from the Jewish historical consciousness. And this does not mean merely the absence of religious belief or ritual observance. The change is one that reaches to the very marrow of their cultural identity and collective memory. Meanwhile, at the other pole of Israeli society, a definite segment of the population is endeavoring with all its might to fulfill Veblen's diametrically opposite prophecy. These people aim to effect a complete break with everything external, Western, universal, modern—a list which includes Zionism and its role as the initiator of a modern, nationalist revolution among the Jewish people.[4]

Let me illustrate the point with an anecdote. A few years ago, around Passover time, the daily newspaper, *Yediot Aharonot*, published an interesting interview with a matzah baker from Tel Aviv. In the article, the man stated that each year the volume of sales tallied by him and his fellow bakers across the country consistently registered a two percent drop. His explanation for the trend is revealing. Non-observant young couples who discontinued their parents' practice of eating matzah during Passover—something that was done, not so much out of religious obligation, but as an expression of cultural and national identity—accounted, he thought, for half the decline. Responsibility for the other half lay with young religious couples, who had grown up in households where regular matzah was deemed acceptable, but who now insisted on consuming hand-baked, *shmurah* matzah throughout the holiday. Thus, he concluded, the poor bakers get pinched on one side and squeezed on the other.

Regardless of whether the baker's analysis stands up to rigorous statistical standards, it contains insight into the cultural dynamic at work in Israel today. This dynamic, interestingly, placed professors of Judaic Studies at Israeli universities in the same boat as matzah bakers, at least until recently. For more than a decade, student interest in subjects such as Bible, Talmud,

Jewish philosophy, Jewish history, and Hebrew literature was on the wane. While the trend seems to have been arrested as of late, it did reflect a process analogous to that perceived by the matzah baker.[5] Twenty or thirty years ago, a sizable number of secular students sought to learn about the history of their nation, its creativity, and thoughts. The next generation of secular students appeared, however, to be much less interested in classical Jewish sources and texts. (It sometimes seems as if a kind of fear arises in this group, lest the classical Jewish sources be used to deny them their spiritual and political liberty.) At the other end of the spectrum, many religious youths, who had formerly sought to learn about classical Jewish texts in an academic setting, turned away from the university and devoted themselves exclusively to yeshiva studies. Whichever way you turned, therefore, there were fewer students to be found.

This polarization, to be sure, is nothing new. It figures into the Israeli experience from the very beginning. What is different about the situation today is that the split which was formerly manifested on the margins of society is threatening to move into the center and to set the contemporary social and political agenda. And as this demarginalization progresses, it appears that the old public arrangements and agreements between secular and religious Jews are beginning to lose both effectiveness and acceptance among members of both communities.

Should this surprise us? In my opinion, no, and, in due course, I shall attempt to analyze some of the factors involved in this trend. Before doing that, however, I should like to call attention to the internal tensions that characterize the Israeli experience, or should I say, the inherent duality at the core of the Zionist idea and project. To my mind, the polarization process reflects, in large measure, the unwillingness of large segments of the Israeli population to continue to endure this tension; they are striving, I would argue, both covertly and openly, to establish a definite verdict on the long-standing conflict between past and present, between normality and uniqueness, between living in a homeland and living in a Holyland.

FLEEING CONTRADICTIONS

Zionism incorporated many of the attributes that characterize a revolutionary movement. It also contained many features typical of a renaissance movement. And in both of its aspects, the revolutionary and the revivalistic, it revealed radical tendencies.

Zionism set out to effect a sweeping reform, more far-reaching and comprehensive than those attempted by other modern revolutions.[6] Consider, for example, the French Revolution, or even the Bolshevik Revolution. To whom did the insurrectionists appeal, and what changes did they try to bring about? They addressed members of existing nations, who spoke established tongues, and who lived within defined territorial and cultural boundaries. As revolutionaries, they aimed to transform certain aspects of the social reality, such as the political or the economic system. On occasion, these changes were even depicted as leading to salvation. But whatever the program was, it was contained within the bounds of an existing territorial and historical framework. It did not extend to every imaginable sphere of existence. In the case of the Zionist movement, however, it was necessary to generate a far-reaching, almost total revolution. The sons and daughters of the Jewish people had to be transported from their countries of residence, relearn the language of their conversation, adopt new modes of life, and take on new professions. Zionism had to wage its battle on all fronts: the social, the cultural, the political, the legal, and the economic. And the movement operated within a historical context which offered very little continuity with which to work. In the political arena, for example, not only did the Zionists, like other revolutionaries, have to reform a political system and turn out a foreign power. They had to create a new political entity "out of nothing," after nineteen hundred years of the absence of Jewish sovereignty.

In addition to seeking an almost total transformation of the conditions of Jewish life, the main Zionist groups advocated a radical departure from traditional religious practice and belief.[7] And yet, at the very same time, Zionism was a renaissance movement which aspired to restore a bygone reality. Whereas other modern revolutions forged a future-oriented mythos and a forward-looking ethos with symbols suggestive of a better tomorrow, Zionism drew its symbols primarily from the past. While not entirely free of Utopian visions, the main building blocks of Zionism's radical myths and ethos were materials that had been preserved in the historical and collective memory: antique landscapes, old proverbs, kings, heroes, and prophets. Like a boomerang describing a circle, the movement burst forth in quest of a radical revolution, while turning its face towards ancient memories and images.

Admittedly, Zionism was not very different in this from some other nationalist movements which followed a similar trajectory and which utilized historical memory and traditional symbols to build the national awareness and the collective consciousness. Even the use of religious symbols is not unique to Zionism; it can be found in the Polish, Irish, and Czech national movements and, for that matter, in most related movements in Europe.[8] But just as the revolutionary elements of the Zionist movement extend further than those of other revolutions, its retrospective gaze towards revival penetrates deeper and demands more.

This was all to be expected. Unlike other revival movements, Zionism is the product of a nation whose ethnic and religious identities were for countless generations fused into a single whole. The Jewish religion is particular to one nation, and in the present era (as opposed to the messianic one), this religion does not pursue a universal constituency but focuses its messages and meanings in a specific nation, its "Chosen People." Similarly, throughout its history the Jewish people has seldom operated within anything other than a religious context: its memories have, for the most part, been filtered through the prism of classical Jewish texts. Its collective national identity and its religious identity were essentially interchangeable. ("Your people are my people, your God is my God";[9] "I am a Hebrew, and I revere God, the Lord in Heaven."[10]) Its laws, culture, language, politics and social norms were rooted in a joint religious and ethnic heritage.[11] Any attempt to resurrect symbols from the nation's past will perforce disinter certain religious claims. For it is the nature of the religious consciousness to see the past not only as the source of history and existence, but as a source of obligation. It is a spring from which, in addition to memories, beliefs and commandments flow.

Consider the dualistic nature of Israel as a *home*land and as a *Holy*land. Whereas the birthplace and the home bring to mind a sense of intimacy, comfort, and naturalness, providing protection and shelter to its children, the Holy conjures up feelings of reverence and transcendence, awe and fear. The homeland is a distinctly national category; the Holyland a distinctly religious one. Birth is an existential term, while Holiness is metaphysical and laden with demand. Throughout Jewish history, the two have always gone hand-in-hand—with all the internal tension inherent in the coupling.[12] When Zionism reawakened the desire for a concrete homeland, it also aroused from its slumber the yearning for the Holyland. And the latter is now risen and staking its claim.

This dualistic intertwining of nationhood and religion expresses itself in any number of ways: in the relationship between modern Hebrew and the holy tongue,[13] between Herzl's State of the Jews and the classic visions of redemption, or even in the contrast between Tel-Aviv and its life and Jerusalem and its symbols.[14] It is no wonder, then, that a number of Israelis are attempting to escape this immanent strain; they wish for a hard and fast resolution of the contrasts and are no longer prepared—on either side of the aisle—to live with the cultural duality. Paradoxically, the more extreme elements on both sides of this question seem to have reached a kind of hidden understanding. The ultra-orthodox and the ultra-secularist despise the contradiction and are surging towards a decisive and unequivocal resolution of the debate between past and present. Each in his own way reviles the ongoing clash between life in the homeland and life in the Holyland.[15]

NORMALIZATION

The dualistic tension in question is not simply the result of conflict between sacred and profane or between the religious and the national spheres. It is woven into modern Zionism's fabric, and built into the national revolution itself. One of the most central themes of Zionist rhetoric was the "normalization" of the Jewish people.[16] To wit: a normal people should reside in its own land, speak its own language, control its own destiny, be free of political subservience and establish for itself a healthy social order. So all the nationalist movements preached. But what kind of a process did the Jewish people have to go through in order to attain such normality? A singular and "abnormal" process, apparently without precedents in world history.

A short illustration from the annals of academic history will, I think, help to illustrate my point. In 1911, the great linguist, Theodor Noeldeke, published a survey of ancient Semitic languages in the *Encyclopedia Britannica*. There were sections in the article about Akkadian, Canaanite, Phoenician, and the like, and next to them, a special examination of the Hebrew language and its history from Bible times onward. As the modern Zionist movement was just then beginning to grow, the author saw fit to comment on the call of contemporary Zionists to revive the Hebrew language as the everyday spoken tongue of the Jewish people. "The dream," wrote Noeldeke, "of some Zionists that Hebrew—a would-be Hebrew,[17] that is to say—will again become a living, popular language in Palestine, has still less prospect of realization than their vision of a restored Jewish empire in the Holy Land."[18] An objective scholar, without any particular biases, Noeldeke deemed the attempt to revive Hebrew and to establish a political entity in Palestine far-fetched, even fantastic. The historical record, of course, has shown him to be mistaken in his assessment. Is it fair, however, to accuse him of error or poor judgment? One may argue, to be sure, that scholars have no business making predictions of this sort. If, however, they decide to go ahead and speculate anyway, they must do their best to evaluate possibilities rationally and to anticipate developments using existing precedents and historical analogies. Neoldeke could find no precedent for the rebirth of a sacred tongue as an everyday spoken language or for the mass migration of people to an ancient homeland after an absence of many centuries. What alternative did he have, but to pronounce it unlikely?

Since Noeldeke, many rich studies of the revival of spoken Hebrew have been conducted.[19] And to this date, no accurate analogy has been identified. Modern Greek, for example, boasts many similarities to its ancestor, yet a speaker of the current language will struggle to read ancient texts. The modern Hebrew speaker, however, progresses without difficulty through the Bible. Similarly, recent attempts to revive the use of Gaelic in Ireland had only modest success, and the language is used today mostly in poetry.[20]

To repeat, the return to the homeland and the rebirth of the Hebrew language were described by Zionists as steps in the direction of normality, which was accorded a certain moral stature. (Normality was thus conceived as a norm.) To achieve normality, however, it was necessary to undergo a completely unprecedented historical process, unique in human history. What was considered routine, proper, and "normal" to other nations (a national territory and a spoken language) demanded the expenditure of incredible energy and the playing out of a singular historical drama for the Jews.[21] Normality, as it were, was inextricably bound up with abnormality.[22]

Today, centrifugal social forces are seeking to resolve the dichotomies inherent in the Zionist enterprise: old *or* new, sacred *or* profane, particular *or* universal, normal *or* singular.[23] While Zionism did reshape the Jewish public domain, there are movements and individuals that now seek to mold it in different and conflicting ways. Substantive ideological confrontation, dormant for many years, is now threatening to penetrate the general consciousness and infiltrate the public domain. There seems, for instance, to be a growing likelihood of a collision between the state (secular) courts and the rabbinic courts and between an army officer's command and a rabbi's halakhic ruling. To be sure, the very possibility of such conflicts is not new. All we have to do is compare Herzl's Zionist expectation that in the new state rabbinical influence would extend no farther than the walls of the synagogue, with Rav Kook's Zionist expectation of the reconvening of the Sanhedrin in Jerusalem and the assumption by rabbis of the roles of judges and legislators for the Jewish people. (When Kook established the chief rabbinate in Jerusalem in 1921, he intended it as the preparatory first phase of this Messianic project.)[24] The practice so far has been to postpone the conflict and neutralize it as much as possible. But now we see individuals attempting to bring these issues to a head—state law versus Torah law—and to expose all of the latent conflicts. In the past, the exponents of religious Zionism were particularly eager to find ways to mitigate such potential conflicts, determined as they were to live and thrive in both worlds. Of late, however, leaders have arisen among them who have sharpened the horns of the dilemma and who brandish them prominently before their students.

STATUS QUO

In light of all this, must we then conclude that Israeli society is doomed to experience *Kulturkampf*, civil war over cultural issues, and that the Zionist synthesis is marching ineluctably toward its undoing?[25] Before answering that question, let us rephrase it in more sober terms. Let us ask why the arrangements which seemed to work well enough in years past are no longer sufficient, and why they are now rejected by various factions within the Israeli public?

It is a matter of common knowledge, that just after the establishment of the State of Israel the secular and religious communities engineered a kind of compromise, which has been termed the "status quo."[26] More than just a political agreement, this was a kind of unwritten social charter, designed to enable the two sides to live together whatever their theological and ideological disagreements. And despite, or perhaps because of, its internal inconsistencies, the arrangement worked well for some time. For example, according to the agreement, public buses were not to run on the Sabbath (except in "red-flag Haifa"), but travel was permitted in private cars and taxis. While difficult to justify on halakhic grounds or according to secular liberal doctrine, each side could claim in this arrangement a partial victory; thus, no-one came away from the table feeling alienated and defeated. If anything, the (partial) disappointment and (partial) satisfaction that resulted from the deal were what guaranteed its (partial) success. Another example: The Israeli "Declaration of Independence" concludes with the following sentence: "Out of trust in the Rock of Israel, we sign our names." Who or what is the "Rock of Israel"? Is it the God of Israel? Is it the genius of the Jewish people? The disputes regarding the phrasing of the Declaration drove its writers to settle for this intentionally ambiguous term which each individual and camp was free to interpret. At the time, one of Israel's leading thinkers derided this ambiguity and deemed it hypocrisy. In my opinion, however, that very ambiguity is what gives the document its advantage in that it provided a point of identification for people of different factions and denominations. Similarly, what is the "trust" described in the Declaration? In the religious tradition it connotes a belief in God and suggests a passive nod towards the Redeemer of Israel.[27] In modern Hebrew, however, "trust" (the Hebrew word is *bitahon*, which also means security) refers principally to physical and military power. Again the double-meaning has proved most fruitful and has enabled people of different opinions to identify themselves with the text.

An extremely important development is the politicization in recent years of the "religious" and "secular" divide with the evolution of the "religious right" and the "secular left." In this we see a deepening of the two principal rifts that divide contemporary Israel: the question of peace (and territorial compromise) and issues of religion and state. Of the many and various events and developments that have contributed to the heightening of tensions, I should like to focus on three basic factors, which had an especially important influence on the Israeli consciousness.

First, it has been about a half-century since the old status quo agreement was reached. During that period, the Israeli reality has undergone great changes. Consequently, it is almost impossible today for any segment of society to recognize its own social and ideological stamp imprinted on the status quo. An example will serve to illustrate the current situation. Today's secular Jew will claim (and he will be supported in this by most religious Zionists) that when yeshiva students were granted exemption from military service, the exemption applied to somewhere between 400 and 900 young men. Today it extends to tens of thousands, and the number is growing year by year. Who could have imagined in the late forties that the day would come when the vast majority of a significant segment of society would exempt itself from military service? Though the initial terms of the agreement continue to be honored, its spirit and intentions have been wholly distorted, or so the secular Jew claims. A member of the Orthodox community, on the other hand, might raise a counter objection. When it was agreed to permit private transportation on the Sabbath, how many Israelis had access to a private vehicle? Not many. It was their right, therefore, to assume that the public domain would be almost free of open violations of the Sabbath. Who could have anticipated that the day would dawn when the privately owned automobile would become the standard means of transportation? From this angle too, a wide discrepancy has developed between the original agreement and its contemporary implications. As is the nature of things, each side pays less attention to what it has gained, inclining to harp on what it has lost over time. It follows, therefore, that each side feels that its rival has usurped control of the public domain.

Second, I would claim that the original political and social agreement was grounded on a mistake common to both sides. Each assumed, for reasons of its own, that the rival camp represented an ephemeral historical phenomenon. Secular, religious, and the ultra-Orthodox, all adhered to the belief that the "others" were fated to decline in strength and numbers and eventually to disappear. Ben-Gurion and his secular disciples, the Lubavitcher Rebbe and his followers, Rav Kook and his Zionist students, all harbored the same conviction. And while they may not have believed that their forecasts would be realized in the immediate short term, all were sufficiently assured in their expectations that any agreement they reached was bound to have a temporary quality, the character of a tactical compromise rather than a fundamental reconciliation.

From the point of view of secularist leaders, it was inconceivable that the future held any promise for what they considered to be the antiquated world of Orthodoxy. Secularists believed that the sons of that world—observant Jews, yeshiva boys, Hasidim or Mitnagdim—were all fated to be overwhelmed by the normalization process transforming the nation. In the Diaspora, such people had served as cultural guardians. But no longer. Their children and grandchildren would conform to the profile of the new Jew then being molded in the national homeland. And, until that day, why not compromise with these anachronistic representatives of a fading epoch and even show them a degree of nostalgic empathy? The Orthodox, however, far from imagining themselves on the brink of extinction, believed that it was the secular Jews who were doomed to disappear. In fact, to the ultra-Orthodox, the term "secular Jews" was an oxymoron. Some would assimilate, and some would return to God and their faith, but they themselves were not a self-sustaining group. The religious Zionists from the school of Rav Kook, in their own way, subscribed to a similar assumption.[28] True, they said, the secular Zionists declare that they are staging a revolt against their parents and grandparents and are abandoning the messianic faith. But what, in fact, do they do? They return from the exile to the Holy Land; they adopt the holy tongue in preference to foreign languages; and they abandon the option of assimilation in favor of the congregation of Israel. One should expect, therefore, that once the secularists accomplished their political and mundane goals, they would quest for an even deeper return of a spiritual and religious nature. And who could withhold affection and good-will from these potential returnees, who were already in the process of fulfilling an active part of the process which would ultimately lead to the redemption of Israel?

To my way of understanding, it was the very same sort of logic that was responsible for the failure to create a constitution for the State of Israel. A constitution is mandated for a long time and is liable to perpetuate prevailing conceptions and entrench the established balance of power. Thus, each side preferred to hold out, waiting for more favorable conditions which would enable it to formulate a constitution in tune with its own heart and mind. Until then, the status quo and a provisional social truce, would do.

But the "optimistic" expectations have failed to materialize. The fleeting phenomena have refused to disappear or to redefine their religious or secular identities. They even insist on asserting themselves as enduring and vital realities which will continue to reproduce and flourish. No longer, indeed, is it possible to imagine a future free of the "others," who seem as likely as one's own group to go on existing in Israel, and to be fruitful and multiply. This realization has led naturally to an escalation of tensions. It was easy in the past to display tolerance and solidarity towards those who, one imagined, would soon be trading in their colors for our own; today we are being asked to deal similarly with individuals and groups who seem determined and likely to preserve their own identities. This demands a kind of acknowledgement and acceptance much different from what was formerly required.[29]

The Jews of the Diaspora are exempt from these demands. An ultra-Orthodox Jew living in Williamsburg will not encounter a Reform Jew from Manhattan, not in a synagogue, not in a "Temple," and not in a community center. And if the ultra-Orthodox Jew runs into a Reform Jew on the street or in the subway, it will be a chance meeting between two Americans, not between two Jews. Zionist nationalism, however, assembled all of these Jews within a stone's throw of each other. It created a forum, a common public space for them. So long as each appeared to the other as an anachronistic vestige, or an ephemeral historical accident, face-to-face contact did not occur. Today, it would seem, that meeting is finally taking place—out of rancor and anger, perhaps—but, it is taking place.

THE CONTESTED ARENA

The reevaluation to which the status quo has been subjected in recent years is related to a third change that has taken place in the Israeli reality and consciousness. Marginal social groups (Sephardim, the religious, Revisionists), as well as certain streams of thought (ultra-Orthodoxy and Reform) which were once opposed to political Zionism, have been brought into the mainstream of the Zionist enterprise. More and more the Jewish State has taken on the shape of an arena in which the contemporary debate about Jewish identity is played out. Less and less does the state reflect the outlook and principles of a single victorious group.

In the Israel of 1948, it was possible to point to a single prototype of the "authentic" Israeli. In those days it was easy to define what it meant to participate in the collective Israeli experience, and what it meant to deviate from it, to recognize who stood at its center and who on its margins. "The struggle over Israeli identity, synthetic a concept as that might be, was a search for a norm, a foothold and a point of departure for a society that had lost its European and Jewish identity," Gershon Shaked wrote in 1983. He continued:

> There is room for a *religious* Israeli, a *Sephardi* Israeli, an *Ashkenazi* Israeli [emphasis in original], and a "Western" Israeli can co-exist with a "Jewish" Israeli. So long as they have a common identity, there is nothing as important as pluralism in a society as rich in human resources as our own; on condition, that there is a nexus, a common foothold, a mutual point of departure. . . . I will continue to speak out in defense of this Israeli nexus, which seems to have gone missing: we must go back and search it out. There is such a thing as an Israeli secular experience. . . . Without Israeliness— it is difficult to be an Israeli.[30]

Therein lies the rub. The nexus that was supposed to bind all Israelis together was forged according to the mold of one elite Israeli group,[31] while other groups—Sephardim, the religious, Revisionists—were assessed according to their compatability with this model.[32] Only later, did these groups arise and gravitate towards center stage, first by challenging the dominant ethos and its monolithic ideal, and then by penetrating the centers of national culture and government. There is no doubt that this challenge to the hegemony of the once prototypical "new Jew" is exacting a toll.[33] It has unleashed confrontations and conflicts that threaten to disturb the Israeli equilibrium. But if this cost appears sometimes to be great, it can also lead to social liberation and cultural plurality. It grants a "home" to "other" communities, creating for them places of their own within the society, rather than on its margins.

This inclusionary process has not skipped over streams of Judaism which were initially inimical to the Zionist movement, but which have over time become integrated into its historic undertaking. Even those factions that formerly opted to stand to the side or even outside the national enterprise, have joined the project (at least de facto). I will bring this point home by calling to mind the debate spawned by the Law of Return, namely the "Who is a Jew?" question. Who are the principal combatants in this fierce debate which has already brought down more than one Israeli government? On the one side, stand the ultra-Orthodox, led by the late Lubavitcher Rebbe, and on the other, the leaders of the Reform religious movement. That this should be the case is no wonder. The argument, after all, concerns the question of how one becomes a member of the Jewish people, that is, who possesses the authority to convert non-Jews to Judaism. (Most accurately put, the question is, "Who is a rabbi?") This is, of course, an issue that inflames first and foremost the leaders of the competing Jewish streams in

North America, all of whom attach inordinate importance to the question of who will be recognized as a religious authority by the State of Israel, its citizens, institutions, and laws. [34]

Now consider who were the fiercest religious opponents of Zionism in its early days, none other than leaders of ultra-Orthodoxy and of Reform Judaism. The former angrily opposed Zionism, seeing it as a rebellious, secularist movement with anti-messianic intentions. The reformers also greeted the movement with fury, viewing it as a backward nationalist reaction which denied the universal mission of the Jewish people. For example, Rabbi Shalom Duber Schneerson of Lubavitch was an implacable turn-of-the-century foe of Zionism.[35] He could never have imagined that the day would come when his movement would attach decisive significance to the laws of the Zionist state—to the recognition by that state of rabbis and conversions. Undoubtedly, he would have been shaken by such a notion. "What connection," he would have asked, "is there between the Zionist revolution and me?" No less would the leaders of the early Reform movement have been shocked, had they known that today Reform rabbis would engage in a fierce struggle for the recognition by the Jewish national state of their religious authority, for that state to view as legitimate within its borders Reform conversions, marriages, and divorces.

These struggles have come to shape the very image of the Jewish state. That is to say, these two movements, which once fought against the formation of a Jewish state, are today bitterly debating the question of the character of that very state, and how it should decide questions of Jewish identity and of religious authority. Are we to see in this evidence of the failure or the success of Zionism? Israel's founding fathers were indeed disposed to see their creation as a manifestation of the triumph of one (theirs) Jewish outlook as if a decisive verdict had been rendered in the debate concerning the future of the Jewish people. And yet, the Israel of today has become an arena for the continuation of that very struggle. The state has increasingly come to include the various opinions and factions that now argue their positions within the walls of the national home. Again, there is no denying that this inclusivity exacts a toll. And the price may, in fact, be deemed too steep by those who expect Zionism to revive Jewish nationalism and normalize the Israelis. The price, however, is not too steep for those who see the movement as a means of reviving the Jewish people in their entirety.

As it turns out, most of the internal tensions that have been stirring within Judaism throughout history have been carried over to the State of Israel and are reflected in the community that is coming together there. Zionism did not create the fragmentation. On the contrary, from a historiosophical, dialectical point of view, it is possible to depict Zionism as a logical outcome of this division. The Jewish nation was able, until relatively recently, to exist as a nation without territorial concentration and in the absence of a solid political base. The *Shulhan Aruch* (the most widely accepted code of Jewish law) and the prayer book were sufficient to bind the people together. In recent generations, however, halakhic principles and religious faith have become a source of contention. In this sense, it is possible to see the Zionist act as a heroic gesture, an almost desperate measure, to re-establish a common denominator in a non-virtual context, as a political and historical entity; to establish once again a national and existential center, despite theological rifts and ideological divides. If we adopt this point of view, it emerges that the attempt of the founders to shape the culture and identity of a new society using as their model a single, victorious image was itself contradictory. It was destined to alienate various segments of the community. In fact, it was precisely those political and social compromises, the "gray areas" as it were, designed to foster mutuality, which most suited the internal logic of the Zionist entity and the complexities of the contemporary Jewish experience.[36]

With the reconstitution of a public forum for the Jewish people in the Land of Israel, an arena for contests and judgments was also created. Outside of Israel, there are almost limitless opportunities for individualistic and pluralistic Judaism. Every family and community can pitch its own tent. As it is possible to avoid contact, so is it possible to avoid collision. There is no need of public showdowns, or for legal or political verdicts. Not so in Israel, where these occur daily. And as it is impossible to avoid confrontation, it is necessary to agree on rules for dialogue and decision-making, although not necessarily on belief and life style. We must nurture "one language" but not necessarily "a single vocabulary." It is enough to encourage empathy and solidarity on an existential level ("a covenant of fate"), and not necessarily on an ideological and theological one ("a covenant of faith").[37]

CONCLUSION

Here I have written about groups, factions, and camps on opposing sides of the house. This does not, of course, provide a comprehensive picture of the complex Israeli social construct, but only of the potential combatants in a *Kulturkampf*. As many studies have shown, there is great diversity of opinion in Israeli society, and a continuity of religious identification which slopes gradually from one end of the spectrum to the other. Looking at the surveys, the extremes do not appear quite so stark. Using a statistical profile, the scholars at the Guttman Institute for Social Research concluded in a 1994 study that "there is no basis for the rhetoric which maintains that Israeli society is polarized between religious and secular Jews." Their authoritative and comprehensive research concludes that "there is a spectrum, from those who are extremely observant of the *mitzvot* (commandments) to those who do not observe them at all, not a distinct separation between an observant minority and a secular majority."[38]

The study findings are indisputably valid. I beg to differ, however, with the optimistic reading which they have been given. Are polarization and alienation, after all, only the products of a society that is sharply divided into two warring camps? Is it not possible for there to be a social and cultural rift, despite the existence of a spectrum, and despite the existence of people and groups of intermediate persuasions? Consider a citizen of India who ventures forth from his home. As he or she proceeds, he will notice changes in the spoken dialect. Progressing further, he will begin to hear many words he does not understand. If he continues to put distance between himself and his point of origin, it will not be long before he no longer recognizes the language of his fellow citizens, despite the linguistic continuity linking the various villages that line the way. To put it in other words, social polarization does not depend only on the slope of the curve that connects one group to the other; it is also judged by the distance of the gap and the depth of the gulf between one extreme and the other—assuming that each extreme is populated by a significant segment of the population. And there is all the more reason to use this second measure, when it becomes evident that it is actually on the ends of the spectrum that one is likely to find the society's leading groups—that is, its educated elite, its moral and political spokespeople, and the individuals filled with ideological fervor.

That is the situation which prevails in Israeli society. Let us take a look at the sociological data. About one-quarter of the population claims to observe the Sabbath strictly[39] and to put on phylacteries every day (25% of men, that is); more than three-quarters attest to fasting on Yom Kippur.[40] Quite surprisingly, 56 percent of Israeli Jews report that they "believe with all their hearts" in the giving of the Torah at Sinai; fifteen percent "do not believe at all"; and the rest are "unsure" about the matter. According to these statistics, there appears to be a religious orthodoxy on the one hand, and a secular "orthodoxy" on the other, each of which claims a relatively equal following (20-25% of the population). The rest (i.e., the majority of the population) sits somewhere in the middle, expressing different degrees of affinity to, and distance from, the traditions and religious faith.

It is my impression, however, that in terms of both quality and quantity, Israeli society's cultural creativity—be it literary, artistic, philosophical, theological, polemical—derives overwhelmingly from both "orthodoxies," and not from the intermediate group. On the one hand, the volume of rabbinical literature being produced today exceeds that of any period in the history of the Jewish people. High level secular Hebrew literature is flourishing to a no less impressive degree. (The field has produced, in recent years, four legitimate candidates for the Nobel Prize in literature.) It is important, then, to differentiate between the realm of personal observance and religious emotions and the realm of culture and creativity. In the first, there exist today a number of tempering factors which can bridge the gap between the two polarized groups. Here, without a doubt, the intermediate groups play an important role. The in-between groups, however, have less to offer when it comes to dulling the edge of the divisions in the intellectual and cultural realm. And they have very little to do when it comes to bridging political differences. For that to happen, it is necessary for members of both "orthodox" elites to internalize the duality of which they have seized only one half and to come to terms with the "otherness" of their fellow-Jews and fellow-Israelis.[41] I have attempted to explicate some of the current processes which may encourage such a development.

Translated by Joshua Brown

Notes

1 Aruthur Koestler, *Promise and Fulfillment: Palestine 1917–49* (London: Macmillan, 1949), pp. 330–31.

2 See also: Georges Friedmann, *The End of the Jewish People?* (New York: Doubleday Anchor, 1968), pp. 26–37, 251–99; Akiva Ernst Simon, *Ha-im Od Yehudim Anachnu?* [Hebrew] (Tel Aviv: Sifriat Ha-Po'alim, 1983), pp. 46–49; S. Z. Sheragai, *Besugiot Hador* [Hebrew] (Jerusalem: Mosad Ha-Rav Kook, 1970), p. 110.

3 Thorstein Veblen, "The Intellectual Pre-Eminence of Jews in Modern Europe," in *Essays in Our Changing Order*, ed. Leon Ardzrooni (New York: M. Kelley, 1934), pp. 219–31; R. Ginge, ed., *American Social Thought* (New York: Hill and Wang, 1964), pp. 219–39.

4 Aviezer Ravitzky, *Messianism, Zionism, and Jewish Religious Radicalism* (Chicago: University of Chicago Press, 1996).

⁵ Interest in classical Jewish texts seems to have been recently rekindled among certain segments of the secular Israeli society, an interest distinct from the return of religion. In fact, in many cases this intellectual involvement seems to stem from a feeling that the classical legacy should not be forfeited to the religious.

⁶ S. N. Eisenstadt, *Jewish Civilization* (New York: SUNY, 1992), pp. 141–52.

⁷ David Vital, *The Origins of Zionism* (Oxford: Clarendon, 1975); idem, *Zionism: The Formative Years* (Oxford: Clarendon, 1982).

⁸ Hedva Ben-Israel, "The Role of Religion in Nationalism: Some Comparative Remarks on Irish Nationalism and on Zionism," in *Religion, Ideology and Nationalism in Europe and America*, eds. Hedva Ben-Israel, et al. (Jerusalem: Zalman Shazar Centre, 1986), pp. 331–39; idem, "Nationalism in Historical Perspective," *Journal of International Affairs* 45 (1992): 79; idem, "From Ethnicity to Nationalism," *Contention* 55 (1996): 54–56.

⁹ Ruth 1:16. The biblical text is not necessarily used here with its original connotation.

¹⁰ Jonah 2:9.

¹¹ Thus, there is a basis to the portrayal of Judaism as an integral civilization which transcends the national or religious sphere in itself. This description was put forth, in different directions, by Rav Kook, Mordecai Kaplan, and Arnold Toynbee. See: Yehezkeel Dror, "Bignut Hanormaliut" [Hebrew], *Kivunim* 12 (1995): 9.

¹² See Aviezer Ravitzky, "Eretz Hemda Va-Harada" [Hebrew], in *The Land of Israel in Modern Jewish Thought*, ed. Aviezer Ravitzky (Jerusalem: Yad Yitzhak Ben-Zvi, 1998).

¹³ Gershon Scholem, *Od Davar* [Hebrew] (Tel Aviv: Am Oved, 1988), pp. 59–60.

¹⁴ Zali Gurevitch and Gideon Anand, "Al Hamaqom: Anthropologiya Yisre'elit" [Hebrew], *Alpayim* 4 (1991): 41–45; idem, "Never in Place: Eliade and Judaic Sacred Place," *Archives de Sciences Sociales des Religions* 87 (1994): 4–14.

¹⁵ The religious side of this equation is discussed at length in my *Messianism, Zionism, and Jewish Religious Radicalism* (see n. 4 above). For the secular side, see A. B. Yehoshua, *Bizchut Hanormaliut* [Hebrew] (Jerusalem and Tel Aviv: Schocken, 1980); Gershom Weiler, *Theokratia Yehudit* [Hebrew] (Tel Aviv: Am Oved, 1977); Yosef Agassi, *Bein Dat Uleom: Likrat Zehut Leumit Yisre'elit* [Hebrew] (Tel Aviv: Tel Aviv University, 1984); Prat (Avigdor Levontin), *Boker VaErev* [Hebrew] (Jerusalem: Sheshar, 1991).

¹⁶ See, however, Shmuel Almog, *Leumiut, Tziyonut, Antishemiyut* [Hebrew] (Jerusalem: Ha-Histadrut Ha-Tzionit, 1992), pp. 126–36; Arik Carmon, *Mamlachtiyut Yehudit* [Hebrew] (Tel Aviv: Ha-Kibbutz Ha-Me'uhad, 1994), pp. 44–50.

¹⁷ It is worth noting that recently Eric Hobsbawm has claimed that modern Hebrew is nothing but a Zionist invention, bearing little resemblence to the original! This coheres with his general claim that nationalism is a fictive creation. See E. J. Hobsbawm, *Nations and Nationalism Since 1780* (Cambridge: Cambridge University Press, 1980); cf. idem, ed. *The Invention of Tradition* (Cambridge: Cambridge

University Press, 1983); See also, Hedva Ben-Israel, "He'arot Hashva'atiyot al Hatziyonut" [Hebrew], *Kivunim* 10 (1977): 5.

[18] Theodor Noeldeke, "Semitic Languages," in the *Encyclopedia Britannica* (New York: Britannica, 1911), vol. 24, pp. 617-30.

[19] Ze-ev Ben Chaim, *Bemilhamta shel Lashon* [Hebrew] (Jerusalem: The Israeli Academy of Sciences and Humanities, 1992); Shlomo Morag, "Ha'ivrit Hahadasha Behitgabshuta" [Hebrew], *Cathedra* 56 (1970): 70–92; Mordechai Mishori, "Tehiyat Halashon—Ha-omnam Nes?" [Hebrew], *Leshonenu La-am: Kovetz Shnat Halashon* [Hebrew] (Jerusalem: The Academy for the Hebrew Language, 1990); Moshe Bar-Asher, "Some Observations on the Revival of Hebrew," in *European Regional Development Conference of Jewish Civilization Studies* (Jerusalem: International Center for University Teaching of Jewish Civilization, 1992); pp. 2–30; Haim Blanc, "The Israeli Koine as an Emergent National Standard," in *Language Problems of Developing Nations*, ed. J. A. Fishman (New York: J. Wiley, 1968), p. 237; S. H. Herman, "Explorations in the Social Problems of Language Choice," in *Readings in the Social Problems of Languages*, ed. Joshua A. Fishman (The Hague, Paris: Mouton, 1968), pp. 492–511.

[20] On the failure of governments, including the Irish Republic, to reestablish national languages, see Punya Sloka Ray, "Language Standardization," in Fishman, ed., *Social Problems of Languages*, p. 763.

[21] Binyamin Harshav, "Tehiyata shel Eretz Yisrael Vehamahapechah Hayehudit Hamodernit" [Hebrew], in *Nekudat Tatzpit: Tarbut Vehevrah Be'eretz Yisrael*, ed. Nurit Gretz (Tel Aviv: The Open University, 1993), pp. 31–37; idem, "Masa 'al Tehiyat Halashon Ha'ivrit" [Hebrew], *Alpayim* 2 (1990): 32–39.

[22] A considerable number of Zionists described this anomaly as a continuation of Jewish singularity throughout history. In the words of David Ben-Gurion: "Our very historical existence, nearly 4,000 years old, all of Jewish history up to and including the creation of the State of Israel, is, essentially, a singular occurrence for which it is difficult to find the like in all of human history." *The World Congress of Jewish Youth 1958* (Jerusalem: W.Z.O., 1959), p. 187. See Ze-ev Tzahor, "Ben-Gurion Kime'atsev Mithos" [Hebrew], in *Mithos Vezikaron*, eds. David Ohana and R. S. Wistrich (Jerusalem: Ha-Kibbutz Ha-Me'uhad, 1997), p. 139.

[23] Elsewhere I have dealt extensively with the tensions between the historical and messianic outlooks and between the search for partial and final solutions (see note 4 above).

[24] Rav Kook's successor as chief rabbi, Rabbi Y. I. Halevi Herzog, was vexed by the question of two hypothetical systems of justice in the future Jewish state and corresponded on the subject with the head of pre-Holocaust Europe's Council of Learned Scholars (Rabbi H. O. Grodzinski). See Y. I. Halevi Herzog, *Tehuqa LeYisra'el al pi HaTorah* [Hebrew], ed. Ithamar Warhaftig (Jerusalem: Mosad Ha-Rav Kook, 1982), p. 25.; idem, "Din Hamelech" [Hebrew], *Talpiyot* 7 (1948): 18–24; Aviezer Ravitzky, *Al Da-at Hamaqom* [Hebrew] (Jerusalem: Keter, 1991), pp.

108–11, 124–25; idem, *History and Faith: Studies in Jewish Philosophy* (Amsterdam: J. C. Greben, Publisher, 1996), pp. 50–58, 69–72.

25 Eliezer Shweid, *Hatziyonut she-aharei Hatziyonut* [Hebrew] (Jerusalem: Ha-Histadrut Ha-Tziyonit, 1996), pp. 100–109; Erik Cohen, "Yisrael Kehevra Post Tziyonit" [Hebrew], in Ohana and Wistrich, *Mithos Vezikaron*, pp. 156–66.

26 Menahem Friedman, "The Chronicle of the Status-Quo: Religion and State in Israel," in *Transition from 'Yishuv' to State, 1947–48: Continuity and Change*, ed. Varda Pilowsky (Haifa: Mosad Herzl Le-Kheqer Ha-Zionut, 1990), pp. 47–80.

27 Moshe Greenberg, *Studies in the Bible and Jewish Thought* (New York: Jewish Publication Society, 1995), pp. 63–74.

28 Rav Kook developed a complex historiosophy with respect to the place for secular Zionism. I deal with this theory at length in my book cited above (see note 4 above), pp. 86–110. Here I will address only one aspect of his theory, which was very popular among his students. See also, Eliezer Schweid, *Hayahadut Vehatarbut Hahilonit* [Hebrew] (Jerusalem: Ha-Kibbutz Ha-Me'uhad, 1981), pp. 110–42; Binyamin Ish Shalom, "Sovlanut Bemishnat Harav Kook Veshorasheiha Ha-Iyuniyim" [Hebrew], *Da-at* 20 (1988): 151–68.

29 Sometimes tolerance entails de facto acceptance and at other times de jure recognition. For examples of mutual recognition from a secular perspective, see David Grossman, "Ani Tzarich Etchem, Atem Tezerichim Oti" [Hebrew], *Yediyot Aharonot*, 23.11.95. For the religious perspective, see Uriel Simon, "Shutafut Hilonit Datit Bivniat Medina Yehudit Demokratit" [Hebrew], *Alpayim* 13 (1997): 154–66.

30 Gershon Shaked, *Ein Maqom Aher* [Hebrew] (Tel Aviv: Ha-Kibbutz Ha-Me'uhad, 1983), p. 29.

31 Yonatan Shapira, *Ilit Lelo Mamshichim* [Hebrew] (Tel Aviv: Sifriat Ha-Po'alim, 1984); Dan Horovitz and Moshe Lissak, *Miyishuv Limedina* [Hebrew] (Tel Aviv: Am Oved, 1987); Anita Shapira, "Dor Ba-aretz" [Hebrew], *Alpayim* 2 (1990): 179–203; Zvi Tzameret, *Yemei Kur Hahituch* [Hebrew] (Beer Sheva: Ben-Gurion University of the Negev, 1993), pp. 56–63.

32 Amnon Raz-Karkotzkin, "Galut Betoch Ribonut" [Hebrew], *Theoria Uvikoret* 5 (1994): 125–30.

33 Amnon Rubinstein, *MeHertzel ad Gush Emunim U-va-hazara* [Hebrew] (Tel Aviv: Schocken, 1980), pp. 77–79.

34 David Landau, *Parashat 'Mihu Yehudi'* [Hebrew] (Ramat Gan: Havaad Hayehudi Ha-amerikai, 1996); Moshe Samet, *Mihu Yehudi?* [Hebrew] (Jerusalem: Chemdat, 1986).

35 Rabbi Schneerson predicted certain defeat for the nationalist, Zionist initiative: "Their presumptuous goal of gathering [the exiles] together on their own will never come to pass." See also Shalom Duber Schneerson, *Igrot Kodesh* [Hebrew] (New York: Ozar Ha-Chasidim, 1982), p. 110; Aviezer Ravitzky, "The Contemporary Lubavitch Hasidic Movement: Between Conservatism and Messianism,"

in *Accounting for Fundamentalisms*, eds. M. E. Marti and R. S. Appleby (Chicago and London: University of Chicago Press, 1964), p. 34.

[36] Dafna Barak-Erez, ed., *Medina Yehudit Vedemokratit* [Hebrew] (Tel Aviv: Tel Aviv University, 1996).

[37] Rabbi J. B. Soleveitchik, "Kol Dodi Dofek" [Hebrew], in *Ish Ha'emuna* (Jerusalem: Mosad Ha-Rav Kook, 1971), pp. 86–99; idem, *Hamesh Derashot* [Hebrew] (Jerusalem: Tal Orot, 1974), pp. 94–95. See also, Michael Rosenak, "Haadam, Hayehudi Vehamedina" [Hebrew], in *Sefer Yovel, Lichvod Rabi Yosef Dov Halevi Soloveitchik*, eds. Shaul Yisraeli, Nahum Lamm, and Yitzhak Raphael (Jerusalem: Mosad Ha-Rav Kook, 1984), pp. 163–69.

[38] Shlomit Levi, Chana Levinson, and Elihu Katz, *Emunot, Shemirat Mitzvot, Viyahasim Hevratiyim Bekerev Hayehudim Beyisrael* [Hebrew] (Jerusalem: Guttman Institute for Social Research, 1994), p. 1.

[39] This seems trustworthy, as only 16% of the population, fewer than the Orthodox component, claimed to observe the laws of *midah* and *tevilah*.

[40] This statistic was later supported in surveys conducted in 1995 and 1996.

[41] This article has dealt exclusively with the cultural tensions present in Jewish society. The co-existence in Israel of Jews and non-Jews raises a different question, and requires recognition of a duality and otherness of a different nature.

7

'AHAD HA'AM, HERZL, AND THE END OF DIASPORA ZIONISM

Hillel Halkin

Item: In August of 1996, *Commentary* magazine published a special symposium, the subject of which was "What Do American Jews Believe?" Forty-eight contributors, all active in the American Jewish community, took part—intellectuals, academics, rabbis, and communal leaders. About half mentioned the state of Israel either not at all, or so casually that its importance to them appeared marginal. Four or five of the remaining half attributed to Israel a great significance in their lives; the others referred to it as one of several components in their Jewish identity, never the first in order of importance.

Item: I recently received for review a volume published by the University of Wisconsin Press entitled *People of the Book: Thirty Scholars Reflect on Their Jewish Identity.* These academics differ from the *Commentary* contributors in that few are active in organized Jewish life and many feel uneasy or unfocused about their Jewishness, although none to the point of outright repudiation. Of the thirty essays, Israel is a central and not entirely positive concern in only one.

Item: For the past five-and-a-half years I have been writing for the *Forward*, a Jewish weekly published in New York that is considered by many to be the best of its kind in America. Staunchly pro-Israel in its editorial policies and allotting to Israeli subjects a fair proportion of space, it is a small newspaper with a full-time staff of about a dozen, mostly young journalists. In the years I have worked for it, to the best of my knowledge, none of these journalists has visited Israel.[1]

Clearly, something has been happening to the place that Israel occupies in the minds of American Jews; and the further down the ladder of age and Jewish identification one goes, the greater the slippage. If twenty-five years ago Israel could be proclaimed without challenge "the civic religion of American Jews," today, in the centennial years of the publication of Theodor Herzl's *The Jewish State* and the convening of the first Zionist Congress in Basel and the jubilee of the state, this faith is losing its congregation.

There are obvious reasons for this. One can list among them the spread of assimilation in the Diaspora; the passage of time that has distanced Israeli and Diaspora Jews from their common roots in a shared Jewish tradition; the discrediting in the contemporary West of nationalism and the values associated with it; the rise of a constellation of attitudes, characterized by a cultural, sexual, and moral relativism and a granting of primacy to individual gratification and fulfillment, at odds with what has been seen as the Israeli ethos. Other factors include the weakening of this ethos in Israel itself; the attrition of Israel's international image between 1967 and 1992 and, once again, since the elections of May 1996; the contemporary disillusion with secularism and the notion of secular Jewish culture; and finally, the complementary revival of interest in Jewish religious expression and spirituality as the central core of Jewish existence. One could discuss each of these factors separately. And one can also, I believe, discuss them together as the exhaustion of 'Ahad Ha'Amism in Jewish life.

It was 'Ahad Ha'Am who, in the words of Arthur Hertzberg's admiring 1991 tribute to him, first "began the debate a hundred years ago" about "the continuing struggle to define a modern Jewish culture"—which he did by staking out a Zionist position that was harshly critical of Herzl. And in the two men's lifetimes there was no more agitated public moment in this debate than that following 'Ahad Ha'Am's review of Herzl's second book, the utopian novel, *Altneuland*, which appeared in 1902. In *Altneuland*, Herzl had taken two imaginary characters, the elderly English misanthrope, Kingscourt, and the young Viennese Jew, Friedrich Loewenberg, and removed them to a shangri-la in the Pacific. Upon their return to civilization twenty years later, there, to their Rip-Van-Winklish amazement, they discover a super-modern and ultra-progressive Jewish society flourishing in Palestine. Although written in the light style that had characterized him as a successful feuilletonist, the novel was Herzl's first and only major statement of his conception of the practical reality of the Jewish state he was laboring to create; and true to the anti-Herzlian stance that he had consistently taken since the first Zionist Congress, 'Ahad Ha'Am attacked this conception soon after its publication.

Little more than a mockingly accurate summation of *Altneuland*'s plot, 'Ahad Ha'Am's review nevertheless contained in concentrated form all of his major objections to Herzl's Zionism.[2] The review referred scathingly to

Herzl's political grandiosity; to his belief that a Jewish Palestine could absorb a majority of the world's Jews and thereby eliminate the Jewish problem in the Diaspora; to his assumption that the country's Arabs would not oppose massive Jewish immigration; and above all, to his vision of a Jewish society that, culturally, seemed to have little specifically Jewish about it—or that, as 'Ahad Ha'Am wrote elsewhere, might solve "the problem of the Jews" who lived in it, but not "the problem of Judaism." The review sufficiently angered Herzl that he asked Max Nordau, his second-in-command and the Zionist Movement's best known Western intellectual, to write a counter attack—which Nordau did in so virulent a manner that it brought even many of 'Ahad Ha'Am's opponents to 'Ahad Ha'Am's defense.[3] The *Altneuland* affair might have gone on longer had it not been overtaken by the even stormier controversy over Herzl's Uganda Plan in 1903, which in turn was cut short by the leader's death in 1904.

Reading *Altneuland* today, one feels that 'Ahad Ha'Am—who no doubt refrained from criticizing the novel's papier-maché quality only because of his own far from sophisticated literary taste—was in some ways too kind to it. Certainly, he was correct in pointing out that anyone considering the "New Society," as Herzl's Zionist community was called in the novel, "will perceive (a point that the author himself makes innumerable times as if herein lay the whole glory of his book) that its Jews have . . . added nothing of their own; they have simply imitated and combined what they found in different places among the most cultured nations of Europe and America." Over and over in his book, Herzl, as if reassuring his readers that he is writing practical futurology not science fiction, stresses that nearly every feature of his utopia—from its huge department stores and telephone advertising campaigns to its elevated railway lines and underground cables, from its progressive welfare and prison systems to its technologized agriculture and profitable farmers cooperatives—is simply a successful adaption of some already existing development in the West. As David Litvak, the New Society's president-elect, tells Kingscourt: "There is nothing new in Palestine; it only has a new look."[4] With minimal changes, 'Ahad Ha'Am remarked in closing, the New Society could just as well have been planned for American blacks returning to Africa.

For 'Ahad Ha'Am, such a society was insufficiently distinctive to justify the collective effort of Zionism—which, he felt, had legitimacy as a movement only if, albeit in a secular guise, it served as modernity's main vehicle for the continuity of Jewish tradition. And indeed, in contrasting the two Zionisms, Herzl's and 'Ahad Ha'Am's, the so-called political and cultural, we tilt the scales when we customarily call the former bold, visionary, and romantically ambitious, and the latter sober, practical, and conservatively restrained. Of course, Herzl's political program was far-reaching in comparison with that of 'Ahad Ha'Am, who never appears to have envisioned more than Jewish autonomy in a Palestine run by the Turks, the English, or even the Arabs. If, however, we skim off its utopian icing, which meant more to Herzl (who was in love with technology and sometimes remarkably prescient about its uses) than it need mean to us, Herzl's conception of an ideal Jewish society was the more modest of the two. As opposed to 'Ahad Ha'Am, who demanded that Jewish life in Palestine reflect fully the ethical and cultural genius of the Jewish people, Herzl was willing to settle for a well-run, European-style social democracy, based on enlightened self-interest, that, as Kingscourt exclaims admiringly at one point, might be mistaken for Italy.

To judge by his writings, Herzl had little interest in the future of those Diaspora Jews who would decline to emigrate to his Jewish state, to which he did not envision their maintaining a relationship; and while his cultural minimalism was dictated by his political and demographic maximalism, with 'Ahad Ha'Am it was the other way around. If, as 'Ahad Ha'Am believed, even a thriving Jewish community in Palestine would physically accommodate but a fraction of the world's Jews, it could be central to their lives only if it served them as a social and cultural model. A Jewish Palestine offering no more than superior department stores and elevated tramways—a Palestine that did not, as Louis Brandeis was to state two generations later in formulating a credo for American Zionism, "develop the best in us through the ennobling effect of its strivings"—was hardly worth the emotional or financial investment of a Jew from New York, London, or Odessa.[5]

Even had 'Ahad Ha'Am never existed, therefore, some kind of "'Ahad Ha'Amism" would have become the dominant form of Diaspora Zionism in a democratic West where Herzl's call for mass emigration to a Jewish state went unheeded. True, 'Ahad Ha'Am's very name, as Arthur Hertzberg laments, is today largely unknown in the Diaspora. Yet, "when they are challenged to explain their relationship to Israel," as Hertzberg puts it, millions of American Jews have traditionally "invoke[d] the spirit of 'Ahad Ha'Am, not that of Herzl."[6]

This invocation has not been a stable or consistent one. It has, historically, gone through shifts of content, several of which I would like to explore here. Although they have by no means been the only paradigms and have overlapped more chronologically than a merely schematic treatment indicates, they represent well the basic tendency of "'Ahad Ha'Amism" to move progressively further from 'Ahad Ha'Am's actual thought, each stage of its development, as it were, attempting to preserve the functional element in his approach while progressively discarding its intellectual substance.

Not long ago I chanced upon a book published in 1925 by Ludwig Lewisohn, a well-known American Jewish intellectual and a fervent new convert to Zionism—although, as was the case with most American Zionists, not quite fervent enough to consider the possibility of settling in Palestine himself. In the early 1920s, he did, however, visit there. He was not uncritical of what he saw; there were things he disliked and was skeptical of; yet wherever he went, he discerned in a Jewish community numbering barely 100,000 souls the "original moral qualities" of a Jewish people that was "passionate for a Messianic kingdom on earth." Practically everything he witnessed—from the new Hebrew University on Mount Scopus, with its message, "the nations are waiting," to the experiments of the Jewish farmer that were "adding to the wealth and garnered wisdom of mankind"—was invested with universal significance. "The life that streams forth from Palestine," he believed, would be "in the largest possible measure a life immediately intelligible to great masses of the Jewry of the world." The one thing he feared—"the practical danger" posed by which, he estimated, was "happily small"—was the Herzlian "romantic idealists in Zion [who] plan to substitute national assimilation for personal assimilation. We are to go to Zion [they say] and be a folk like other folk." On the contrary, the author insisted, "We do not desire renationalization in the romantic sense. . . . It is just this sort of thing that as a people we have transcended. . . ."[7]

Lewisohn may never have read a word of 'Ahad Ha'Am, almost nothing by whom had been translated into English at the time. This, however, was 'Ahad Ha'Amism in its purest form. Indeed, in an 1899 essay entitled "The National Morality," in which he chided both Herzl and Nordau for writing plays in which Jews un-Jewishly challenged gentiles to duels mistakenly fought in the name of Jewish honor, 'Ahad Ha'Am had argued that it was precisely the Jewish moral sense, different from and more advanced than that of any other people, that could best inform Zionism with the unique Jewish content it required.[8]

Lewisohn's portrayal of Jewish Palestine was not solely a Diaspora projection: a socialist and utopian idealism was a powerful force in those years in the Palestinian Jewish community itself, particularly among the left-wing *halutzim* or pioneers. Yet for these *halutzim* 'Ahad Ha'Am was an irrelevant bourgeois thinker. What was characteristically 'Ahad Ha'Amist in Lewisohn's formulation was Lewisohn's interpretation of their lives, not in their own Marxist or Tolstoyan terms, but in those of the Jewish prophetic tradition. When Lewisohn declared that Palestinian Zionism "not only offers a home to our homeless . . . but offers to all the world the first example of a national community that exists, in the old eternal words of Zachariah, 'not by might, nor by power, but by the spirit,'" and thus "fulfills our mission among the peoples of the earth," he was addressing concerns less those of a Palestinian *halutz* than of a Diaspora Jew like himself, eager to see validated a concept of Jewish existence—one curiously akin to that of the anti-Zionist Reform movement in which he was educated—that could not possibly assume a fully lived form in the Diaspora.[9]

More romantic in its way than any of Herzl's techno-fictional fantasies and mocked from the beginning by that strain of Herzlian Zionism represented most forcefully by Jabotinsky and the Zionist right, such a view of Jewish nation building was a central motif in Diaspora Zionism practically up to the establishment of the State of Israel. As late as 1944, when news of the enormity of the Holocaust had already reached America, one still finds it typically expressed in a far from naive observer like Maurice Samuel. Samuel wrote that, "The opening of Palestine to millions of Jewish refugees has a greater purpose even than the saving of so many lives; it is part of the world's reconstructive program . . . [the Jews] have come to Palestine to be an ethical people . . . in the setting of a world vision."[10]

This vision had the ability to inspire Diaspora Zionists with the sense of more than merely parochial importance that their self-image demanded, but it could not survive the transition from a small, voluntaristic community of pioneers to a state created in violence and maintained in siege in a real world. An actual—as opposed to an imaginary—Israel caught up in a prolonged conflict with its Arab neighbors and in the social and economic tensions among different sectors of its own largely immigrant population, was necessarily implicated in the same coercive uses of force and institutional defenses of privilege that are found even in the most progressive of societies. This lesson in reality would have spelled the end of 'Ahad Ha'Amism as an ideology of Israeli-Diaspora relations had this ideology not retreated to more fortified ground that 'Ahad Ha'Am himself never anticipated.

Thus it was that the Holocaust and Israel's war with the Arab world were used, rightly or wrongly, not only as justification of the sweeping exercise of Israeli power, but were also spontaneously invoked in the years after the establishment of Israel to shift 'Ahad Ha'Amism to a new fulcrum at the historical point at which its previous base had foundered. If the Holocaust, that is, represented the attempt of absolute evil to exterminate the Jewish people, and if the Arab states sought to complete the task that Hitler had only partially carried out, then in the name of resistance to evil, no higher task than which was conceivable, survival became not only a necessity but a supreme Jewish and human value; and Diaspora support for Israel was this value's outspoken assertion. At the moment that the "old, eternal words of

Zachariah" appeared to have become uneternally anachronistic, the tough Israeli paratrooper took the place for Diaspora Jews of Ludwig Lewisohn's pacifistic pioneer. A country determined to live at all costs was hailed as the emblem and inspiration of the Jewish will-to-live everywhere, of the "614th commandment" of "not handing to Hitler a posthumous victory," elevated to the status of a first commandment by a Diaspora Jewish theologian like Emil Fackenheim for whom a Jewish state was not compensation for the Holocaust, but a *tikkun*, an act of primal restoration, coming after it.[11]

A Zionist ethic of survivalism reinforced by the Israeli-Arab wars of 1967 and 1973, which left behind deep traumas of feared catastrophe despite military victory on the battlefield, thus dovetailed with the growing concern for Jewish demographic and cultural continuity in the Diaspora that first surfaced as a major issue in the 1970s. It also corresponded to the mood of a significant part of the American Jewish public which, after the liberal harmonies of the 1960s, felt increasingly beleaguered on the American scene. To this public, Israel might still be a beacon of morality shining its light on the Diaspora, but the only moral imperative was now to fight and win.

Yet, even as Holocaust consciousness continues to grow among American Jews sometimes to the point of becoming a new civic religion in its own right, a tough survivalism as a secondary form of 'Ahad Ha'Amism is on the wane. Brought to the fore by history, it has been undermined by it, first in the form of the Israeli-Egyptian peace treaty of 1979, which removed any military threat to Israel's immediate future; then, more fundamentally, by what Nietzsche would have called "the feminization"—what we might more colloquially speak of as the "anti-machoism"—of contemporary Western and American culture; and finally, by the Oslo accords between Israel and the PLO. An Israel reconciled with its neighbors—assuming that, despite its continuing ups and downs, that is indeed the final destination of the current peace process—is not an Israel that can mobilize Diaspora emotions based on Jewish fears of annihilation and the felt shame of Jewish passiveness, especially when it is in the process of being culturally "feminized" itself.

The Oslo accords are also likely to represent the beginning of the end for the last and final form of "'Ahad Ha'Amism," that most removed from its original roots in 'Ahad Ha'Am's own writings—the Zionist triumphalism ushered in by the Six Day War. Like the survivalism that it in large measure replaced, this triumphalism—which, apart from the 1967 war's immediate aftermath, has taken hold mainly in Orthodox religious circles—has been a celebration of might. The might it celebrates, however, has not been simply that of the Jewish will-to-live, but rather that of the fulfillment of divine promise—or, if one prefers, of ancient national myth. Here is a characteristic formulation of this view expressed by another Jewish philosopher and theologian, Eliezer Berkovits, writing a few years after June 1967:

> For Israel, history is messianism on its way to the Kingdom of God on earth. Because of that, Israel knows Auschwitz, because of that Israel, all though its history, has been on the way to Zion. In our days it has arrived there.... What was not granted to any other generation was awarded to the people in Zion—an encounter with all Jewish history, a very real communion with all the generations.[12]

Written a mere twenty-five years ago, and describing thoughts and emotions that many of us can remember from the time, these words already sound as archaic as those of Ludwig Lewisohn. For Berkovits, as for many other Diaspora Jews, the Israel of 1967 was precisely the objective validation of Judaism that Lewisohn found in the Palestine of 1924—the Judaism in question, however, being of a very different nature. A Jew could live in Philadelphia or London, Buenos Aires, or Toronto: Through the repossession of the biblical land of Israel, miraculously restored to the Jewish people by Israeli military power, he was now part of a great redemptive theodicy, heralded, as the book of Deuteronomy puts its, "with a mighty hand and an outstretched arm, with great terror, signs, and wonders."

I do not know precisely to what degree such a theological reading of Israeli history still has its tenacious supporters in Kiryat Arba or Crown Heights now that a Likud prime minister is negotiating with the PLO. Perhaps the spiritual cataclysm predicted by some observers as befalling the theological triumphalists upon the rupture of their dream—one often analogized to the collapse of Sabbatianism after the conversion of Shabbetai Zvi—will not take place. Yet whatever political solution is reached between Israel and the Palestinians, and however ephemeral or long-lived its consequences for the inner lives of those Jews who for years saw the hand of God or of national destiny in Israeli rule in Judea and Samaria, the ideology by which they sought to persuade the Diaspora that Israel is center stage of a cosmic drama in which Diaspora Jews too have their supporting role, has come, or is coming, to an end.

It is played out; and with it, I believe, is the 'Ahad Ha'Amism that distantly fathered it and that in it has become the historical reversal of its own self: 'Ahad Ha'Am's ambitious program for an evolutionary secularization of Jewish religious tradition turned into a revolutionary re-theologization of Zionist secularism, the last paradigm by which Israel could be imagined to confer a higher meaning upon the Jewish life of the Diaspora.

"But," the objection will be voiced, "all you have said is on the level of abstraction! The Jewish moral genius, the Jewish will to live, the Jewish rendezvous with cosmic destiny—Diaspora Jews don't actually need such grand justifications. They care about Israel because it's theirs, regardless of what it does or doesn't stand for. They pride themselves in it; they worry about it; and it remains a source of inspiration for them even if they know it isn't perfect. A Shabbat in Jerusalem . . . a street full of Hebrew signs in Tel Aviv . . . the Kinneret seen from the hills of Galilee . . . a group of tired Jewish soldiers waiting for a ride . . . these things speak to them. And they speak to their children too, which is why there is no better investment in the Jewish future than for a young man or woman of an impressionable age to spend a year in Israel. That's what the centrality of Israel is about, not some Platonic idea of a Jewish state!"

Far be it from me to deny the beauty of the Kinneret or—when you can still find a street not clogged with traffic—the special atmosphere of Shabbat in Jerusalem. But it is only the strong light of an idea that can keep such things, if they are not woven into the fabric of daily life, from fading into the pallor of old pictures in a photograph album. This is something that 'Ahad Ha'Am, though he did not live in the age of congregational tours to the Land of Israel, understood.

"Yet 'Ahad Ha'Am," the objecting voice persists, "did not have only ideas in mind. He had in mind institutions, creativity, schools, universities, literature, arts, religion, the Jewish street—an entire Hebrew renaissance that would radiate its influence into the Diaspora. Surely this is the kind of cultural center that Israel still is and will continue to be."

I repeat: Without the glow of an idea, no Jewish state can cast its light from afar. There are Hebrew schools and universities in Israel; they strive to be as good as their leading European and American counterparts and do not quite succeed; even in the field of Jewish Studies they must now strive to compete with the Diaspora, to which they continually lose talented scholars. There is a flourishing Hebrew literature, which emulates the best Western models; a small number of Diaspora Jews even follow it in translation, since a smaller percentage of them today read Hebrew than at any previous time in Jewish history; it does not appear to move them greatly. Israel has thousands of crowded synagogues; they are less innovative and creative than the synagogues of America, and American Jews who want their tradition undiluted can find that, too, in the Diaspora. There is in Israel a busy Jewish street; its signs now say "McDonalds" and "Burger King." Those things that were once most distinctive about secular Israeli culture—the kibbutz, the youth movement, the citizen army, the fierce patriotism, the simplicity of taste, the disdain for bourgeois values and bourgeois ostentation—are already the estate of the past or soon will be as much as khaki shorts and the *kova tembel,* swept away by a tidal wave of Western fashions, Western food, Western music, Western commerce, Western culture. This is not what 'Ahad Ha'Am was thinking of.

Herzl, though eccentric about many things, saw this aspect of the future more clearly. Unlike 'Ahad Ha'Am, he grasped not only technology's power to change the world beyond recognition at a vastly accelerated pace, but its inexorable universalism and culturally leveling effect that would increasingly obliterate the individuality of countries. He was a mistaken optimist in his conviction that, starting with the benefit of a clean slate, a Jewish state would use modern technology more rationally and effectively than Europe or America. He was a historically vindicated realist in believing that the new society built there would not differ greatly in its essence from other technologically advanced states and would quickly absorb the latest influences from them.

But let us give 'Ahad Ha'Am credit, too: He understood better than Herzl that such a society could solve the problems of Jews but not the problem of Judaism. That insight remains as true today as it was a century ago. Israel offers the Jews of the world, as it has done since its creation, a truly enormous, albeit severely restricted, opportunity: that of living in a society with a Jewish majority, located in the Jewish historical homeland, in which Jews have responsibility for every aspect of their lives. This is, by definition, an opportunity that cannot be exercised in the Diaspora. It cannot travel. Ideas can—but, 'Ahad Ha'Amistically speaking, Israel has run out of them. By living in it you can choose to share your problems with other Jews, but the problems themselves will increasingly be those of human beings everywhere. And the problem of Judaism not only remains in a Jewish state, it grows more vexed and painful from year to year.

In the final analysis, Israel is ceasing to be central to the Jews of the world for the simple reason that they have chosen not to live in it, and no community can exist indefinitely by means of a vicarious identification with life lived elsewhere. There is a naiveté in the plans and strategies of the Jewish technocrats who think they can reverse this trend by means of some gimmick, however simple or complex. Issue a voucher to every Jewish teenager to visit Israel, suggests Labor politician Yosi Beilin! But when, voucher in hand, young Bruce or Jennifer steps off the plane and finds a nation of Yosi Beilins, what profiteth him or her to have left Philadelphia?

We will not drift totally apart. As Jews, we will continue to share interests, problems, concerns, emotions, projects. We may even share again, as we have shared in the past, emergencies and crises. But we will more and more live our own lives and go our own ways, and both Israel and the Diaspora will be central first and foremost to themselves. This is a consequence of what has been called post-Zionism; it is more or less the happy ending that Herzl had in mind. Perhaps no Jewish figure in the past one hundred years has been so wrong about so many things, yet so right about the essentials.

Notes

1 In all fairness, I should add that, having learned of these remarks, the *Forward*'s publisher, Seth Lipsky, has subsequently sent several staff members to Israel at the paper's expense.

2 'Ahad Ha'Am [Asher Ginsberg], "Altneuland" [Hebrew], in his *Kol Kitvei Ahad Ha'am* (Tel Aviv: Hotza'at Dvir, Jerusalem, Hotza'ah Ivrit, 5725 [1965]), pp. 313–20. Originally published in *Hashiloah* 10:6 (1903).

3 Ernst Pawel, *The Labyrinth of Exile: A Life of Theodor Herzl* (London: Collins Harvill, 1990), pp. 472–73.

4 Theodor Herzl, *Altneuland* (Haifa: Haifa Publishing Company, 1960), p. 75.

5 Louis D. Brandeis, *Brandeis on Zionism: A Collection of Addresses and Statements by Louis D. Brandeis* (Washington, D.C.: Zionist Organization of America, 1942), p. 29.

6 Arthur Hertzberg, "Ahad Ha'am, 100 Years Later," in his *Jewish Polemics* (New York: Columbia University Press), 1992, p. 93.

7 Ludwig Lewisohn, *Israel* (New York: Boni and Liveright, 1925), pp. 128–30.

8 'Ahad Ha'Am, "The National Morality" [Hebrew], in his *Kol Kitvei*, pp. 159–64. Originally published as "On the Issues of the Day. V" [Hebrew] *Hashiloah* 5:1 (1899).

9 Lewisohn, *Israel*, pp 128-30.

10 Maurice Samuel, *Harvest in the Desert* (Philadelphia: Jewish Publication Society, 1944), p. 314.

11 Emil Fackenheim, *To Mend the World* (Bloomington: Indiana University Press, 1994), pp. 299–300.

12 Eliezer Berkovits, *Faith After the Holocaust* (New York: Ktav Publishing House, 1973), p. 153.

PART
3

THE FUTURE OF
JEWISH CULTURES
IN THE DIASPORA

8

THE FUTURE OF JEWISH CULTURES IN THE DIASPORA: AN INTRODUCTION

Seymour Mayne

In his essay on faith and religion (see chap. 4), Rabbi W. Gunther Plaut, with an ironic poetic touch to pique our interest and sharpen our awareness, figuratively depicts the role of the synagogue in North American Jewish life as that of a filling station. We like the synagogue to be on the side of the highway for those special life cycle occasions; we maintain it with the patronage of membership so that it is there when we need it to serve those Jewish rites of passage, but it is not on the map as an essential station on our daily journeys. How can we encourage more people to pull up to the synagogue, seeing it as a frequent destination in Jewish life, he reflects.

But if the synagogue is to be compared to a filling station, where do we find culture in present day Jewish life in Canada and the United States? Is it that small heritage shop that we pass just down the road from the gas station, where only a few stop by to windowshop? If the synagogue is no longer as central in our communities as it once was, what then has happened to Jewish culture? The majority of Jews will stop in at the synagogue from time to time for a social or spiritual fill-up—a bar or bat mitzvah, a marriage, for instance—but who wants to park in front of the less conspicuous cultural depot when there are the real shopping centers to draw us in three hundred and sixty-six days a year!

Without the synagogue, there is no communal Jewish life, some would say. And without what the synagogue and Jewish education provide, it is nearly impossible to maintain Jewish cultural life. Recently, a major revival in Yiddish culture in the United States was initiated by a group of dedicated young women and men under the leadership of Aaron Lanksy of the National Yiddish Book Center in Massachusetts. Not only are they dedicated to the ingathering of thousands of Yiddish books and directing them to libraries and educational institutions where the texts are required for courses and study, but from the new center they recently built they also plan to extend their self-declared mandate. They are committed to including other aspects of Jewish American cultural life that are seen as an outgrowth from and a link to the thriving Yiddish-centred activity of just a few decades ago. Preserving and renewing as of old, they seek to move forward!

The contributors to this volume have been brought together, not only to contemplate and speculate about the future of Judaism and Jewish life, but also to bring the insights and perspectives of scholars and teachers to bear upon the ongoing life of our communities. We do not, however, have to look south to find ways to ensure the vitality and vigor of Jewish cultural life. For those of us in Canada, the National Yiddish Book Center need not serve as the model for reinvigorating and reinventing Jewish culture in our community life. We have an institution—if that is the right word for this very special place—which remains unique in Jewish Canadian life, and has served one community, not only as a repository of books and documents, but also as a center for writers and as a meeting place for audience and creator. Specifically, I have in mind the Jewish Public Library of Montreal, an institution that has continued to renew itself from generation to generation since its official founding in 1914. Close to a century of Jewish cultural life in Montreal would have been inconceivable without the Library and what it has provided for thousands of members of the community year in and year out. For this writer and educator, the Library has been an intellectual home second to none other. In all matters literary it was the center which helped nourish my interests and invigorate my commitment to literature, not only to pursue writing, but also to understand from the very beginning that books require the reverberations and resonance of tradition and community in both their genesis and dissemination, if they are to live and have relevance.

While we speculate and discuss, there remains the imperative to educate and sustain the audiences who are nourished and thereby help maintain our cultural life. How can this be done? That is the question we ask and wish to clarify. Where do we turn next? What should we do? The first step is to take stock and, with that typical Jewish reflex, we turn to the past in order to find a guide or a key to the perennially perplexing future.

Professors Gerber and Stanislawski speak from their fields of special interest and expertise. As Jane Gerber puts it, historians by training are focused on the past, not on predicting the future. We cannot, however, help but look into the future with the blueprints and records of the past. What does the history of Sephardic Jewry reveal to us as we examine the transformations and changes it underwent for centuries? Are there lessons for us to consider as we go back to our communities? What strategies can we devise to preserve Jewish culture in the most open societies we Jews have encountered over our long history? Michael Stanislawski takes a complementary view when he reviews the crisis of Jewish secularism and its failure—in its various streams—to transmit itself as a sustaining vision for Jewish life. Without the symbiotic relationship to Jewish religious life, can secularism guide and sustain us into the future? Should Jewish life be bifurcated between these two visions? Where do we go next? These are urgent questions.

If we are to maintain our cultural life, we know at the start that we cannot fall back, alas, on the ideological fervor and commitment of earlier generations. But, we have institutions in place—especially libraries—in most of the major population centers across the country. Could we not establish useful working links among them, so that they could develop a lecture and learning program for inviting the numerous writers, artists, and scholars who are scattered across the country? And from time to time supplementing these visiting speakers by bringing over writers and thinkers from the wider Jewish world? Why is it that so few visit the larger and smaller communities, lecturing on their current work, and helping to expand the horizons not only of students but also of the public in general? Can we not devise a stimulating list of essential subjects and set up institutes for learning and culture at Jewish libraries and Jewish community centers from the Atlantic Provinces to Vancouver Island? Few of our writers and artists, for instance, are invited on a consistent basis to present their work and ideas to the Jewish community at large. We leap to invite the "star" from the U.S., Europe, or Israel, but there are more than a few dozen intellectually engaging speakers in Canada who could do much to maintain a bridge between members of our communities and the resources and riches of Jewish Canadian culture.

An association of writers and speakers could be set up under the aegis of an umbrella of libraries and community centers in the country. Reading groups, lecture venues, and small *"shabbaton"* (retreat) programs could be initiated to draw in young and old alike. These contacts and activities can only have a beneficial effect; in particular, we may be able to draw in a neglected group in our community, our university students, who are poised at this time in their lives to be brought more fully into an awareness and appreciation of Jewish Canadian or Jewish American culture.

There is a need to draw the community at large into the small corners of the shop on the heritage highway next to the filling stations. Let us explore and find the ways and means to put our *schoireh*, our cultural goods, before our communities so that we enrich our cultural possibilities, and even stimulate further traffic between the shops and the precious filling stations, thereby enhancing the routes and traffic of Jewish life in our communities.

9

LESSONS FROM THE SEPHARDIC PAST
Jane S. Gerber

Until the eighteenth century, Ashkenazim and Sephardim lived in autonomous communities, governed by Jewish law and their own traditional leaders. Their lives were guided by Jewish ritual and ancestral obligations. Slowly, often in fits and starts, the modern world and Western society began to beckon, opening up a multiplicity of once unimaginable options leading to radical transformations. For the modernizing Jew, the process of change was sometimes liberating and heady. For the more traditional, it was often traumatic and demoralizing. But no community was left untouched by the assumptions and innovations of modernity.

A comparison of Ashkenazic and Sephardic responses to modernity reveals a great deal about the contrasting postures of the two major segments of the Jewish people. Ashkenazic responses ranged over a very broad spectrum, from outright rejection of Jewish tradition at one extreme, to self-imposed isolation and fundamentalism at the other. By and large, Sephardic reactions to modernity tended to be more subtle, cautious, and moderate; Sephardim did not repudiate their traditional leaders nor lose their traditional moorings. Their embrace of Western forms was enthusiastic and selective but not overwhelming, and Sephardic approaches to modernization and Westernization may offer some fruitful guidelines to any discussion of creating Jewish cultures in the Diaspora today.

Much of the large body of literature dealing with the modernization of Jewish life focuses on the Ashkenazic response with its examples of dramatic rejection and radical reformulations. The central challenges posed by secularism, science, and technology (as well as many of the other "isms" associated with modernity) proved to be profoundly destabilizing to Ashkenazic Jews, producing a wave of innovations in synagogues, rituals, and daily behavior as well as mass defections from Judaism and the Jewish people. The Sephardic experience, however, provides a fascinating counter-weight to the Ashkenazic revolutionary posture, one that can enrich our understanding of Jewish options in the present era of increasing malaise over the high cost of freedom and secularism.[1]

The "winds of change" did not reach the Sephardic masses in Ottoman lands until well into the nineteenth century. For a long time, Sephardim remained between what has been described as a declining position and a still fragile modernity. The agent of change was not a revolutionary event like the French Revolution which dramatically swept aside old boundaries separating Jews and non-Jews. Nor was change introduced by a rebellious or subversive class within the Sephardic communities. Unlike Europe, no emancipation debate occurred in Muslim lands during which the Jews were forced or cajoled into concluding that sweeping communal transformations and religious reforms would lead to greater prosperity and acceptance by the wider society.[2]

During the course of the nineteenth century, certain reforms were pressed upon generally reluctant Ottoman authorities by the European powers. The granting of broader rights to non-Muslims in Turkey was of paramount concern to the British as a means of pacifying rebellious minorities who were turning to England's rivals in the Near East. The nineteenth century Turkish reform movement known as the *Tanzimat* introduced such improvements in the status of non-Muslims as the elimination of dual standards of justice for Muslims and non-Muslims and mixed courts, and old boundaries separating Jews and Muslims began to blur. Still, a person's status continued to be defined by his or her religion. Citizenship for Ottoman Jews was a totally alien concept; there was no possibility of a Jew becoming a Turk or an Arab in the way one could become a Frenchman or a German citizen in Europe. Thus the atmosphere of quid pro quo in which the European Jew transformed himself and his community in exchange for the benefits of civil emancipation was not an option for Sephardim in the world of Islam. At best, Western powers hoped to eliminate the most egregious humiliations associated with *dhimmi* status. Only in Algeria, where French control was most advanced, did Jews undergo a process of rapid secularization and eventual naturalization with the promulgation of the Crémieux Decree in 1870. Elsewhere, Jews remained a more or less oppressed and second class population; reforms were perceived largely as a means of improving Jews' economic plight or of rationalizing decaying communal structures.

A second distinction between the Sephardic and Ashkenazic confrontation with the modern world should be noted here. The modernization of the Jews in Europe was part and parcel of a broader program of secularization of European society. During the French Revolution and its aftermath, religion was marginalized in the life of the individual and the state. But secularism was totally alien to Islam and Muslim states; it is still anathema to most Muslim spiritual leaders. Even today, it has not been accepted as the norm of any Muslim state except Turkey, and even there, a fragile secularism required the revolutionary charisma of an Ataturk and the cataclysmic defeat of World War I to make any headway among the conservative population. Reforming politicians have been compelled to pay lip-service to Islam. Sephardic Jews, who were exposed to Western Jewish notions such as religious "reform," Zionism, and the secularization of communal institutions were required to react diffidently and cautiously within a much more conservative ambience.

The first Sephardic Jews to encounter Western ideas in the nineteenth century were Jewish merchants of Italian (particularly from the city of Leghorn or Livorno) origin, known as *francos*, who had sought their fortunes in Ottoman lands in the seventeenth and eighteenth century and had maintained close economic ties with Europe. Often they found active employment as agents of Ottoman merchants or of foreign noblemen in the metropolitan centers of the Islamic world, and gained protection under the umbrella of European consular authorities. These merchants were only partially Westernized, but they recognized that Western "connections" were often keys to commercial success and political protection. The ideological content of Western politics was generally of secondary interest to this native class of Jews, who often gained their first exposure to the tenets of the Enlightenment and the innovations of the *haskalah* in the course of travels. On the whole, such isolated individuals did not serve as a force for revolutionary change among the Sephardic subjects of the Ottoman Empire. Still, in some respects, the *francos* and their western European (especially French) Jewish colleagues did play the role of catalyst for change in the East that the nation-state had played in Europe. Local elites and European Jewish reformers joined forces to enhance the status of the Jews through a rationalization of the Jewish community, through reforms of Jewish community organizations, and, above all, through the introduction of modern educational institutions.

In 1860, French Jewry founded the Alliance Israélite Universelle, an international organization which aimed to defend, protect, and uplift downtrodden Jewry. The charter of the Alliance represented a peculiar mixture of *noblesse oblige*, imperialism, and Jewish solidarity. Men like Adolphe Crémieux, a founder and the first president of the Alliance, embraced their Sephardi co-religionists with almost missionary fervor, hoping to protect them against such local outrages as blood libels or the *corvée*, while uplifting them economically and spiritually. Alliance programs and personnel blended the aspirations of newly emancipated French Jewry with nineteenth-century notions of advancement and personal transformation through education and social engineering.[3]

The well-meaning French reformers who sought to "civilize" their Middle Eastern Jewish brethren chose the educational system as their main weapon for effecting change. The patrons of the Alliance hoped that they could bring about permanent change by integrating Sephardic Jewry into Western culture. They sought to establish a network of schools with the French language and French civilization at the heart of the curriculum. Many valid criticisms have been leveled against both the assumptions and the results of the work of the Alliance. One of the immediately apparent and most controversial results of the Alliance's success was to widen the cultural gap between Jews and their Christian and Muslim neighbors. This resulted from immersing Sephardic Jews in French language and French culture. At the end of the nineteenth century, it is estimated that approximately one-quarter of the 250,000 Jews of the Ottoman Empire spoke French, while fewer than 1,000 spoke Turkish. The most poignant expression of deracination caused by French education among Sephardic Jews was expressed by Albert Memmi in his autobiographical memoir, *Pillar of Salt*:

> I am ill at ease in my own land and I know no other. My culture is borrowed and I speak my mother tongue haltingly. I have neither religious beliefs nor tradition. . . . To try to explain what I am, I would need an intelligent audience and much time. I am Tunisian, but of French culture. . . . I am Tunisian but Jewish, which means that I am politically and socially an outcast. I speak the language of my country with a particular accent and emotionally I have nothing in common with Muslims.[4]

Simultaneously with the spread of French and Western-style schools, a veritable flowering of Ladino literature occurred in the Balkans, Turkey, and Egypt. Western classics, indigenous drama, journalism, and the collection of Ladino folk traditions were all by-products of the cultural changes transpiring in the Sephardic communities of the East. It should be noted that this literature was generally conservative socially, bearing little of the reforming polemic or lacerating critique of contemporary Jewish society that permeated German or Yiddish literature of that period. The tensions between faith and community already manifest in the works of Moses Mendelssohn were absent from enlightened Sephardic circles.

The Ottoman government kept a low profile in these developments, as it had done traditionally with regard to Jewish community affairs. It looked kindly upon moderate reform of the community since a streamlining of Jewish self-government and centralization of authority among the various minorities tended to give Istanbul greater control over them. The central government even played a hand in supporting advocates of change within the community, appointing those candidates for the rabbinate who would work harmoniously with the modernizers. Since the Jewish moderniza-tion program focused on educational reform, not religious innovation, it was relatively easy to pursue change once the initial opposition within the community had been quelled. Additionally, even foes of Westernization were fully aware that Jewish youth needed the educational tools that only modern schools could provide. The desperately poor masses of Jewish youth of the Ottoman Empire could not be competitive with the more Western-ized Greeks and Armenians unless practical subjects like languages and ac-counting were taught. Thus poverty and aspirations joined with official acquiescence to soften resistance to the new educational agenda. French classes and vocational training for boys and girls, while radical for their time and place, were a good deal less threatening to the traditional way of life than were the rabbinical conferences and synagogue reforms that punctuated the process of emancipation of the Jews in Europe. The net result was that West-ernization in Ottoman lands was partial and generally peaceful. With a few notable exceptions, severe splits within the Jewish community were avoided.

How is it that the Alliance schools, notwithstanding the very real iden-tity crises that they inculcated in many of their graduates, could play such an effective and generally positive role in the process of change? From the beginning, Alliance authorities tried to stress the reforming, rather than revolutionary, nature of their innovations. The new curriculum was im-parted primarily by Sephardic Jews who were natives to the communities in which they functioned. Many of the young men, and especially women, who were trained in the Alliance's special École Normale in Paris came from Balkan and North African families and were expected to return to Muslim countries to work in Alliance schools after their training. It is sig-nificant that the apostles of Westernization were local products who had obtained intense first-hand knowledge of Europe in a controlled setting. Generally, these Alliancists did not harbor grandiose projects of political reform or social restructuring.[5]

Opposition to the Alliance schools was usually local and temporary. The outstanding example of a community which successfully resisted the introduction of Alliance schools was that of Djerba in Tunisia, a unique island community with a vigorous tradition of Jewish learning and a prolific local publishing industry that disseminated the works of its venerated rabbis. Usually, rabbinical opposition was overcome through negotiation and politicking.[6] To smooth the path of its innovative schools, the Alliance received the endorsement of traditional authorities by including them on the faculties as instructors of Hebrew language, Jewish history, and the festivals. In fact, most of the rabbis were only too happy to find a new source of gainful employment. But the most compelling factor for meeting traditional opposition to the Alliance schools was the enthusiasm for them shown by parents who correctly perceived that their children would acquire useful skills there. Moreover, the aggressiveness of mission schools in recruiting Jewish students in Turkey, and especially Egypt, undercut the arguments of Jewish foes of the Alliance schools.[7] It was better to send one's children to a modernizing Jewish school than to expose them to the wiles of the missionaries.

In contrast to sharply negative rabbinical responses to modernizing currents in Europe, the Sephardic rabbis of the Ottoman Empire tended to be supportive of the new currents. They did not merely pay lipservice to the new schools; they enrolled their own children! In his book, *She'eirit Hanahal*, Rabbi Israel Moses Hazzan, Chief Rabbi of Alexandria from 1857 to 1863, presents a fictitious dialogue between two scholars and a merchant on the subject of the study of foreign languages by Jewish youth. While Hazzan, naturally, emphasizes the importance of studying Hebrew and Arabic, he endorses—through the two scholars—the newer curriculum claiming that "it was never forbidden at any place or any time for the sons of Judah to learn the language[s] of the nations."[8] And it was true, that foreign language had been an integral part of the Sephardi curriculum in the great medieval yeshiva at Lucena, and doubtless also a staple of the intellectual diet of students in medieval Kairouan and Baghdad. Sephardi intellectual traditions had been sensitive to Greek, Arabic, Castilian, and Italian currents of thought for centuries.

Westernization among Sephardim, as among Ashkenazim, went beyond questions of curriculum and foreign language. New modes of dress and home furnishings and new roles for women in the family and the economy followed. Just as European Jews pondered what constituted the Jewish language in an age of entry into general society, Sephardim began to question if they should speak Ladino, Judeo-Arabic, or French in the future. Should they abandon Ladino for a European language or simply modernize it by switching from the Hebrew alphabet to the Latin? Some Sephardim participated in the revival of Hebrew as a national language of all Jews, debating the merits of Ladino in terms quite similar to East European debates regarding the status of Yiddish. The late nineteenth century witnessed an explosion of Ladino newspapers, especially in the Balkans. At the beginning of the twentieth century a number of novels were translated from French, Italian, Russian, and even Yiddish into Ladino. In contrast to Europe, Sephardic *maskilim* (enlighteners) did not develop assimilationist ideologies but instead, engaged in the writing of Sephardic history. Among the literati in Salonica and Sarajevo, enlightened leaders emerged who advocated the protection of the Sephardi heritage. They recognized that the legacy of *romanceros* and ballads which had survived hundreds of years of dispersion was in danger of being lost with Westernization and became the guiding spirits in the collection of Sephardic folk traditions. [9]

The relatively smooth pace of Westernization of the Jews in Turkey may be partially explained by the proximity of Europe and the presence of major Christian communities which were also undergoing some of the same intellectual transformations. Yet, at the other end of the Mediterranean, in conservative Morocco where Jews were the only non-Muslims in the population, traditional rabbis also tended to be moderate and accommodating in their receptiveness to Westernizing trends. Rabbi Isaac Bengualid of Tetouan, an early nineteenth-century scholar from the North where Spanish influences prevailed, endorsed the permissibility of studying secular subjects including foreign languages and permitted the acceptance of government subsidies for language instruction.[10] In his first year as Chief Rabbi of Tripolitania (modern Libya), Rabbi Elijah Hazzan set about modernizing the curriculum of the Jewish community schools to include Arabic, Italian, mathematics, and vocational subjects. He did not ignore the implications of modernization, particularly the unprecedented freedom of choice which it presented, and he tried to offer guidance to the observant and the no-longer observant Jews.

Historically, the Sephardi rabbi in recent centuries was the spiritual leader of the entire community and sought to lead by consensus. In the new era, unlike the European Orthodox rabbis who sought to ostracize the modernizer, Sephardic rabbis remained leaders of the entire community, unwilling to repudiate the modernizers or the no-longer observant. This crucial distinction between the rabbis of Europe and those of Islamic lands has been the subject of several important studies by the contemporary scholar, Zvi Zohar.[11] Through a careful analysis of rabbinic responsa in Egypt and Syria, Zohar reveals the extent to which Sephardic rabbis understood and appreciated the implications of technology. Rather than rejecting it out of hand, as the Muslim *'ulema* usually did, the rabbis understood how technological innovations could become a positive force for preserving the Jewish people and in implementing *halakhah*. Furthermore, they sensed that the anonymous bureaucratization that is a hallmark of modern Westernization could be exploited to extend rabbinical jurisdiction in matters of personal status such as divorce.[12]

Sephardic Jews have traditionally adopted a deferential attitude toward their rabbis. This behavior has continued even with the demise of the ancient communities through emigration to Israel and the West. Conversely, Sephardic rabbis have tended to be less confrontational and less ideological. Zionism among Sephardim was less radical, more rooted in traditional Jewish spirituality. Hence there was almost no opposition to it among Sephardi rabbis as there was among Ashkenazi rabbis at the turn of the century, even though Jews in Muslim lands had little experience with political and social activism. When rabbinical opposition to Zionism did occur, it appears to have been based upon the realization that participation in Zionist activities posed a real danger to Jews in Muslim countries because of the rising tide of Arab nationalism.

How can we explain this moderate response to modernization among Sephardim, a moderation which succeeded in avoiding the tragedy of the deep and irreconcilable polarization of Jewry which has splintered the Ashkenazim for more than one hundred years? Is the relaxed religiosity, so typical of Sephardim in the past, also operative today in the face of the continuing corrosiveness of secularism?

As one examines the Sephardic experience over the past millennium, one can cautiously state that there is a distinctively Sephardic way of confronting other cultures. While it would be exaggerated to speak of a Sephardi "national character," historical forces did create an alternative manner of confronting and coexisting with foreign cultures distinct from that of Ashkenazim. Throughout their history, Sephardic Jews tended to regard various branches of human knowledge with more liberality than the Jews of northern Europe. Perhaps the most dramatic example of this liberality is the curriculum of study from twelfth-century Spain preserved in Joseph b. Yehuda ibn Aqnin's *Tibb al-Nufus* (*Healing of the Soul*). This remarkable document reveals that the Sephardic male was not restricted in his formal studies to Torah, Mishnah, and Gemara; he also studied Hebrew, grammar, rhetoric, calligraphy, philosophical observations on religion, astronomy, astrology, natural sciences, and music.[13] This broad, humanistic curriculum, produced in Iberia while Jews were still at ease, outlasted the so-called "golden age of Spain" by hundreds of years. Multilingual and multifaceted leaders were not confined, moreover, to one century or one country of the Sephardic Diaspora. Geniza lists of books in the possession of Mediterranean businessmen in medieval Cairo reveal a similar breadth of outlook. The harmonization of Judaic and secular culture appears to have been common among Sephardim throughout the Mediterranean world. The long tradition of serving as cultural intermediaries, so prevalent in Umayyad Cordoba or Nasrid Granada, typical of their service at the court of Alfonso the Wise in Christian Toledo or of Suleiman the Magnificent in Ottoman Istanbul, stood the Sephardim in good stead when Western notions began to penetrate the Near East. Foreign cultures were not *a priori* subversive.

The cultural heroes of the Sephardic world have bequeathed a particular legacy of the courtier/rabbi which has no peer in pre-modern Ashkenazic circles. Who else but a Sephardic rabbi like Samuel ibn Nagrela could write a lyrical poem on the bouquet of a good glass of wine or the heat of a chilling battle and *also* compose Talmudic treatises? Who else but a Sephardic poet like Solomon ibn Gabirol could compose the most intense religious poetry and the most skillful imitations of Arab motifs and metrics? The creative tension that flowed from the combination of secular and religious currents in the same Jewish leader created a fascinating personality type unknown outside the Sephardic world before modern times. These complex personalities were not only exceptionally ambitious, but their spiritedness appears to have enabled them to live with the contradictions between religion and their frequently sophisticated social reality, contradictions and tensions which would come to characterize the new era of secularism.[14]

The Sephardic experience raises probing questions about the dynamics of acculturation in Jewish history. How do individuals and entire communities acculturate? How much can be absorbed from the external environment without permanent loss and dilution? Jews have always borrowed from the general culture in which they found themselves, often creating new and surprisingly original amalgams of the two. The annals of Jewish life in Iraq, Egypt, Turkey, Tunisia, and Yemen, as well as Spain, reveal how dynamic the process of cultural borrowing can be. The end product of this process in Cordoba, Izmir, or Fez was a lively and frequently literate Diaspora, dedicated to the service of God and the enjoyment of this world, perhaps not in equal measure. Sephardic Jews were not fearful of interaction with broader cultures or wider environments.

Several modes of response to foreign cultures have been characteristic of Jewish history. One response has been retreat and withdrawal, building up the proverbial fence around the Torah to heights that would constitute an almost impregnable fortress. The second response is that of wholesale imitation, characteristic of such movements as nineteenth-century, classical Reform Judaism in America with its Sunday prayer service and *trefah* (non-kosher) banquet. The third mode of response, that of selective appropriation of foreign elements and creative adaptation of those elements, was the historic path of Sephardim. Their response, at its best, included adoption and adaptation, both imitating and competing with foreign cultures. They did so most adeptly in the early Middle Ages, somewhat less easily in recent centuries of advancing poverty. Given this historic stance, it should not come as a surprise that Sephardic Jews confronted Westernization, Zionism, and increasing secularization with a degree of equanimity that avoided revolution, neo-Orthodoxy, and ultra-Orthodoxy.

Sephardim may not have been quite as mellow as this reconstruction suggests. Unquestionably, however, they perceive themselves as moderates and non-ideological. And yet, the contemporary situation of Sephardic Jews shows troubling signs. The paradigm of harmony that existed during the past two hundred years has been severely shaken by the new realities of life in the State of Israel. The Sephardic traditions of respect for home and family and veneration of rabbis have tended to withstand the great trauma of upheaval and immigration. Most Sephardim have avoided the current religious polarizations, retaining a traditional piety that is without tensions, enabling them to embrace the larger world while remaining tied to some traditional family and religious practices. At least some Israeli Sephardim, although few Ashkenazim, are able to pray in a traditional synagogue on a Saturday morning and drive to the beach on Saturday afternoon, handling the contradictions between the two modes of behavior with equanimity. And yet, the earlier spirit of religious tolerance and moderation has broken down to some extent. Israeli Sephardic Jews did not build their own educational institutions in the period of rapid immigration during the past forty years. Instead, they have sent their children to Ashkenazic institutions. One result has been the unprecedented proliferation of Ashkenazi-style fundamentalism. The Sephardi spirit of openness to the outside world is currently under attack. It can be argued that a phenomenon such as the Shas Party is part of a broader, postmodern backlash against modernity or a delayed response to modernization. Perhaps it would be unrealistic to suppose that contemporary Sephardim, a generation which has witnessed one of the greatest upheavals and transplantations in its history, would be able to glide smoothly and tranquilly into a Westernized Israel without violent reactions on many levels.

Wrestling with foreign cultures has been an exercise that Sephardic Jews traditionally enjoyed immensely. The tension between rootedness and rootlessness of modern Jews is not a new phenomenon for them. Their names, their lullabies, their genealogical bent and traditions tie them to other lands in the distant past reminding them on a daily basis of those ties. Thrice exiled, from ancient Jerusalem, from medieval Spain, and in our generation from one of the Muslim states of North Africa or the Middle East, the Sephardic Jews face the contemporary world with some trepidation. They fear that the old memories are dimming, that former communities are disappearing.

The past generation has witnessed a spirit of Sephardic renewal simultaneous with the more problematic emergence of Sephardic extremism. The Sephardic presence of several hundred thousand relative newcomers in France has led to a remarkable proliferation of Jewish institutions and a communal posture of greater activism and visibility. At the same time, increasing assimilation is ubiquitous in France. Canada is host to a new Sephardic community of approximately 40,000 to 50,000 Jews, primarily from Morocco. Being francophone, these Sephardim have found a niche for themselves, especially in the province of Quebec. Their synagogues and day schools are scenes of involvement and youthful vitality. The largest North American community, that of the United States, presents perhaps the greatest challenge to the survival of a distinctive Jewish culture. Deeply divided among several ethnic groups, possessing only a few day schools (notably, although not exclusively, in the Syrian community), the 250,000 American Sephardim tend to have little knowledge of their cultural roots. Their Sephardic loyalties are either ethnic—to the community of origin in the Muslim world—or familial and synagogal. One wonders how long they will remain immune to the ferment sweeping the Ashkenazic community generated by such issues as liturgical reform and feminism. That they have avoided meaningful discussions of these issues until today is a sign that they have yet to integrate themselves fully into either the American scene or the American Jewish Ashkenazic subculture. Sephardic Jews possess perhaps the most potent keys to Jewish survival—pride in their past, respect for Judaism and its traditions, and deep familial attachments that even the corrosive forces of modernity have not managed to obliterate. These traits may, ultimately, provide precisely the antidotes that Jewish communal organizations are seeking to counteract the loneliness of the modern Jew in a skeptical world.

As we have suggested, Jewish history has been characterized by multiple approaches to major issues for thousands of years. Rather than regarding multiple approaches as a divisive force, the Sephardic way has often provided a viable alternative. The Sephardic response to modernity is one such case. Much more needs to be learned about how Sephardic Jews have confronted the challenges of the modern world. It is just possible that in their responses lie important sources of strength from which all Jews facing the challenges of the twenty-first century can learn.

Notes

1 Few studies examine the challenges of modernity among Sephardic Jewry. An early study of the modernization process among Sephardic Jews is still valuable; see Jacob Katz, "Traditional and Modern Societies," *Megamot* 10:4 (1960): 304–11 and idem, "Traditional and Modern Society," in *Jewish Societies in the Middle East*, ed. Shlomo Deshen and Walter Zenner (Washington, D.C.: University Press of America, 1982).

2 On the *francos* in Turkey see Abraham Galante, *Histoire des Juifs d'Istanbul depuis la prise de cette ville en 1453*, vol. 2 (Istanbul: Impr. Hüsnüt-abiat, 1942), pp. 213–24, reprinted in Abraham Galante, *Historie des Juifs de Turquie*, vols. 1 and 2 (Istanbul: Isis, 1987); and Attilio Milano, *Storia Degli Ebrei italiani nel Levante* (Florence: Casa Editrice Israel, 1949). On North Africa, see Michel Abitbol, "The Encounter between French Jewry and the Jews of North Africa: Analysis of a Discourse (1830–1914)," in *The Jews in Modern France*, eds. Frances Malino and Bernard Wasserstein (Hanover and London: University Press of New England, 1985), pp. 31–53. An outstanding exemplar of the reforming Jew in Ottoman lands is analyzed in Aaron Rodrigue, "Abraham de Camondo of Istanbul: The Transformation of Jewish Philanthropy," in *From East and West: Jews in a Changing Europe 1750–1870*, eds. Frances Malino and David Sorkin (Oxford: Basil Blackwell, Ltd., 1990).

3 The best analysis of the activities of the Alliance in Turkey is Aron Rodrigue, *French Jews, Turkish Jews* (Bloomington: Indiana University Press, 1990).

4 Albert Memmi, *Pillar of Salt* (Chicago: J. Philip O'Hara, Inc., 1955), p. 331.

5 Aron Rodrigue, *Images of Sephardi and Eastern Jewries in Transition, 1860–1939: The Teachers of the Alliance Israélite Universelle* (Seattle: University of Washington Press, 1993); Esther Benbassa, "Education for Jewish Girls in the East: A Portrait of the Galata School in Istanbul, 1872–1912," *Studies in Contemporary Jewry* 9 (1993): 163–73.

6 One notable instance of community resistance to the introduction of a Western-style school was the spirited resistance to the earliest such school which occurred in Istanbul in the mid-nineteenth century. Its guiding spirit, the *franco*, Abraham de Camondo, was ultimately compelled to leave the Ottoman Empire entirely, living his remaining years in great oppulence but as a broken man in Paris.

7 See Jacob Landau, *Jews, Arabs, Turks: Selected Essays* (Jerusalem: Magnes Press, 1993), pp. 49–59, for a discussion of the teaching of Hebrew in the Egyptian schools of the Alliance Israélite Universelle.

8 See Norman A. Stillman, *Sephardi Religious Responses to Modernity* (Luxembourg: Harwood Academic Publishers, 1995), pp. 29–47, for a fuller discussion of Elijah Bekhor Hazzan and Raphael Ben Simeon and their gradualist approach to modernization in Egypt and Morocco, respectively.

[9] See Harvey Goldberg, ed., *Sephardi and Middle Eastern Jewries: History and Culture in the Modern Era* (Bloomington: Indiana University Press, 1995), for wide-ranging discussions of modernity in the Middle East.

[10] Marc D. Angel, *Voices in Exile: A Study in Sephardi Intellectual History* (Hoboken, New Jersey: Ktav Publishing House, 1991), pp. 182–83.

[11] Zvi Zohar, *Tradition and Change: Halakhic Responses of Middle Eastern Rabbis to Legal and Technological Change (Egypt and Syria, 1880–1920)* [Hebrew] (Jerusalem: Ben Zvi Institute, 1993).

[12] Rabbi Hazzan issued an extremely significant ruling on the problem of the *agunah* and recommended that during the wedding ceremony, the bridegroom should make a statement indicating that the marriage was conditional. That is, if in the future, he and his wife were divorced civilly, he would give her a *get* in a specified period of time; if he failed to do so, the marriage would be considered null and void. This moderate and humane position is only now gaining acceptance in courts of law in Israel. See Stillman, *Sephardi Religious Responses*, pp. 43–44.

[13] Norman Stillman, *The Jews of Arab Lands* (Philadelphia: Jewish Publication Society of America, 1979), pp. 226–28.

[14] The best description of the courtier/rabbi is still Gerson D. Cohen's discussion in his introduction to the *Sefer ha-Qabbalah: The Book of Tradition of Abraham ibn Daud* (Philadelphia: Jewish Publication Society of America, 1967). For a sophisticated discussion of the creative tensions among the worldly Spanish poets, see Ross Brann, *The Compunctious Poet* (Baltimore: Johns Hopkins University Press, 1991).

10

THE CRISIS OF JEWISH SECULARISM
Michael Stanislawski

On November 3, 1935, at the age of fifty-five, Vladimir Jabotinsky, the founder and head of the Revisionist Zionist movement, and perhaps the most controversial Jew of his day, wrote his last will and testament. Virtually penniless, he had few material possessions to allocate to his heirs; of greater concern to him, then as always, was his political legacy, which he expressed in clear and precise instructions in the English language: "My bones, if I be buried outside the Land of Israel, should be transferred to the Land of Israel only at the express order of the Jewish government of that country when it will be established."[1] In other words, even in anticipation of death Jabotinsky was the ultimate statist Zionist, dedicated beyond all else to a Jewish polity in Palestine. In the vociferous public debate over his views both during his life and ever since, much attention has been given to the controversy over Jabotinsky's version of militant Jewish nationalism and the bitter animosity that had prevailed between him and the leaders of the Leftist and Liberal Zionist movements, a personal and ideological hostility which still serves rather to define the basic political divides in Israeli society between the Left and the Right.

But very little attention has been paid to the first line in Jabotinsky's instructions concerning his bodily remains, twenty-two words which speak volumes about his deepest philosophical and personal beliefs: "I wish to be buried or cremated (it is the same to me) at the place in which death shall find me."[2] In other words, Jabotinsky's Jewish nationalism was so unremittingly secular, that he cared not a whit about transgressing perhaps the ultimate taboo of Judaism, cremation, shunned and avoided by even the most alienated and atheistic Jews.

I can think of no better introduction to the subject of this chapter—an attempt to sort through the crisis of Jewish secularism through the prism of a Jewish historian. In the past century many attempts have been made to create a secular Jewish culture built on the Hebrew or Yiddish language, the political vision of Zionism, or the social ideology of Marxism. What can we say about the past, present, and future of such ideologies, and in the process, what can we learn about creating the Jewish future? To answer these questions in their entirety would require at least a semester's worth of lectures at Columbia; how can we go about summarizing a plausible response on one foot, as the Hebrew cliché has it?

Let me begin, as I probably ought not, with a personal anecdote: In the mid-1970s, as a graduate student at Harvard, having just returned from a year of doctoral research in Israel, I decided for some mysterious reason that it was terribly wrong of me not to belong formally to any Jewish political party. I therefore opened the Boston telephone directory and found the address of the local branch of the organization that seemed closest to representing the ideas with which I sympathized on the Israeli scene—the Labor Zionist Alliance. I was a bit troubled by the fact that officially, at least, the Labor Zionists were still a socialist party, but nonetheless I began my trek to the headquarters of the Boston Labor Zionists. I was a bit perplexed by the address I had found. It was not, as I had expected, the Zionist House on elegant Commonwealth Avenue, just opposite the Ritz Carleton Hotel and the Boston Public Garden, nor even the far less majestic, but multifaceted, edifice of the Combined Jewish Philanthropies, a stone's throw away from Filene's Basement—but some dark, dank, and anonymous building in the midst of what then passed for Boston's Financial District. After wandering around for half an hour, I finally found my way to the tiny office which was the object of my quest, presented myself to the two nice little ladies behind the door, and blurted out my request: "May I please have some information on joining your organization." Barely able to contain their laughter at the sight of a young person in a tweed jacket and chinos asking how he could join the Labor Zionist Farband, they explained to me that in the twenty years they had worked in that office they had never faced such a situation. While it is true that this was the Boston—nay, the New England—headquarters of the Labor Zionist Alliance, their job, truly, was to work on the Histadrut campaign. If I really wanted to get information on becoming a Labor Zionist, I would have to call a Mr. Goldberg, the secretary of the Boston Farband. But I ought to be warned, they concluded as I slinked out the door in embarassment, that I might not feel entirely comfortable in Mr. Goldberg's group, whose members' average age was seventy-five. I never did become a Labor Zionist.

Although always extremely wary of generalization from anecdote—the greatest pitfall of east European Jewish historiography—my tale does, I think, graphically depict an unassailable truth in North American Jewish life: the decline and fall of the ideologies of Jewish secularism which were either transported to these shores from eastern Europe or developed indigenously by east European Jewish immigrants in North America. The plethora of organizations and parties based on the varieties of modern Jewish secular politics—Zionist, socialist, communist, Yiddishist, Hebraist, and their multitudinous permutations and combinations—are now slowly but surely dying out along with their original adherents. To be sure, here and there we see isolated and eccentric exceptions to the rule, but these curiosities do not add up to any substantial continuum of the movements they adhere to, and oftentimes seem only to mimic their grandparents in a fit of anti-Establishment post-counter cultural nostalgic mimesis. Historians and sociologists of North American, and particularly United States, Jewry have amply documented this demise, tracing the abandonment of the ideologies of Jewish secularism on the part of the very next generation of American Jews on their seemingly implacable rise into the upper middle class and its natively American and American-Jewish ideological preoccupations. If the children and grandchildren of all these Bundists and Labor Zionists and Revisionists and Communists and Territorialists retain an identification with the Jewish community (and we truly have no way to establish to what extent they do), it is overwhelmingly in the classic form of what is often called the "civil religion" of North American Jews: attenuated synagogue affiliation, UJA contribution, voting and marriage patterns, and the like.

Historians and sociologists have most often attempted to explain the progressive death of the ideologies of Jewish secularism in the United States and Canada by focusing primarily on the processes of immigrant absorption that have rendered all these ideologies inherently incompatible with the cultural, social, and political ideals, norms, and behavior of the New World. These processes are rather self-evident: the unassailable magnetism of the English language and monolingualism in American and Anglo-Canadian culture; the failure of any socialist movement to establish itself in American political life; the self-destructive imperative of North American Zionists-in-exile after the establishment of the State of Israel.

Though certainly correct on one level, these explanations of the demise of Jewish secular ideologies and movements in North America are immensely complicated by the fact that a very similar process obtains not only in the Jewish communities of Great Britain, France, and Latin America—all of whose social and political cultures are substantially different from the American or Canadian way—but more importantly, in the State of Israel itself, the grandest creation of nineteenth-century Jewish secularism.

Few readers would be surprised to hear that Israel today is grappling with acute ideological malaise, at least on the part of its secular majority. (I shall not here discuss the parallel story of the crisis of Israeli Orthodoxy.) In sum, the attempts at creating an Israeli civil religion based on secular Zionism and Hebraism (and, in most cases, socialism) are assailed today by an utterly unexpected crisis of conscience. All the famous kibbutz Passover *haggadot* which do not mention God but only the exodus from Egypt and the rites of spring, the Shavuot ceremonies which celebrate the agricultural harvest but not the Revelation at Sinai, the Hanukkah menorahs lit without blessings in recollection of military victory rather than miraculous intercession, have all but failed to sustain the spiritual and ideological needs of the first generation of Sabras (nativeborn Israelis) born after 1948. Thus, in addition to their substantial material and physical woes, young secular Israelis suffer increasingly from the lack of a clear commitment to a Jewish identity beyond love of land, and even lack a profound understanding of the history and meaning of Zionism itself. Every other year, it seems, the Israeli Ministry of Education comes up with another program for raising "Jewish consciousness" in its secular school system, but invariably the crisis continues, the complaints recur, the curricula are replaced, the effort fails.

The cause of this crisis, it must be understood, is perhaps not so paradoxical as it may first appear: The secular Zionist ideologies that motivated and inspired the fight for the establishment of the Jewish state have to a substantial extent lost their hold as a consequence of their very success. On the left, the selfless sacrifice to labor, to *"kibbush ha-'adamah*—conquering the land," had reaped unheard of fecundity, to the extent that Aaron David Gordon or the other founders of Degania, the first kibbutz, could not possibly recognize their beloved settlement today, not least of all because hard manual labor has been rendered all but superfluous by automation and by an international economy that has caused many, if not most, of the kibbutzim and moshavot to shift their emphasis away from agriculture to light manufacturing or high-tech, computer technology. The children and grandchildren of the original *halutzim* (pioneers) are now not suffering from malaria and mosquitoes in the swamps, but leading the comfortable life of upper-middle-class suburbanites who know, in their heart of hearts, that a new dream, a new vision, a new *raison d'être* is absolutely essential to their future, if frustratingly elusive. Similarly, if not so overtly, on the right, the Revisionist movement as it has been legitimized into the Israeli mainstream, has lost a good part of its original constituency and relies almost exclusively on support from an entirely new population with a view of the world and of Judaism which would make Vladimir Jabotinsky spin in his grave.

The results of this crisis are clear: on the one hand, an unprecedented level of emigration from Israel, caused not only by financial woes and the burden of military service, but also by a perceived lack of reason to stay, to bear the financial, physical, and psychic burdens in the absence of a compelling ideology; and on the other, a marked movement back to religious Orthodoxy, oftentimes of the most fundamentalist stripe. Not only do former pop stars, soccer players, and drug addicts flock en masse to black-hatted yeshivot, the rumor had it some time ago that no less than Leon Trotsky's grandson was studying in a yeshivah on the West Bank. And in between the extremes of abandonment and fanaticism, there extends a vast gulf of confusion and anomie.

How can we explain the crisis of Jewish secularism which is manifest, albeit in different forms, in Cleveland and in Hadera, in Toronto and in Tel Aviv, in Buenos Aires and in Beersheva?

The answer—or at least the beginnings of an answer—may lie in a critical reappraisal of the very beginnings of modern Jewish political and intellectual history, from the middle of the eighteenth century to the end of the nineteenth. That was the time when a shattering crisis of identity and faith tore many (and ultimately most) Jews away from their ancestral moorings and led some of them to create compelling new philosophies and ideologies to guide them through the dizzying maze of the modern world. This revolution resulted, of course, from the spread of the ideas of the Enlightenment. First and foremost this meant the acceptance of a new conception of the primacy of the individual: Each human being was deemed to hold the same natural rights, to deserve equal treatment regardless of station in life, family, or origin. This conception made possible the emancipation of the Jews as equal citizens of the modern nation state. But the premise of inherent and unalienable equality had a fateful corollary as well. All philosophical or religious traditions which were based on inequality or claimed unique divine inspiration were forcefully attacked; no one religion had a monopoly on the truth, proclaimed the Enlightenment. Rather, all religions shared the same philosophical and spiritual premises clothed in different garb. Religion, therefore, was to be a matter of individual conscience and to be relegated to the private sphere where it could not perpetuate restrictions on individual liberty. The notion prevailed, in other words, that church and state, the realm of the sacred and the realm of the secular, religion and nationality, were distinct and separate entities. Along with Roman Catholicism and the various Protestant denominations, Judaism was forced to defend itself against this new way of thinking and to respond creatively to the severe criticisms levelled against traditional religion by the Enlightenment. For Jews, moreover, the Enlightenment's relegation of religion to the private domain raised another, quite different, problem: the definition of a Jew. Until this time, everyone—Jew and non-Jew alike—had agreed that Jews constituted both a nation and a religious group. But now that the concepts of religion and nation were separated, the question was posed: "Are the Jews simply adherents of a faith parallel to all other faiths, or are they members of a distinct national group?"

To simplify matters substantially, but not unfairly, in the first half of the nineteenth century, western European Jews responding to the unprecedented opportunities and attractions of emancipation redefined themselves in the terminology of the Enlightenment as members of a religious confession without any specific national traits. The Jews in Germany, France, England, or America were not members of the Jewish nation, but simply Germans, Frenchmen, Englishmen, or Americans of the Jewish faith (or of the Mosaic persuasion, as the charming phrase went), parallel to Germans, Frenchmen, or Americans of the Christian persuasion. The most radical consequence of such a redefinition was proposed by the Reform movement, many of whose nineteenth-century proponents argued that Judaism's uniqueness consisted not in specific rituals or laws but in its essential religious truths, its teachings of ethical monotheism. To be a good Jew meant not to obey any outdated ritual laws, but to live according to the Hebrew Bible's moral and ethical precepts; and the task of the Jews as a group was to spread these lessons to the world at large. This new type of Judaism had no national boundaries or implications; any references to national exclusivity were expunged from the liturgy and the theology; the Messianic hope was transformed from a belief in a personal Messiah who would lead the Jews back to Zion to a commitment to universal brotherhood and freedom; all references to the Land of Israel were to be deleted; and German, or any vernacular language, was acceptable as the language of Jewish prayer. This basic formulation of "German-Frenchmen-Englishmen-American of the Mosaic persuasion" was soon adopted—if with far less radical theological or liturgical consequences—by the two other new forms of Jewish religiosity in the West, Positive Historical Judaism, the forerunner of Conservative Judaism, and Neo-Orthodoxy.

A few decades later, a different group of Jews, in different political circumstances that placed them outside the purview of emancipation, began to argue the other side of the coin of the Enlightenment's dichotomy between religion and nationality. That is, for the first time, Jewish intellectuals began to argue that the Jews as a group were not a religious community at all, but a nation—perhaps a nation different in some ways from other nations, but a nation nonetheless that ought to be regarded, and in time to become, just like all the other nations. This new self-definition of the Jews began to be articulated not, as is often claimed, only in the aftermath of the pogroms of the 1880s, but in the 1860s and 1870s. These decades, of course, were the period of the greatest successes of the new movements of nationalism which swept through Europe from Russia to Greece and from Serbia to Ireland, and resulted, most dramatically, in the unification of Germany and Italy and the transformation of the self-perception of dozens of smaller ethnic and religious communities.

At precisely the same time, and for parallel reasons, large numbers of Jewish intellectuals began to be influenced by the rising socialist movement in the West and the so-called Populist movements in Russia. Some of these men and women ceased to regard themselves as Jews or were utterly indifferent to the fate of their erstwhile community, believing that they were simply members of the new revolutionary *avant-garde*. (The latter-day bearers of this mentality included such famous stars of international communism as Trotsky and Rosa Luxemburg.) But already in the 1870s, other young Jewish radicals began to bring socialism to the Jewish street (to use a later slogan); some brave souls even began to forge a new, radical Jewish identity, synthesizing their socialism with their Jewish nationalism. These Jewish versions of modern nationalism and socialism and their intersection guided more and more adherents, for rather obvious reasons, in the decades that followed the pogroms of 1881. By the late 1890s, these trends had essentially crystallized into two distinct camps: the Bund, the Jewish socialist party, founded in Vilna in 1897, which argued for a synthesis between socialism and Jewish nationalism based on a commitment to Yiddish as the national language of the Jews, and the Zionist movement, founded in Basel that very same year, which united liberals and socialists in faith in the return of the Jews to their ancient homeland to build there a third Jewish commonwealth based on the Hebrew language.

These two movements quickly became bitter enemies, often denouncing and battling one another more passionately than outside forces. Yet the objective student of modern Jewish politics must understand that both Zionism and Bundism—and their linguistic offshoots, Hebraism and Yiddishism—were, in fact, variations on the same theme of modern Jewish nationalism. (One famous Russian radical made the same point, to the fury of the Bundists, by denouncing them pithily, as "Zionists afraid of sea-sickness.") Not only did both these movements stem from one common source, they shared a profoundly and aggressively secularist bent, a post-Enlightenment areligious modernism premised on a break with the ideological and spiritual traditions of both east European Orthodox Judaism and the emancipated Judaisms of the West. The pre-condition of either form of modern Jewish nationalism, in other words, was the secularization of a significant part of the Jewish people. Perhaps it is not in the least coincidental, therefore, that the prime fathers of both Zionism and Bundism were utterly secularized, areligious, if you will, "assimilated" Jews. Moses Hess, Leon Pinsker, Theodor Herzl, Max Nordau, Nahum Sokolow, Vladimir Jabotinsky, and Vladimir Medem were all men who had absolutely no interest in, or commitment to, the religious or spiritual aspects of Judaism but who, in Herzl's words, "found their way back to the Jewish people" through the door of modern Jewish nationalism. (Medem, the founder of the Bund, was actually baptized and raised in the Russian Orthodox Church; and Zionist historians are always discomfited by a rather purple passage in Herzl's diaries, written before he stumbled into Zionism, which advocated the pilgrimage of the entire Jewish people to St. Stephen's Cathedral in Vienna to be baptized en masse, thereby solving in one fell stroke the "Jewish Problem.") When these men returned to the Jewish community, they did not want to come back to the old Jewish way of life, not that of the Vilna *bes midrash* or the Berlin Chorschul; they were determined to build an entirely new Jewish life, a new, secularized notion of the Jew, a new Jewish personality, a new Jewish culture, even a new Jewish body, that would result in the creation of a healthy, productive, Jewish national organism.

The radical break with the Jewish past demanded by both these movements is easier to understand in regard to the Bund than to Zionism. For the Bundists, of course, the rejection of the religious or spiritual nature of Jewishness was total and absolute; traditional religion was the opiate of the masses and the tool of the clerical-bourgeois oppressors. The holidays and sancta of the Jewish life cycle and year cycle were to be marked with totally secular celebrations in the Yiddish tongue. The fathers of Yiddish literature and socialist politics were to supplant the patriarchs of the Bible (even the famous Yiddish translation by Yehoash).

For the Zionists, the solution was not so clear-cut. From the beginning, the leaders of the movement recognized that they depended on a broad spectrum of opinion on matters both political and spiritual to gain any momentum, and they frequently invoked the language, metaphors, and symbols of traditional Jewish religious culture, all the while infusing them with radical new meanings. But Zionism, no less than Bundism, was not an easily accepted, natural, normal, "establishment" outgrowth of Jewish history and belief. On the contrary, it was a revolutionary movement, a radical break with the past, in all its manifestations, whether left-wing, right-wing, or centrist. This is difficult to explain today, for the simple reason that an ideology which merely one generation ago was adhered to, in truth, by only a small part of the Jewish people, has now become the universally accepted bastion of faith of the vast majority of Jews. To my generation, born after 1948, the state of Israel is simply a fact of life, as natural a part of world geography and politics as France or Japan; to my students at Columbia—all of whom were born, believe it or not, after the assasination of John F. Kennedy—Zionism is as much a part of the "Establishment" as the Chase Manhattan Bank or the Columbia Business School.

An illustrative anecdote is in order here. Periodically I teach a course on modern Jewish ideologies that surveys all the political movements invented or happened upon by Jews since the beginning of the nineteenth century. As part of the exercise, I have my students—basically, nice, bright, well brought-up kids from Scarsdale or Newton or Shaker Heights—read Theodor Herzl's classic utopian novel, *Altneuland*, his fascinating, if rather peculiar, fantasy of what a Jewish state in the Land of Israel would be like. All of my students read the book and understand its futuristic vision, but rarely, if ever, does any one of them ever notice, or at least remember, the entire first section of the novel, the dramatic crux of the story, which is a devastatingly sharp and angry critique of bourgeois Jewish society in Vienna at the end of the nineteenth-century. It is really a *Goodbye Columbus* type of satire written when Philip Roth's grandfather was merely a tot. My students don't mark the sarcasm, don't understand the satire, for a simple reason: they cannot for a moment conceive of Theodor Herzl as a devastating critic of Jewish society or of Jews, as a pained and furious outsider denouncing Jewish life and mores. Herzl as a critic of the gentile world or of antisemitism they eminently expect, but the dissent of Herzl and his disciples, their often vitriolic attacks on established Jewish life and religion are simply too far beyond my students' realm of experience or expectations even to be noticed without prodding and explication. Essentially, the compromise that was agreed upon by the Zionists in regard to the role of religion in the Jewish future was the solution preached at the very beginning of the movement by one of its earliest theoreticians in Russia in the 1880s, Moses Leib Lilienblum. For all the importance of the religion in Jewish culture, Lilienblum argued, religious questions cannot, under any circumstances, be allowed to interfere with the movement for settlement of the Land of Israel. That goal—which is synonymous with the question of whether the Jews will once more be a living nation—overwhelms and renders insignificant any other issues.

Listen to Lilienblum's words, written in 1882, which formed the basic political strategy of the new Zionist movement in regard to religion:

> Be silent, all sectarian squabbles, before the salvation of Israel! The nation as a whole is far dearer to all of us than the obdurate rulings of legalists or the religious conscience of freethinkers. In [the national struggle] there are no *misnagdim* or *hasidim*, no traditionalists and modernists, no Orthodox or heretics, only the children of Abraham, Isaac, and Jacob! Any Jew who does not abandon his nation is a Jew in the fullest sense, one of the chosen people.
>
> May everyone among us understand—*Hasidim, misnagdim*, enlighteners, freethinkers—that only in vain do the moralists always complain that we are not all united in one belief. Such a unity never existed among us and never will, just as it never obtained among any other nation. Only sheep can be so united, not intelligent human beings; there is no nation in Europe that is not divided into clericalists, conservatives, liberals, progressivists, radicals, orthodox, freethinkers, heretics, materialists, and the like. We, too, always experienced similar divisions . . . for it is said that just as men's faces are different so are their ideas. Therefore, there is no sense to hope that when we return to the land of our fathers all Jews will be of the same religious cast. May every individual there follow his own conscience . . . orthodox will send their children to schools just like those in Lithuania and Poland, and the enlightened will establish European schools, and neither side will oppress the other. *Our political life will* reconcile all *problems.* . . .
>
> All individual problems, be they religious or economic, must be stilled in favor of the one overriding goal—the permanent salvation of the Jews! Let us unite, come together, gather our dispersed and ascend to our Land in joy. All those on the side of the Lord and His nation must proclaim: I am for Zion![3]

For Lilienblum and his comrades, then, arguments over the religious complexion of the new Jewish homeland in Palestine were not only destructive to Jewish unity but utterly superfluous. In the future Jewish state, religious, cultural, and economic pluralism would result naturally from the very fact of Jewish political self-determination; in the present, what was essential was a pluralistic banding together of disparate points of view, a broad coalition of rabbis and freethinkers, socialists and liberals, all committed to the same overarching goal of creating an autonomous Jewish polity in Palestine.

What Lilienblum and his colleagues did not or could not fathom was a two-fold truth that is only observable now through the great luxury of both hindsight and the existence of a sovereign Jewish state. First, in the absence of religious freedom religious pluralism can easily become a self-obliterating mirage. It is not only dangerous, but self-contradictory, to expect religious pluralism from those convinced that they alone hearken to the voice of the Lord. Second, and possibly more importantly, the bond between religion and nationhood seems to be too profoundly etched in the character and culture of the Jews blithely to be wished away. Neither the Zionists nor the Bundists could fathom that the rendering asunder of Jewish nationality and religion was an act of self-denial and spiritual deracination which could not, in the end, fructify a long-lived, new form of Jewish identity. What seems to have happened, quite simply, was that the ideologies of Jewish secularism created in eastern Europe in the nineteenth century could not survive more than two generations of rupture from Jewish religious tradition and behavior. It was one thing for children born in traditional Jewish homes to reject their parents' religiosity and the culture and spiritual succor which went along with that religiosity; it was far more difficult, but possible, for the rebels to raise their own children on purely secularist spiritual food. But it has proven exceedingly difficult, if not impossible, to sustain a third generation of secularized Jews—for the very simple reason that the original distinction between nation and religion demanded by the Enlightenment was naive and inappropriate to the Jewish condition, if not to humankind as whole. This analysis does not lead to the conclusion that the only form of Jewish identity that can sustain itself through the generations is the pre-Enlightenment variety which rejects the basic premises of modern Western civilization. On the contrary, it is abundantly clear that for the vast majority of identifying Jews the world over, the only possible version of Judaism that can sustain itself in the future is one that seeks to harmonize Jewish nationality with Jewish faith and Jewish civilization with the concepts and teachings of Western culture. Thus, for example, gradually the anti-nationalism of the Reform movement was worn thin by the realities of modern Jewish history, and especially by the rise and success of the Zionist movement, to the extent that all but an insignificant extreme wing of the movement made their peace with and began actively to support the return of Jews to Zion.

What no one—and certainly not a mere historian—can predict, is how exactly those raised in the now troubled and exhausted ideologies of Jewish secularism will solve the dilemma of reintegrating themselves with the spiritual core of Judaism, how they will reunite their Jewish nationalism with its Siamese twin, the Jewish religious tradition. But I am left only with the most poignant articulation that I know of that grueling dilemma—the words

of one of the most eloquent and most pained spokesmen of the religion of
Jewish secularism, the Yiddish poet, Jacob Glatstein:

> My beloved God,
> How many prayers to him I've profaned,
> How often have I blasphemed
> In the nights
> Warmed my fearful bones
> At the firepot of knowledge. . . .
> The God of my unbelief is beautiful.[4]

Notes

[1] A Hebrew translation of Jabotinsky's will can be found in his *Ketavim* (Jerusalem: Eri Jabotinsky Publishing Co., 1947), correspondence volume, p. 18. I have examined the original English version in the archives of the Jabotinksy Institute in Tel Aviv.

[2] Ibid.

[3] Translated in Arthur Hertzberg, *The Zionist Idea* (New York: Atheneum, 1959), pp. 170–71.

[4] The original Yiddish is reproduced with this translation in Binyamin and Barbara Harshav, *American Yiddish Poetry* (Berkeley: The University of California Press, 1986), p. 323.

PART
4

EDUCATING
FOR THE
FUTURE

11

EDUCATING FOR THE FUTURE: AN INTRODUCTION

Alex Pomson

An ancient Chinese philosopher is supposed to have said:

Those who think in terms of months - sow seeds.
Those who think in terms of decades - plant trees.
Those who think in terms of centuries - become teachers.

Perhaps it is not too rash to suggest that this particular philosopher may have been overly pessimistic in his estimation of the time needed for educational change, while the more optimistic Jews may have got it right. This suggestion is made in light of the life and work of the two contributors to this section of the volume. Together they demonstrate that it is possible to effect change through education, both in individuals and in whole groups of people, over a much shorter space of time. Indeed, the influence of their work over the last thirty years is rivaled by few in the worlds of either Jewish or general education.[1]

Their shared topic is entitled "Educating for the Jewish Future." At first sight this phrase appears tautologous. After all, one would assume that all of education is inherently future directed. However conceived, education is surely concerned with the change, growth, or development of people, and with the transmission of knowledge or culture from the present generation to future ones.

Certainly, this is self-evident from the perspective of progressives who see education as about becoming rather than being. From their standpoint, education is about the transformation of individuals and of society, and is valued, as John Dewey argued, in terms of how well it supplies the conditions which ensure growth. Indeed, even from a more conservative perspective, education is predicated on a recognition of the inevitability of change or, at least, of human mortality. It is, as Ralph Perry showed, founded on an attempt to enable those who will be alive in the future to know of the past and of its accumulated knowledge. For both progressive and conservative theorists, then, education is driven by a conception of the future and by an attempt to prepare for it.

In practice (and sadly), this is not always so. Much of general and Jewish education is straitjacketed by the past. In the world of Jewish education, policies have been profoundly shaped by inherited prejudices about, for example, relationships between Jews and non-Jews or about the challenges facing Jewish survival. Thus there are many who would respond to contemporary problems of Jewish continuity by trying to recreate models of Jewish education that were successful in earlier, if somewhat different, circumstances. Pedagogy, too, is often crippled by past practice. Teachers of Jewish Studies, for example, use techniques or texts because "that is how things have always been done." Such a mindset exacerbates what is already an endemic problem. Research has shown that, in general, teachers tend to act in a conservative fashion reproducing the pedagogies to which they were exposed in their own education. In the case of many Jewish educators, such studied reproduction has been elevated to a principle, either because they believe change to be halakhically (that is, according to Jewish laws) forbidden or because they believe ancient knowledge to be qualitatively superior to the fruits of contemporary enquiry.

In some ways, Jewish education has also been entirely driven by the present. Schools have been built, for instance, to respond to short-term demographic needs, even if longer term predictions would make them hard to justify. One can think of a number of examples from around the Jewish world where, within a few years of a school's opening, children have had to be bussed long distances to avoid the costs of closing down a recently built institution and starting over in another place. In many fields of education, curricula have been developed in knee-jerk response to urgently felt and present-time difficulties, with a limited sense of the larger pedagogical or financial problems such initiatives might face. The most oft-cited case in the world of general education is the rapid and poorly planned introduction of the new mathematics in America in the wake of Sputnik. Within the realm of Jewish education, a similar and most painful instance was the convulsion following the Rabin assassination, wherein many calls were heard and heeded for the swift introduction of new curricula for "moral education," with little consideration to the broader or longer-term educational context.

This, of course, is not to dismiss the requirement that education be relevant or responsive to the present needs of students and society. Neither is it to ignore the value of rooting Jewish education in Jewish tradition or in the often painful experiences of the Jewish past. The problem, we are suggesting, is that of finding a balance among loyalty to the past, sensitivity to the present, and readiness for the future.

This is the context within which the chapters of Professors Rosenak and Schiff should be seen. In considering how we should educate for the future, they offer two ways to navigate a difficult route. Professor Rosenak, as so often in his writings, maps a powerful conceptual framework within which to consider the content of Jewish education. He takes the concepts of language and literature which he has developed in his most recent book, *Roads to the Palace: Jewish Texts and Teaching*, and shows how they might be used to clarify differences between major orientations towards Jewish education from the past and present.[2] He subsequently demonstrates how these concepts might also help in charting the possibilities that exist in the future treatment of central Jewish educational questions, such as those relating to the nature of Jewish peoplehood or to the meaning of Talmud Torah (the study of sacred texts). His is a masterclass in applied philosophical analysis from someone who has the distinction of having established the philosophy of Jewish education as a serious academic field.

Professor Schiff sets out a different route to the future by portraying the systems and strategies that would go some way towards meeting the future needs of the Jewish community. This paper, like so much of Schiff's work over the last three decades, is grounded in a combination of research, hands-on experience in managing innovative Jewish educational institutions, and an uncanny knack for reading the contemporary educational scene. It is typically global in scope and impressively comprehensive in its grasp of what are depicted as the most urgent challenges.

Together, Professors Rosenak and Schiff constitute a formidable double bill. One analyzes the content, while the other describes the shape which Jewish education could and, in fact, should take in order to secure a healthy Jewish future. Implicitly, they demonstrate why schemes such as York University's Jewish Teacher Education Program are integral to that future. For without teachers capable of meeting the challenges which each of them sets out in his paper, the Jewish people would need the patience of the ancient Chinese before they see an improvement in their present condition.

Notes

1 A somewhat different version of the papers in this section appeared in *The Journal of Jewish Education* 63 (Fall 1997): 23–47.

2 Michael Rosenak, *Roads to the Palace: Jewish Texts and Teaching* (Oxford: Berghahn Books, 1995).

12

INSURING EFFECTIVE
JEWISH EDUCATION
Alvin I. Schiff

The *Midrash* informs us that there are essentially two kinds of future: יש מחר עכשיו ויש מחר לאחר זמן. There is an immediate future—the day after today; and there is a distant future—that holds the many morrows (*Mekhilta* 22). This suggests that in educating for the future, we must engage in both short-range and long-range planning. For each of these levels, the approach must insure both *individual* Jewish identity and Jewish *group* continuity. The latter term—"Jewish continuity"— has been used much too glibly by the Jewish community. "Continuous Jewish group vitality" may be a better way to identify the group need for future survival. Whatever the term, both concepts—individual Jewish identity and Jewish group continuity—are interdependent. If effective, they reinforce each other.

Using a classical Judaic formula to address the theme of this essay, we might say about educating for tomorrow: על חמשה דברים החינוך לעתיד היהודי עומד. Educating for the Jewish future depends on successfully addressing five challenges: (1) bringing the goals of family and school into harmony; (2) finding the proper confluence of the affective and cognitive domains; (3) promoting Hebraic cultural literacy; (4) transmitting both universalistic and particularistic Jewish values; and (5) using appropriate instructional technology.

Why these five items? Because they all address the needs of the target populations of Jewish education. These populations can be differentiated by level of Jewish identity and participation. For lack of a better terminology, I refer to them by the descriptive language currently used to label the various levels of Jewish identification—the affiliated, the marginally affiliated, and the unaffiliated. The classification *affiliated* refers to committed Jews, generally observant Orthodox, Conservative, Reform, or Reconstructionist Jews who participate regularly in synagogue and Jewish communal life, visit Israel, and provide their children with an intensive Jewish education. The *marginally affiliated* category includes Jews who belong to a synagogue and/or a Jewish Community Center and/or contribute to Jewish charities, and/or are involved in Jewish communal work, but are not fully involved in any area. Marginally affiliated Jews generally send their children to a Jewish supplementary school through *bar/bat mitzvah*. A small percentage of them have visited Israel. *Unaffiliated* Jews, who constitute the largest segment of the Jewish population, are just what their classification implies. Generally, they do not belong to Jewish organizations and are not involved in Jewish life activity at home or elsewhere. They have not visited Israel, and their children do not receive a Jewish education. Marginally affiliated and even unaffiliated Jews sometimes may experience forms and feelings of Jewishness in their social, vocational and leisure-time settings. These do not, however, represent significant involvements.

Toward whom should we target our funding and efforts, the unaffiliated, the marginally affiliated, or the affiliated? Should we try to respond to the needs of each group, and in what order? To do so would require a great deal of talent, knowledge and financial resources, perhaps more than the community can marshal. For several decades I have stressed the need to be concerned with all of these categories of youth and adults. Given the current availability of funding, however, it is necessary to prioritize the investment of effort and funds into the most promising and productive activities. Priority support should be provided to those programs with the greatest potential for insuring Jewish continuity. This translates, in the first instance, into aid for Jewish day schools, where most of the students are recruited from the ranks of the affiliated.

The combination of quality Jewish schooling, a good, positive Jewish home, and sound informal Jewish educational experiences is the best guarantee for Jewish continuity. Accordingly, more support must be forthcoming for the day schools, including the funding of family education programs for marginally affiliated parents of pupils and of informal educational programming, particularly Israel experiences, for day-school teenagers. Second-level priority funding should address the needs of Jewish supplementary school pupils and their marginally affiliated parents. As with day school families, this means improving and intensifying school programs, providing family education and encouraging informal educational activities, especially the Israel experience for synagogue school post *bar/bat mitzvah* students. Third-level funding should be targeted for the unaffiliated and made available only after the needs of the affiliated and marginally affiliated are met adequately. Insufficient support for the affiliated, and, certainly for the marginally affiliated, might lead to their joining the growing ranks of the unaffiliated. We must build on what already exists.

The 450,000 Jewish day school and supplementary school pupils in North America and their parents are a ready audience; it is much less difficult to insure their Jewish continuity than that of the unaffiliated. Here, the message for the future is: "Galvanize the core as a Jewish communal priority." Addressing the five challenges with which I began this essay will help insure the future of the core and of many other Jews as well.

THE JEWISH FAMILY AND THE JEWISH SCHOOL

A fascinating study of talented people by Professor Benjamin Bloom of the University of Chicago found that there are two features common to the background of top performers in the arts, music, sports, academia, and science fields. The first is *home support*. Bloom notes:

> The parents of the talented individuals varied greatly in the level of education they had completed, the type of work they engaged in, their economic level, and their avocational interests and activities. However, they were all genuinely concerned about their children and wanted to do the best for them at all stages of their development. To a large extent, they could be described as child-oriented and willing to devote their time, their resources and their energy to giving each of their children the best conditions they could provide for them. Almost no sacrifice was too great if they thought it would help their children's development. . . . It is clear that to be successful, education must be a synergistic experience. Teacher effectiveness depends upon parents and parent effectiveness depends upon teachers.[1]

This kind of synergy does not exist in our Jewish supplementary schools—certainly not for the vast majority of parents.

Most recently, Dr. James P. Comer, after thirty years of clinical involvement with school children at Yale University's Child Study Center, observed that, in successful schools, there is home-school social congruence. He stressed that, to be effective, schools must allow for "the empowerment and full partnership of parents and staff as true partners in addressing the children's psycho-educational and developmental needs."[2] In the context of Jewish education, home-school congruence and the empowerment and partnership of parents and teachers must be Jewishly based.

The school has become a necessary component of every civilized society and a dominant factor in technological, industrial and cultural progress. This fact, however, does not discharge the home of its basic tutorial obligations in the area of subculture and ethics. Modern research clearly demonstrates the need for the home to act as an educational instrumentality. We cannot deal with students if we disregard their family background, since school is, at best, a reinforcer of attitudes, behavior patterns, and even skills acquired in the home environment. In the most comprehensive analysis of American schools ever undertaken, James Coleman and his associates concluded (in 1966) that unless unfavorable home environments were changed, nothing the urban schools could do would have any effect on how much their pupils learned. The Coleman Report claimed that "schools bring little influence to bear on a child's achievement that is independent of his background and social contacts."[3] Another researcher, David Cohen, formerly of Harvard University, argued that "Daily contact with family and peer group society is the most crucial influence on educational attainment and eventual adult behavior."[4]

These findings are even more salient for religious than for secular schooling. The role of the home in contributing to the success of Catholic education, for example, was underscored by the findings of the national study of Catholic schools in America several decades ago.[5] The researchers in that study found that Catholic education exerted an impact only upon students who came from religious homes. The schools, by themselves, had almost no significant effect on the religious behavior of other children. Regarding Jewish behavior, my recent study of graduates of Jewish day schools in the United States shows the influence parents have upon their progeny.[6] It demonstrates that Jewish schools, like Catholic schools, are considerably more effective with pupils from observant or committed homes.

Similarly, in research done at Harvard University, Geoffrey Bock shows that "Doing well in [the Jewish] school depends on the learning environment, the congruence of school values with home values, with the school culture, and [with] other noncognitive effects of education."[7] Jews have always believed that the influence of the home is paramount in the lives of children. The traditional home is best characterized by the spirit of Jewish practice "from the *mezuzah* on the doorpost to the observance of dietary laws in the kitchen." It is the center of religious activity, the means by which children learn to behave Jewishly. Family practices, such as placing coins in the charity box (*pushka*) before lighting Shabbat candles on Friday eve and feeding the family pets and domestic animals before the family members sit down to eat, serves to transmit the social and humane values of Judaism. Children of all ages acknowledge the pedagogical role of the home by blessing their parents as educators—("my father my teacher," "my mother my teacher")—in the Grace after Meals.

In fact, in Jewish tradition, primary responsibility for Jewish education lies in the home. Parents are responsible for the education of their off-spring. "And you shall teach your children" (Deut. 11:13) is a command-ment taken literally. In biblical times, and later in the post-biblical period, elementary level instruction was left in the hands of the parents, particu-larly the father. In the second century C.E., Rabbi 'Akiba instructed one of his disciples: "When you teach your son, teach him out of a well-corrected book," suggesting that the father has an awesome responsibility to teach his offspring properly.[8] When teachers were hired to help parents fulfill this responsibility, they were accorded the same respect due to parents. "He who teaches his friend's son—it is as if he sired him," noted our sages (*Sanhedrin* 19b). Even after the school became a recognized institution in the post-Talmudic era, parents continued to teach their children. The home was the natural place for religious and moral training. Jewish tradition was ahead of its time in ascribing an educational role to parents.

The powerful bond between Jewish parents and children, exemplified by mutual responsibility and mutual respect, made the home a bulwark able to withstand the numerous pressures and stresses from without. If there are reasons for the mysterious ability of Jews to survive against so many odds, they are the family and the school. More than any other people, Jews have recognized their life-sustaining role. Indeed, in calling for Christian-Jewish cooperation in 1960, the Archbishop of York asserted: "We can learn from the Jews about education, about the richness of their home life, and the enormous influence it [sic] had upon their people."[9]

And now, the Jewish family in America is in crisis. One need only cite the all-too-well-known findings of the 1990 National Jewish Population Survey to confirm this observation.[10] With the exception of a very small percentage of homes—mostly Orthodox—the traditional relationship be-tween education and family has broken down.

This brings us to the critical role of the school. The singular focus of schooling—including the Jewish school—has been the education of the child. It is clear, now, that the current challenge of continuity requires that the school broaden its scope to include the whole family. This will change the relationship of the educator to pupils, to parents, and to the community. It will also change the nature of the synagogues that sponsor schools. The last decade has seen some small movements towards change, as creative Jewish educators have developed programming for entire families, but there must be more.

Confluence of the Cognitive and Affective Domains

There are basically two aspects to the process of Jewish identification: *identity formation* and *identity reinforcement*. For children, youths, and adults having no or little home involvement with Jewish life, the *formation* of identity is a necessary first level of education. For those having varying degrees of affiliation, knowledge and experience, *reinforcing* their Jewish identity is the appropriate mode.

Learning takes place in various ways. Different things are learned best in different ways. Learning outcomes depend in part upon the nature of the learning processes. Essentially, there are two types of learning process—*cognitive* and *affective*. Cognitive processes pertain to the acquisition of facts and the comprehension of ideas. They help the learner analyze and articulate concepts and communicate information. Cognitive learning has been, and is, the chief—and often the only—ingredient of formal education. For identity formation, however, cognitive learning is not enough. Affective processes which involve emotions, attitudes, interests, preferences, and values are needed. The affective domain is indispensable in helping learners develop receptiveness to new ideas and behaviors to assure commitment to particular values. Working in confluence with the cognitive domain, the affective process reinforces the school's work with the family as it helps fashion the Jewish identity of young people.

No matter how successful the school is in its family education programs, for the vast majority of students in the Jewish supplementary school and for a significant percentage of day school pupils as well, the school must serve as an alternative Jewish environment. The most important characteristic of the Jewish day school with its longer day and two sets of teachers is its full-time, all-encompassing Judaic climate. This feature is lacking in the supplementary school where it is most urgently needed. The recommendations of the three-year study of Jewish Supplementary Schools in Greater New York, which I directed in the 1980s, respond to this challenge in a variety of ways.[11]

The recommendations fall into a pattern of thesis, antithesis, and synthesis. Supported by current research, the thesis contends that the family, more than any other agency, is the crucial factor in influencing the eventual outcomes of schooling. The antithesis, deriving from Effective Schools Research activity in the public arena, suggests that, notwithstanding societal or family influences, the school can become the crucial, overriding force transmitting knowledge and values to children and youth. The synthesis incorporates both approaches, as it stresses the importance of the family and the school and recognizes the role of the home and the classroom and the impact of both parents and teachers on pupils.

The New York Supplementary School Study recommends that the synagogue school change its education focus from schooling of the young to education of all members of the family. To enhance the affective quality of synagogue education, it suggests that a new structure be developed in which all professionals, including the rabbi, principal, teachers, youth leaders, and cantor, will become members of a family education team, with the rabbi assuming the role of Judaic content leader.[12] Furthermore, the study recommends that the congregational supplementary school provide pupils with opportunities for increased formal and informal educational exposure. This would mean integrating informal educational activities into every level of the school curriculum emphasizing summer educational camping and weekend fellowship programs (one *shabbaton* or weekend retreat per month for upper grade students in lieu of their weekday and Sunday classes during that week).[13] For high school students, this means integrating an Israel experience with appropriate pre-tour and post-tour educational components.

This new mode of synagogue school operation would require the training or retraining of all synagogue professionals. For some teachers, shifting the focus of the school to families would mean full-time educational career opportunities where none or almost none currently exist in the supplementary school system.

EFFECTIVE HEBRAIC-JUDAIC TEACHING AND LEARNING

The second common characteristic of top performers in the Bloom study is quality time-on-task.[14] In the first instance, this means that you cannot really succeed in study unless you invest sufficient time in it. The time invested, moreover, must be *quality* time.

This dimension—quality time-on-task—imposes upon the Jewish community the awesome responsibility of insuring that Jewish school supervisors and teachers are qualified to achieve quality teaching—learning conditions. Among other things, this challenge means making the Jewish education profession attractive to the most talented persons. It means providing high quality in-service education to the current educational professionals and enforcing high standards of practice. These matters deserve full-length, detailed attention much beyond the scope of this chapter.

Unlike the supplementary school, which is seriously deficient in the amount of time available for learning, the day school generally provides a sufficient number of hours for Jewish Studies. Here the challenge is the quality of learning and the lasting effect of instruction.

It is to the credit of the yeshivot throughout North America that over the years they have increased their emphasis on the study of Judaic sources in the original, especially the Pentateuch, the Talmud, and their respective commentaries. The ideological bent of most yeshivot limits their curricula to these subjects plus the study of *Shulhan ʿArukh* (Code of Jewish Law). They pay little or no attention to the Hebrew language as a subject, to the Prophets and Writings, to Jewish history, Jewish philosophy, and Israel. Neither the immediate nor the long-range future holds any prospect for change in their curricula.

The emphasis on the study of Talmud is accompanied by increasing stress on ritual practices as viewed from a fundamentalist, sectarian perspective. In this way the ultra-Orthodox, *Haredi* segment of the Jewish community, seems to be successful in reinforcing the narrow, intensive identity of its youth. Thus its continuity seems well assured. Virtually all the *Haredi* students continue their yeshiva studies through high school and beyond.

While the modern Orthodox day schools and the somewhat less intensive Solomon Schechter (Conservative) schools differ in religious and textual emphases, they all provide balanced Hebraic curricula for their students. The Jewish Studies programs in most communal day schools are not as intensive as in the Orthodox or Conservative schools, and the Judaic programs in day schools under Reform auspices are less intensive still.

My recent research on graduates of Jewish day schools clearly points to the superiority of all-day education. It is clear that young adults who studied in a day school are more likely to observe the Sabbath and *kashrut*, to be involved in the community, and to visit Israel than those who did not. They also intermarry much less frequently.[15]

Further, my research shows beyond a doubt, that young adults who graduated from a day *high* school demonstrate significantly higher levels of adult Jewish behavior than those who completed only an elementary day school. And the intermarriage rate of graduates of Jewish day *high* schools is much lower than that of alumni of elementary schools.[16] These findings challenge the communal leadership to provide greater support to day schools, particularly high schools, to enable all who wish to complete twelve grades of Jewish education to do so.

We must be concerned with the content of Jewish schooling in its entirety as well as its extensiveness. The content of Jewish schooling relates directly to the language of the texts and the language of instruction of Jewish Studies. The Midrash informs us that the Israelites were redeemed from Egypt because, among other things, they did not change their language

(*Midrash Vayikra Rabbah* 32:3). They continued to speak and use Hebrew while in Goshen and during their servitude. The Hebrew language, broadly interpreted to include its use in study, prayer and daily conversation, is one of the key reasons for the miraculous survival of the Jewish people during the last two millennia against unbelievable odds. There are cases of individual Jews who assimilated and whole communities which disappeared, because, among other things, they lost contact with the Hebrew language. The total assimilation of the Jewish community of Alexandria, Egypt, some fifteen hundred years ago is a prime example of the results of this tragic neglect. A working knowledge of Hebrew for the study of texts and for prayer is an imperative for Jewish group survival, since Hebrew is the bearer of Jews' spiritual identity. It is a vehicle of a sacred past, of eternal Jewish values, and, at the same time, a major expression of contemporary Jewish vitality. The mystique of Hebrew underscores the individuality of the Jew, differentiating him from his environment, but not estranging him from it.

Hebraic cultural literacy is one of the most important goals of Hebrew language learning. Even though Hebrew was not a spoken language of the vast majority of Jews during their long Diaspora history, the average person used as many as twelve hundred Hebrew words and terms to denote familiar Judaic concepts and practices. These expressions continue to be an essential part of Judaic-Hebraic literacy, and a literate, well-educated Jew should possess this unique linguistic baggage.

As I note in my book, *The Mystique of Hebrew*, one of the characteristics of Jewish life from the times of the Second Temple until the beginning of the twentieth century was its trilingual dimension. Jews had an internal or Jewish language, an external language, and a sacred language. Their Jewish language was the vernacular of their home (Yiddish, Ladino or other Jewish languages, punctuated with Hebraic religious terminology). The language of the country in which they lived was their external, non-Jewish language for business activity and association with non-Jews. And Hebrew was their sacred language for prayer and study.[17] In educating for the future, Hebrew must become both the vernacular and the sacred language of Jews.

A variety of new instructional efforts including the production of Hebrew language texts and materials and teacher training courses was initiated in the 1980s to improve the teaching of Hebrew language. Hebrew literacy initiatives for adults, moreover, have gained momentum in the 1990's. Yet the revival of the Hebrew language in America is still an elusive goal for the overwhelming majority of Jews. We need a comprehensive plan which takes into consideration: (1) the realities of North American Jewish life and education; (2) the various roles of the Hebrew language in the configuration of Jewish continuity patterns; (3) the potential resources that can be utilized in developing effective Hebrew language programs; (4) the variety of approaches to transmitting Jewish values, reinforcing Jewish identity, and strengthening Israel-Diaspora ties; and (5) the best possible ways to coordinate, modify, and improve current efforts aimed at improving Hebrew language education.

A Jewish community of active Hebrew language learners and regular users is not an unattainable goal. The key is to find the ways to teach Hebrew effectively both as a modern language and as the essential link to the Judaic heritage. It may be helpful to examine those foreign language teaching programs on the university level which do not begin with instruction in conversation. Similarly, we might pursue the modes and goals of teaching Hebrew reading comprehension as a first step in Jewish elementary schools. The program would continue on to text learning, and, then, for a select number of students, to conversation, and finally to writing.

There is strong feeling among many academicians and practitioners that Hebrew "spokenness" is not an attainable goal for the North American Jewish community—that it is certainly not achievable for students in Jewish supplementary schools, and it may even be difficult for many pupils in day schools. This issue must be examined carefully. But the goal of Hebraic cultural literacy for the Jewish masses must not be abandoned; it surely is at least partially achievable. The combination of both goals—Hebrew cultural literacy for the Jewish community, at large, and Hebrew speaking for an elite segment of the Jewish population—may be the best answer to the question of what is the most appropriate role of Hebrew in American Jewish life.

Jewish Values

On the third day of the month of Tishrei, Jews observe the Fast of Gedaliah, commemorating the assassination of the Jewish governor of Jerusalem appointed by the Babylonians after they destroyed the First Temple in 587 B.C.E. "And who killed him?" asks the Talmud (*Rosh Hashanah* 18b). "Ishmael, the son of Netaniah, killed him," comes the answer. "This teaches us that the death of the righteous weighs as heavily as the burning of our Temple." A fast day commemorates each event.

In our time, we have witnessed the murder of an Israeli prime minister. The causes and consequences of this abominable crime thrust upon the educational community in Israel and the Diaspora a major responsibility regarding the moral/ethical education of our youth—an obligation that could change the face and future of Jewish schooling. Rabin's assassination has to change the Jewish education agenda everywhere, for all time. The challenge is to confront irreverent feelings, uncontrolled passion, misdirected energies, and inflammatory language wherever they may be found—on the Right or Left, in the hearts and homes of the fervent opponents of the peace process or of its passionate proponents. The educational challenge is to demonstrate that extremism of any kind is dangerous, that the misuse of language can set the stage for unspeakable acts against humanity.

First, we must note the precedents in Jewish history. Our ancestors were not immune to crimes of fratricide. When 'Avner ben Ner was killed by Yoav (Samuel II 3:27), King David and the Israelites were in shock. "You well know," mourned David, "that a prince and a great man has fallen this day in Israel." Jeremiah was killed by fellow Israelites in Egypt, because they could not bear his unrelenting remonstrations. The Second Temple was destroyed along with Jerusalem and many lives were lost, because relationships among Jews had deteriorated to the point where, our sages inform us, the people of Israel deserved to be destroyed, even though they were meticulous in other Jewish observances. *Sin'at hinam* (baseless hatred), the Talmud suggests, brought about the destruction of the Second Temple.

Rabin's death reminds us that one of the greatest dangers the Jewish people have faced throughout history has been ourselves. There are numerous other lessons we must now teach in all our schools. Foremost is the value of human life, the worthwhileness of every human being. This lesson should be part of a campaign to promote tolerance, understanding, and love of fellow human beings. Jewish education must be in the forefront of reviving the ethical/moral dimension of Jewish life as expressed in the *mitzvot bain adam lahavero* (commandments concerning relationships among people). We must teach our students that one can disagree without being disagreeable, that dissent is a good Jewish tradition. Jews are no strangers to controversy. One needs only to note the sharp differences between Bet Hillel and Bet Shammai, between 'Abaye and Rava in ancient times. Their disputes, however, were "for the sake of Heaven." They all sought to establish the truth and bring about higher standards of Jewish living. Today we must instruct that dissent in a civil manner is a much needed and valuable social and political instrument in a democratic society.

Schools must place emphasis on the idea of ethical role models. In the introduction of his insightful study, *The Prophets*, Abraham Heschel stresses that "the significance of Israel's prophets lies not only in what they said, but also in what they were."[18] Heschel's pithy and powerful description of the prophets provides a meaningful message of modeling for our times. He writes: "The prophet is a person who sees the world with the eyes of God . . . a person who holds God and man in one thought at one time, at all times . . . who suffers harm done to others . . . living in dismay, he has the power to transcend dismay."[19]

The adults in the school community—supervisors, teachers, rabbis, cantors, youth leaders and clerical staff—must all be able to serve as models. Parents must be sensitized to the importance of adult members of the home serving as models of Jewish behavior within the framework of Jewish family education. Moreover, Jewish history is replete with "heroes" whose biographies could well serve to inform and inspire. This form of teaching should be highlighted in our schools.

Students must be taught to appreciate and practice *ahavat hinam* (selfless love) as advocated by the saintly, Chief Rabbi of Palestine, Abraham Isaac Kook. If the Second Temple was destroyed because of *sin'at hinam* (gratuitous hatred), he asserted, the Third Temple will be built because of *ahavat hinam*. In each school, curricularizing Judaic ethical teachings is a programmatic imperative on three levels: moral education as a separate subject; integration of ethical lessons into the ongoing subject matter of the school; and the development of a moral climate.

The Jewish educational establishment has a responsibility beyond the classroom walls to help provide moral/ethical instruction in formal and informal settings. Educational leaders everywhere must organize for moral education through conferences, seminars, teacher training, the development of text materials and guidelines, and pilot school programs. In our thrust to highlight Jewish moral/ethical education, we must take care to insure that all points of view—from the political Right to the political Left, from ultra-religious to ultra-secular, from zealous sabras to Jews committed to Diaspora living, from ardent Zionists to non-Zionists whose support for Israel is expressed solely in financial terms—are considered with civility, fairness, and honesty.

Modern Educational Technology

It is impossible in the latter half of the last decade of the twentieth century to speak about "Educating for the Future" without urgent consideration of the implications of the technological revolution for Jewish schooling. The computer has revolutionized modern civilization. It can improve teaching and learning in school and home dramatically. Since the arrival of the cyberspace age, the classroom will never be the same. The computer permits teachers and students to go beyond the classroom walls and become part of a larger, exciting Jewish world. The remarkable information superhighway can benefit education, as it has the corporate and business worlds.

It can make teaching easier and increase student productivity significantly. It can initiate new Jewish learning and reinforce the classroom through the internet, which allows teachers and students to access information from libraries and other on-line sources with ease. It makes possible desk-top video conferencing. In addition, the internet permits the development and use of new educational tools like e-mail and chatrooms, where students all over the world can talk to each other, and it allows asynchronous learning, which simply means that information can be accessed at any time from any place. Colleges in North America are moving rapidly into this form of learning. Jewish education must do the same. Talking to Jews all over the world would give Jewish students a sense of Jewish connectedness. The global village will help Jewish students to see that "the whole world is Jewish." New computer-based multi-media can extend, expand, modify, and strengthen teaching and learning at home and school. Interactive, computer-based instruction can help students discover new knowledge; students can pace themselves according to their specific learning needs.

For the young and young-at-heart, using the computer is fun. As of this writing, forty-one million Americans are connected to the internet, and three hundred synagogues in North America have their own websites or e-mail addresses. These numbers are constantly growing. All Jewish youth movements are on-line. The Council of Jewish Federations, in cooperation with other major Jewish organizations, sponsors the Jewish on-line network.

A recent study shows that 11- to 14-year-olds are the most frequent individual computer users. The Jewish educational community must insure that Jewish programming is available on the computer for this critical group. It is at their age that Jewish identity is often challenged as their peers replace the influence of their home and as they themselves become increasingly involved in the larger society. The only electronic equipment needed by a school for internet involvement is a computer and a modem.

AFTERWORD

Here I have described five urgent Jewish educational challenges that confront us as we contemplate the future. There are obviously many more education needs that should be addressed both for the *mahar achshav* and the *mahar l'ahar zman*—in the immediate and distant futures. Increasingly, in the open North American society, the Jewish school must be able to respond effectively to new societal developments, new communal conditions, new problems, and even new threats, if future generations are to face the future. If these five challenges are dealt with adequately the Jewish community will be well on its way to a bright future.

Notes

1 Benjamin Bloom, *Developing Talent in Young People* (New York: Ballantine Books, 1985), p. 117.

2 J. P. Comer, N. M. Haynes, E. T. Joyner, and M. Ben-Avie, eds., *Rallying the Whole Village* (New York: Teachers College, Columbia University, 1996), p. 51.

3 James Coleman, *Equality of Educational Opportunity* (Washington, D.C.: Office of Education, 1966), p. 262.

4 David Cohen, "Why Curriculum Doesn't Matter," *The New Leader* 54:22 (15 November 1971): 7.

5 Andrew M. Greeley and Peter H. Rossi, *The Education of Catholic Americans* (Chicago: Aldine, 1966), p. 145.

6 Alvin I. Schiff and Mareleyne Schneider, *The Jewishness Quotient of Jewish Day School` Graduates: Fortifying and Restoring Jewish Behavior: The Interaction of Home and School* Research Report 3 (New York: Yeshiva University, 1994), p. 47.

7 Geoffrey Bock, "The Jewish Schooling of American Jews: A Study of Non-Cognitive Educational Effects" (Ph.D. Dissertation, Harvard University, 1976), p. 78.

8 Rabbi Akiba, *Avot Derabbi Natan*, 6:2.

9 Quoted in Alvin I. Schiff, "The Jewish Family and the Jewish School," *Amit Woman* 59:3 (Jan./Feb., 1987): 9.

10 Barry Kosmin, Sidney Goldstein, et al., *Highlights of the CJF National Jewish Population Survey* (New York: Council of Jewish Federations, 1991).

11 Alvin I. Schiff, *The Jewish Supplementary School—A System in Need of Change* (New York: The Board of Jewish Education in Greater New York, 1988).

12 Ibid., p. 136.

13 Ibid., pp. 134–35.

14 Bloom, *Developing Talent*, p. 68.

15 Schiff and Schneider, *Jewishness Quotient* Research Report 1 (New York: Yeshiva University, 1994), pp. 11–12.

16 Schiff and Schneider, *Jewishness Quotient: Far Reaching Effects of Extensive Jewish Day School Attendance* Research Report 2 (New York: Yeshiva University, 1994), p. 4.

17 Alvin I. Schiff, *The Mystique of Hebrew* (New York: Shengold Publishers, 1996), p. 89.

18 Abraham Heschel, *The Prophets* (Philadelphia: Jewish Publication Society, 1962), p. xiii.

19 Ibid.

13
BETWEEN TEXTS AND CONTEXTS: HOW MAY TOMORROW'S JEWISH EDUCATION BE DIFFERENT?

Michael Rosenak

Predicting the future is always risky. All really significant developments, the sociologist Robert Nisbet once wrote, are the discoveries or inventions of geniuses, prophets, or madmen, and these are all highly unpredictable.[1] Yet, no one can deny that we always find ourselves in the midst of trends. There are various assumptions at work; and all around us there are activities in progress, based on attitudes and orientations. These invite examination and awaken the urge to conjecture, to theorize, and to hope. That is what I plan to do in this chapter, rather than outline a curriculum or suggest specific syllabi; these, I believe, may cogently "take off" from a theoretical springboard such as this.

THREE POSITIONS

What do people think today about the tomorrow of Jewish education? There are, I think, three basic positions or attitudes.[2]

The first is what may be called "the righteous remnant" view, which celebrates a small but growing group of the faithful who are intensely and comprehensively Jewish, whose devotion is ever becoming more intense and more consistent. These faithful set themselves emphatically apart from the modern world and almost certainly will keep their distance from the post-modern one. For ultra-traditional Jewry, Jewish education in the twenty-first century will be a dedicated, but not necessarily reflective, thrust toward more of the same; this group's leadership education will rest on a conscious and ideological decision towards greater spiritual segregation and more vigilant self-defense. Ideologically, this group's position will remain what it is now: that nothing of substance has changed, for nothing of substance can change. Neither modernity nor post-modernity raises intrinsic questions for Jewish life and education. The only questions are tactical ones concerned with overcoming the subtle and devious opponents of faithful Jewish existence. And the motto, born of determination and faith, is: "We shall overcome the menace of contemporary culture."

Two distinct groups uphold the righteous remnant approach. First, are the members of the *Haredi* (ultra-Orthodox) community, and second, the non-*Haredi*, and even non-observant, well-wishers who support *Haredi* positions and institutions. These well-wishers consider the Jewish future assured through zealous ultra-Orthodoxy alone. The existence and vitality of ultra-Orthodoxy takes the sting out of the grim sociological facts in the well-wishers' own streets and backyards, where intermarriage and assimilation are in virtual control of the ground.

A second approach is that held by those I term "secular naturalists."[3] Their position is that the survival of the Jews is assured as long as there are people who wish to remain such, or who feel that they have no choice but to be Jews. Thinkers and educators associated with this group assure us that, largely thanks to Israel, Jewish survival is relatively certain, but they caution against insisting that this survival be based on any sacrosanct assumptions, sacred beliefs, or traditional regimens of living. Judaisms have emerged, changed, and withered in the past, and new ones, radically different from what we now know, are likely to emerge in the years to come. The postmodern Judaism of the future, like all significant realms of feeling and belonging, will depend more on consciousness than on objective values to be transmitted by education. Since choice and consciousness are not transmitted but individually experienced, the enterprise of education for this group will increasingly be concerned with cultivating the intelligence and autonomy of the young, so that they can competently and freely create their own realities. This education will not be overtly Jewish. Nevertheless, Jews who live in the (largely) Jewish collective of Israel or in Jewish communities which maintain broad allegiance may refer to the schools, camps, and clubs through which they are helped on the road to maturity as "Jewish ones."

The third orientation is the "religious-cultural" one.[4] Its adherents point out that Judaism and the Jews have managed to be contemporary with ancient, classical, medieval, and modern civilizations. True, the Jews are a very small people, for in each period they are threatened with annihilation or assimilation. Not everyone, nor every community "made it" from one epoch to the next, and the physical destruction of our age was admittedly the most horrendous and demographically the most threatening. The freedoms and opportunities for Jews in Western countries are also unprecedented. Nevertheless, now as in the past, there is abundant testimony that the people of Israel still lives. Jewish energies are not exhausted. Jews are now, as in the past, adapting and retaining what they consider essential in their faith and identity, in the entire religious and spiritual enterprise with which Providence (however perceived) has entrusted them. They are reinterpreting and developing new forms and asserting new emphases.

Among adherents of this position are people of various religious commitments and concerns and even some who define themselves as largely secular. Their secular-naturalist fellows, however, are likely to refer jokingly to the non-religious in this group as "secular rabbis."

A PRELIMINARY STATEMENT OF FAITH

I believe that the position of "the righteous remnant" becomes plausible only if Judaism is stipulatively defined as "what *haredim* do." I cannot agree that a Judaism that either has no message for the world or simply refuses to be communicative with others about that message represents God's will for His people. I suggest, moreover, that the secular naturalism that speaks for Jews without any recognizable and communicable Judaism is viable only where Jews are socially and culturally excluded or exclude themselves, in other words, in an environment that is more oppressive than that in which most contemporary Jews find themselves.

My thesis is that the third orientation, the religious-cultural position, articulates the truths of Jewish existence. Yet this position is vulnerable and easily corrupted. Being open to change, it may blur all distinctions between the essential and the innovative. Its adherents always confront bothersome questions and dilemmas: "What must be transmitted in all cases and circumstances? What are the limits of adaptation and adaptability? When does Judaism 'learn' from a social or intellectual situation that is new and unprecedented? When must it reject that which seems enticing or even persuasive, lest Judaism be robbed of its identity? What is this identity?" On these and similar questions, we are today, as for the past one hundred and fifty years or so, in the midst of an intensive, and at times harsh, controversy between the trends or "denominations" of religious-cultural Judaism. In the generation to come, this controversy is likely to become, at least for some, even more acrimonious. For reasons I shall give below, I also believe that, paradoxically, in the generation to come, the divisions within religious-cultural Judaism will be perceived as existentially less central and threatening.

LANGUAGE AND LITERATURE

To explain the basic mindset of the large, yet ideologically divided and variegated, religious-cultural group, I refer to an educational theory developed in my recent book, *Roads to the Palace*.[5] That theory articulates a distinction between the *language* of a culture, a civilization, or a faith, and its *literature*.

These terms are not to be taken literally. By *language* I do not mean English or Hebrew or French; likewise, *literature* does not refer simply to novels, poems, or essays, though the structure and assumptions of a national tongue may well be an intrinsic part of "language," and poetry is certainly part of what generally constitutes "literature." My usage, based on models developed by such philosophers as R. S. Peters and Michael Oakeshott, is broader and generic:

> The *language* of a culture sets down its basic assumptions, problems, aspirations and understandings. It establishes its forms of rhetoric, its methods of inquiry, its patterns of community, its symbolic expressions, its paradigms of order, coherence and norm. . . . *Language*, gives us our collective identity, our stores of what is self-understood among us, our forms of articulation and communication.

As for literature, it is what those who know and use the language do when they are expressing themselves within it, when they communicate and create within it. "In literature they show the power of their language to shape reality and to provide a home within reality for those who speak it. As ever, new literature is created in the language, its funds of meaning are explored and broadened: simultaneously, those who speak are expressing themselves, revealing sides . . . of themselves that they can or wish to bring to light only in that language."[6]

Language makes it possible for people to make clear what they are doing and talking about. Hence, many jokes of mutual non-comprehensibility are about "language." There is, for example, the famous story of the young Jewish child who dashes excitedly up the stairs of his tenement in New York's Lower East Side one summer afternoon in the 1930s to inform his greenhorn grandfather that the famed baseball star, Babe Ruth of the New York Yankees, has just hit his sixtieth home-run of the season. The grandfather's response, curious and somewhat concerned, is: "Is it good for the Jews?" Though the old man had mastered some English, he did not speak the cultural language. He didn't get the point. He was a stranger to the context of his grandson's excitement. Conversely, his grandson may have already forgotten the language in which it made sense to ask himself, before drinking a glass of milk, "When did we finish our (meat) lunch?"

To understand and use a language is a complex affair, but those within it generally have no difficulty. They understand such questions or expressions as, "When does Shabbat 'come in' tonight? What is the portion of the week? Have you counted the Omer? Is this (bread) *mezonot*?" Hearing these questions, an outsider to the language may look at the door to see when Shabbat will come in, think a portion is the outstanding or carefully measured dish being served that particular week, wonder what the Omer is and how or why it is being counted. He or she does not know what *mezonot* are and how they may be identical with bread. Indeed, some of these questions are quite complicated. For example, in the "language," the last question means several things: "Shall I make one blessing rather than another before eating this bread, because it contains some ingredients that 'simple' or ordinary bread does not? For *mezonot*, I don't have to wash my hands ritually before eating, as is required when bread is eaten, [which is very convenient on airplanes and in deserts]. And, shall I recite a short blessing after my meal rather than the longer Grace after Meals?"

In the Jewish tradition, the "language" is generally identified with the term, "Torah." That which is Torah, is Judaism itself. And "literature" comprises the ways that specific Jews, under particular circumstances, have expressed themselves about Torah, interpreted it, and moved in given directions with it. We may say that the classic Jewish way to speak about what we are calling literature was to identify it with commentary or *midrash*.

The distinction between the two was reasonably clear throughout most of Jewish history. Sacred writings were defined as Torah, as those that presented and represented the commanded and experienced identity of their readers and their realm of ultimate responsibility and meaning. But around the "text" of Torah there were numerous commentaries, each making sense of Torah in its own way. The text had to be defended at all costs, for language is identity, but commentaries, that are discrete expressions of it, could be weighed and then accepted or rejected. There were rationalistic thinkers as well as mystical ones in our tradition. Later, there were Hasidim and Mitnagdim. Though sometimes those in one group branded their opponents as heretics or apostates who had left the language, they eventually came around to seeing the others as wedded to different, even if to them unpalatable, literatures.

While not all language was text, all of it had a textual basis in the very "bookish" language of Judaism. And all literature was a way of exploring the possibilities inherent in that language.

To illustrate: *Eretz Yisrael*, the land of covenant, was traditionally, like covenant itself, an element of language. That meant that you could neither fully understand the elements of Jewish life nor express yourself on many subjects without knowing how to use the term *"Eretz Yisrael."* The language of Judaism would not make adequate sense without it. Now, the modern movement of Zionism is, without a doubt, a creative and imaginative "take-off" on *Eretz Yisrael*. It is literature on the *language* of *Eretz Yisrael*. Hence, to say that one cannot live within the language of Judaism without being a Zionist would not be accepted by most Jews; even most Zionists would take offense at the suggestion. Did the virulent opposition to Zionism of the rebbe of Satmar (the leader of the Hasidic group originally based in the town of Satu-Mare) mark him as an apostate or, as many Zionists would claim, stubborn and ill advised? What is "our" (that is Zionists') problem with him? That he did not accept our language or that he despised our literature?

Amidst the ideological diversity that characterizes modern Jews, it is not always possible to reach agreement about what actually constitutes "language" (to be defended at all costs), what "literature" is, and where the line between them is to be drawn. Take, for example, the piece of bread that is really *mezonot*, that is, (subject to the rules of) cake. Above, we have presented this piece of cake as an integral idiom in the language of Judaism, so that understanding the question and acting in inherent agreement with the logic of the answer means to be within the world of Torah, to "speak the language." But many contemporary Jews will raise the question whether these halakhic minutiae, or even the Talmudic *halakhah* itself, are to be categorized as "language" or as "literature." Are they Judaism, or merely one possible (historical, existential, social) way of expressing its "language?" Perhaps speaking Hebrew and living in the land of Israel with an ethical and prophetic posture is what Torah (the language) really is? Perhaps the stance that makes *halakhah* the main feature of Jewish language is simply the bias of a Talmudic "literature" that passed itself off as language? Would Jeremiah have accepted it? Did A. D. Gordon and Martin Buber?

The argument rages. All Orthodox Jews, most with a vengeance, will insist that *halakhah* is the soul of the language. To paraphrase the late Professor Isaiah Leibowitz: If we were to invite Maimonides, the *Rambam*, to a conference and with him the Holy Ari, Rabbi Isaac Luria, and have the great rationalist encounter the great kabbalist in a theological discussion, they might come to blows within minutes. Maimonides would see Luria as a polytheist; Luria, the *Ari Hakadosh*, would accuse the *Rambam* of atheism. Their theologies, in short, were so different that they couldn't, said Leibowitz, have understood each other. "But then," Leibowitz loved to conclude with an ironic smile, "they would both get up from their debate to *daven Minhah*" (recite the afternoon prayer). Theology, after all, was only "literature." The "language" is davening *Minhah*, the *halakhah*.

THREE TYPES OF EDUCATORS

If we agree that Judaism is indeed a composite of "language" and "literature," then we may define Jewish education accordingly. It is transmitting to children the language and making them familiar, "at home," with a variety of worthy literatures. It is cultivating their loyalty to the language as well as their ability to recognize and choose good literature. At its best, Jewish education will enable young people to create Jewish literature, to be active participants in the "midrashic" enterprise.

This definition of education raises many problems. Who decides what the language is? Who decides what "good" and worthy literature is? Is everyone qualified to make *midrash*?

But these problems arise only within the community, however broad, of the religious-cultural camp. The two other schools of thought do not agree that all culture is a blend of language and literature. Those we have termed "the righteous remnant" basically believe that everything of importance, everything Jewish, is language. Not accidentally did this community develop the concept of *da'at Torah*, of "asking the rebbe" about every important action to be taken. What the authoritative Torah personality says *is* Torah: it is "the language," absolutely committing, the test of Jewish identity and loyalty. And education in this group is understood to be no more and no less than transmitting the language and socializing into it. The very idea of creativity, of exposure to interpretations that are open to deliberation, of various styles and options of authentic Jewish life is anathema and anarchy. Hence all authorities, past and present, are taught as reliable and authoritative.

Secular naturalists take a rather opposite approach. Secular-naturalist educators are not responsible to any core Judaism which may be expanded and perhaps enriched by new literature. For them, all Jewish life (there being no essential phenomenon that they would identify as "Judaism") is "literature" which interprets, revises, or rejects previous literature. There is nothing to be defended in principle. Hence, exponents of "language" will generally refer to a seemingly immoral verse in the Torah as "difficult," for this verse is, for very many of them, part of the corpus of language itself. Secular naturalists, however, are liberated from such inhibitions. They will declare the verse archaic and unacceptable and are likely to explain that an educator's commitment should not be to verses but rather to the free moral development of pupils.

Because of the modern difficulty in deciding what the language is and where literature takes over, the first two educational positions seem more persuasive and comfortable. Indeed, in the contemporary religious-cultural world, much is unclear. For example: Is everything in the Talmud to be seen as language? More specifically: Is a given opinion, say of a specific sage, just "hard to understand" (language) or "off the wall" (literature)? Is the *halakhah* the irreducible practical manifestation of language as mode and message, as Orthodoxy holds? Or is it the prophetic ethic, as classical Reform posits? Because of the fragile balance between language and literature, it has been all too easy in this century for Jewish educators and their disciples to slip into greater consistency, namely, to relinquish literature or language. This has given us the twin phenomena of "Haredization" and naturalistic secularization.

To make the religious-cultural school of thought viable for the twenty-first century, its Jewish educators and other leaders will have to decide where they agree, and where they disagree, and therefore consciously and in principle maintain their own "denominational" affiliations/associations.

Let us explore this issue by looking briefly at some basic questions facing contemporary Jews and Jewish education. In all but the first case, the status of these questions falls squarely, albeit problematically, within the domain of "language." The importance of the first question is that it involves an explicit disagreement about that. Nonetheless, here too, the dispute exposes certain commonalities to view.

"Who Has Not Made Me A Woman"

Neither the ultra-Orthodox nor the secular communities are, in principle, troubled by questions of feminism and egalitarianism. Among the former, there is a continual sharpening of perceptions and standards as to what is appropriate and honorable in social roles and relationships. There, the distinction between men and women is unambiguously drawn and re-drawn in dark hues to ward off modern sexual permissiveness. For the secular naturalist, too, egalitarianism poses no dilemma, though the discrimination against women is recorded as an interesting and unfortunate historical and sociological datum.

It is different in the religious-cultural world, and here the points of view are profoundly diverse. In the liberal wing of this school, gender distinctions and alleged discrimination are a historical, yet deplorable, example of literature; others, specifically the modern Orthodox, will insist that the Torah certainly intended men and women to develop discrete identities and to worship God in distinct and identifiable ways. For them, gender is a matter of language.

This controversy runs along the Orthodox/Conservative-Reform divide. On the one hand, it sharpens "denominational" distinctions. On the other hand, it must be realized that the modern Orthodox approach (within the religious-cultural school) is marked by deep, though not always admitted, discomfort with this feature of language. And, as has been the case throughout the history of interpretation, such discomfort is the well-spring of an ever-expanding and empathetic "literature" on the gender distinction within Judaism. Such modern Orthodox literature has already won Orthodox women the acknowledged right to serious Torah study, accommodated itself to the latent threat to Jewish family life by legitimating the pursuit of careers among women, and created Jewish community life in which traditionalist women play central and sometimes equal roles.

We may expect an even more expansive literature on halakhic and theological planes in the decades to come. For most of the non-Orthodox, gender will become a non-issue, and this will cause Orthodox education to distinguish itself by its insistence that it is a language issue. The result is that Orthodox and liberal Judaism will feel farther apart from each other.

But, on the basis of present tendencies, we may expect a parallel and opposite development. The vastly increased "literature" (halakhic decision making, synagogue and educational policy making, etc.) in the modern Orthodox community on this "language issue" of men-and-women creates empathy with the subject and a more realistic understanding of what most women in the religious-cultural community or communities expect. Certainly, then, we may expect the universal concern with the question in the religious-cultural camp to create unanticipated commonalities, that will probably expand in the decades to come. Members of the religious-cultural camp will thus come to feel closer to one another, both because they have common *Haredi* and secular positivist antagonists, and because they share common concerns, if from opposite sides of the language-literature divide. At the same time, as noted, the divide between the traditionalists and the liberals within the religious-cultural group will become more clearly delineated. As the groups deal with this and related issues very diversely, the issues themselves will enter more deeply into their distinct self-understandings and self-definitions.

"And Who Is Like Your People, Israel . . ."
A People, Not A Confession

An area of crisis for Jewish life and education in the years to come will undoubtedly be the nature of Jewish community and peoplehood. As Jews have increasingly become full-fledged members of their former "host societ-ies," their status as a people has come to seem increasingly implausible or irrelevant to many of them. How can one be a member of the Jewish people when one is so obviously an American or Canadian? Hence, the tendency to assume that Jewish identity and education is properly focused on the individual, his or her search for meaning and faith, and his or her freely chosen or rejected community of religious life.

The *Haredi* school has consistently and coherently defended the peoplehood feature of Jewish language by refusing to exchange their guest status in modern national states for full-fledged membership. The secular naturalists solve the problem by viewing the State of Israel as the natural anchor and address of Jewish peoplehood. Consequently, they posit that those who consider Jewish national life important are best off living in Is-rael, where they may freely explore and develop the contemporary signifi-cance of Jewish nationhood.

The fathers of nineteenth-century Reform viewed the national aspects of Judaism as mere literature, but this viewpoint, as explicit ideology, survives only in such fringe groups as the American Council for Judaism. Except for such outsiders even to mainstream Reform, all who speak for religious-cul-tural Judaism agree in principle that the Jews are, in some sense, a people, and this they assume to be inherent in the character of Judaism, an aspect of language. Many throughout the religious-cultural spectrum will subscribe to Martin Buber's declaration that the revelation that constitutes the foun-dation-stone of Judaism was given to a people, for only as a people can Israel carry out God's charge to be a holy and just community.[7] Most are now aware of the threat to this cornerstone of Jewish life.

Peoplehood is a multi-faceted program for life. It implies that other Jews are not merely "co-religionists," but fellow members of a historic com-munity. Usually, therefore, peoplehood is seen to mandate an inclusiveness of identity that makes room for divergent viewpoints and life-styles, at least in the circumstances of modernity. It requires mutual responsibility among communities throughout the world. And it comes to grips with the reli-gious and cultural meaning of *Medinat Yisrael* for all Jews, wherever they are. Most significantly for contemporary Jews, peoplehood means that the central sociological project, achieving normalization by becoming either "a religion like all others" or "a nation like all other nations," may (providen-tially!) be expected to fail. The people of Israel will remain unique, some-what of a mystery, living alongside the nations even when significantly tied up with them and largely identified with them. Israel will remain a unique faith-people, an *am segulah*.

Given that all religious cultural Jews do consider the peoplehood of Israel an element of "language," they must, with the greatest possible unity, find the educational paths and tools to cultivate such a Jewish identity. Otherwise, those who were Jews, but are now Canadian and French, will continue to leave us as they have already done *de facto*. They will become, fully and without qualifications "given over to another nation."

". . . Who Teaches Torah To His People Israel . . ."

In the Jewish tradition, the "language of Judaism" is taught to Jews by the corpus of Bible and Talmudic-Rabbinic writings deemed to be of supreme value and truth. In the lexicon of the "language" itself, God teaches His people through His Torah.

How does this traditional axiom fare in the contemporary Jewish world? In the *Haredi* community, the centrality of "learning" is so self-understood that the community of ultra-Orthodoxy has been called, with some justice, a community of learners. For secular naturalists, value and truth are unequivocally the result of present need and interest. Automatic reverence for particular texts is condemned as mystification, an existential flight from personal authenticity.

Contemporary Jews of the religious-cultural school are not of one mind as to what in the canon of traditional Judaism is to be identified with language, and this fact occasions much controversy among them. Some view the entire corpus as the words of the living God. Others, more liberal in orientation, see the sacrificial laws and much of presently applicable *halakhah* as ancient "literature." They seek "language" in theologically educative narrative and in ethical-prophetic ordinances and exhortation. For many, the Talmud itself is a composite of language and literature, and perhaps most view the *midrashic* compilations as more than simple literature but less than language. Yet all members of the religious-cultural school strive to understand the language through facets of this rabbinic corpus and probably most seek within it "gems" of literature, which set criteria for excellence in the interpretative and creative tradition of Judaism.

It follows that tomorrow's Jewish education will have to continue an enterprise of educational inquiry and practice that has already been seriously addressed in our generation: namely, rethinking and restoring the tradition of learning, of *Talmud Torah*. For those who live critically but unapologetically in Western culture, it has already become clear that more is required than "books about" or even anthologies of Torah. Nor do computers offer comprehensive or magic cures for the ills of ignorance and indifference.

Our rich tradition of study, of *limmud Torah*, suggests insights that may be crucial for the success of the enterprise and that should be translated into modern "literature," that is, idiom, style, and method. One of these historical insights is that learning is best conducted in *havruta*, with another within communities. Also not to be forgotten is the famous adage: whenever the good impulse urges Jews to the study of Torah, the evil impulse suggests *talking about* Torah. I believe that Jews of tomorrow's generation will continue a process already in full swing in the traditional wing of the community to make day school education standard, and to make some kind of *yeshiva* experience available for young Jews entering adulthood. Current plans and pilot projects for establishing Reform yeshivot in Israel and the Diaspora suggest a direction of today that may become a norm of tomorrow.

". . . Who Has Sanctified Us Though His Commandments . . ."

The *halakhah* traditionally determined what one, though able to do, was proscribed from doing, and what sometimes seemed difficult but was mandatory. Philosophically, it was a mainstay of Jewish "language"; non-observance of commandments was construed as both direct rebellion against God's sovereignty as the law-giver for Israel and for each individual within it, and a denial of the significance of the community which He ruled through His Law.

Yet the *halakhah* has seen sad days since the advent of philosophical enlightenment and political emancipation. The former made religious law seem benighted and irreconcilable with individual autonomy; the latter brought it into competition and conflict with the laws of the nation-state. *Halakhah* was first reduced to customs and ceremonies and then dismissed as tedious and irrelevant. It is not surprising, therefore, that those of "the righteous remnant" transform every custom into an inflexible statute, while the secular naturalist camp relates to *halakhah* as to an ancient and outdated regimen, an almost trivial and sometimes comic "literature" of Talmudic Judaism.

The religious-cultural orientation, throughout its communities, cannot make its peace with either of these approaches. For modern Orthodoxy, the *halakhah* is a central, some would say the dominant, feature of Jewish "language," and its scope and application remain a live issue within Conservative Judaism. Reform Judaism, too, is now addressing the question of normative practice, at least as a guiding principle, even though this creates significant friction with its left-wing faction.[8] Cultural Jews in Israel, too, have increasingly confronted the question of cultural norms that will identity the Jewish society of Israel as historically continuous, if not in the details of practice, at least in its general patterns.[9]

The task for tomorrow's educational leaders is two-fold. First, standards must be set within the separate communities of this school of thought for communal and, to the extent possible, individual practice within a broad perspective. By this, I mean that each grouping will see the *halakhah* in some form, even if mainly as theological principle, as an aspect of language but will keep other elements of language in clear view as well.[10] Thus the Orthodox community will be cognizant of the documented datum that observance too often covers up a dearth of *Yir'at Shamayim* (spirituality), as a larger moral and existential posture vis-à-vis God and fellow humans, and it will come to have a comprehensive and reasoned curriculum of *halakhah*. Conversely, the more liberal wings of the religious-cultural school will increasingly cultivate the social behaviors attendant upon Jewish loyalty and will recognize the dangers of an overly internalized Judaism that consists largely of attitudes but lacks standards for action.[11]

Second, the entire religious-cultural camp will have to address the question of whether there can be behavioral standards that, at least in the public sphere, create a common ground. The achievement of common halakhic principles for the entire community of religious cultural Jews, which could win the silent assent of secular-naturalistic Jews as well, is close to the heart of the enterprise of community schools and such community enterprises as "general" Zionist or communal youth organizations, camps, and community centers. Parenthetically, I may mention my own memories of Young Judea's Camp Tel Yehudah at Ellenville, New York in which I spent several summers. As a young modern Orthodox member of the educational staff, I was impressed, though often shocked, by the halakhic modus vivendi Tel Yehudah had worked out so that "everybody could live with it." I realized then that a pattern of life for all significant-other Jews did not mean merely that everybody gave due consideration to the feelings of the Orthodox, but that there would be significant cognitive and religious bargaining. Others too, had feelings and sensibilities. During the rest of the year, I was glad to be back in my own (Orthodox) community, where "the language" was, to my mind, best spoken. But I had learned not to identify it mistakenly with *klal Yisrael* (the whole community).

"This Is My God And I Shall Exalt Him . . ."

It is admittedly odd to place the Almighty within the aspects of "language" that must be further examined and fostered in tomorrow's Jewish education. After all, by the rules of the language, God is not an item within it but the author of the language, its revealer and teacher. In a secular age such as ours, it may even be opined that the less said about God, the better. Hence, it has been suggested that the best way to "teach" about God may be simply to teach who His friends are. That is, don't talk about God; talk about Abraham, David, Hannah and her seven sons.

It is probably a good idea to speak of God through the prism of His relationships rather than in abstract theological terms. And it is in these contexts that He appears in the Jewish life of individuals and groups. Speaking of God in His relationships is, in a sense, speaking of human potential, as in Moshe Haim Luzzatto's work, *Mesilat Yesharim*, which concerns clarifying what Jews have meant by the love of God and the fear of Him. It is about honing ideals for Jewish education, explicating what we mean by noble character and what we consider worthy intentions.[12]

Perhaps because of the secularity of modern society, God does not come up much in the educational conversation. But there is no certainty that tomorrow's generation will be as secular, nor does Jewish education have to toe the line of the socially acceptable and unexceptionable. Most crucially: When God is not omnipresent in the education of religious-cultural communities, its practitioners may be cutting off the branches on which they sit.

Imagine (or recall) a curriculum in which God is fundamentally absent. There is no discussion of what God wanted for Adam and Eve, what Noah was doing when he "walked with God" or Abraham, when be walked "before" Him and argued with Him about Sodom or failed to argue with Him about the *Akedah* (the binding of Isaac). There is no comparing Psalm 73 with the Book of Job to initiate talk about evil in God's world, and no comparing either with the *hesed* (or love) that takes on evil (rather than discussing it) in the Book of Ruth.[13] There is no study of Rambam on *teshuvah* (repentance) and no real prayer. There is no philosophy of Judaism and precious little *piyyut* (poetry). In fact, there is, even amidst an abundance of posters, pageants, facts and skills, a profound and shattering silence about the meaning of Judaism and the inner identities of Jews.

In the schools of tomorrow, if they are to be liberated from the former generation's embarrassment about God, pupils will learn that there are many "literatures" about the Source of Jewish language: theologies, testimonies, and ways of standing before God within Jewish tradition. "They have figured You in a multitude of visions," the author of "An'im Zemirot," the "Hymn of Glory," declares, "yet You are one in all imaginings."

When the Messiah Comes

One unfortunate consequence of ultra-Orthodox "remnant theology" is that it requires a thorough sectarianism. Sectarianism is easily seen, because it is picturesque, but it cannot be heard, because it is uncommunicative. Since the others won't understand anyway, it is best to be silent. In practice, this means that one cannot profitably enquire of members of this community: "What difference does Judaism make for the world and within it? What is the temporal world to come and what does it look like? What is its human ideal and what is the face of its Messiah?"[14]

The secular naturalist most likely sees the question only in procedural terms: "When human beings are acting intelligently, how are they locating and solving their problems? How do they grow?" Much of what this school of thought deems educative is, in fact, working towards intelligence and growth.

The religious-cultural group is, I think, at one in thinking that messianism is part and parcel of Jewish language, and it is aware that messianism is demanding and usually complicated. In the name of historical significance, it can render all present history insignificant. It can sanction an evasion of social responsibility, and can be reduced to a vengeful anticipation of the correcting of all historical wrongs.

In historical messianism, there is much "literature." But I hope that the twenty-first century Jewish educator will build on different literatures, those that rebel against smugness, and realize that even the modern suburb does not make this the best of all possible worlds. We shall be looking for Messianic literature that teaches us to engage in world repairing, that rejects the comfortable attitude of making peace with what there is, viewing the present world, however flawed, as good enough.

In setting educational goals, we need to raise several redemptive issues: What is the thrust and content and place of idealism in Jewish education? What kind of community do we envision, in which there will be a reconciliation of all schools without erasing the distinctions between them? What will the Judaism of the day after tomorrow look like? How will it confront the world, challenging it yet not shirking from active membership in it?

Once Again, Yir'at Shamayim, the Fear of Heaven

The Talmud brings us the musings of Rabba on the post-mortal judgement of the human soul:

> At the time they bring in a person for judgment, they say: "Have you carried on commerce honestly? Have you set aside time for the study of Torah? Have you engaged in bringing children into the world? Have you anticipated redemption? Have you wisely deduced one thing from another?" (Shabbat 31a)

To this, Rabba adds that all these things are worthy only if accompanied by the fear of Heaven, which, I have suggested elsewhere,[14] is the hallmark of a noble and reliable religious character. In such a character, we find obedience and personal responsibility, divine service, and autonomy. The ideal of *yir'at shamayim* is one of improving the world and making relationships more reliable and enduring. It is a character conception that Judaism can, perhaps uniquely, cultivate, that can be the spiritual "calling card" of religious-cultural education. If we translate the "language" of *yi'rat shamayim* into a literature suitable for our children, a literature of empowerment and anxiety, of hope and uncertainty, without doing violence to the language, then we may proceed to build a curriculum for the Jewish schools of tomorrow.

Our communities have already started, haltingly, to do it, giving us grounds for the hope that we may continue. But half-measures are, perhaps, worse than none. Maimonides, in the "Preface to Perek 'Helek'" of his *Introductions to the Mishnah*, tells us that teachers must be philosophers. They must know which questions to ask of a text and how to approach learners who cannot yet fathom its depths or the importance of what it says.

What was true then is doubly the case now. The way(s) of religious-cultural Judaism dare not look unprincipled, and dialectics should not be made to appear as mere confusion. What should be done is to ensure that the outcome of deliberation is wedded to competence and sensitivity. And yet, in education, time and the need for action wait for no one. Thinking and acting, doing and understanding, always intertwine in this very practical field. As we do today's work, it will be tomorrow before we know it. Then, hopefully, we shall simply continue to think and try out and implement—just as we are doing now.

If we succeed, we shall be building an education for our children and grandchildren that fosters faith without naiveté, pride without parochialism, and fear of Heaven without loss of self. We shall be teaching a language of Torah adorned with resplendent literatures.

Notes

[1] Robert A. Nisbet, "The Year Two Thousand And All That," *Commentary* 45 (June 1968): 66.

[2] As will become clear, each of these basic orientations may accommodate diverse substantive positions, beliefs, and ways of life. In a sense, the cogency of this division is sharpened against the backdrop of Zionism, as a new unifying and

dividing force in modern Jewish history. For each of these orientations understands Zionism differently and draws clear conclusions from these diverse understandings about Judaism, contemporary and perennial. Of the three, two see Zionism as a Jewish challenge and promise, and one, as a threat.

[3] A prominent spokesman of this position in the educational field is Professor Zvi Lamm of the Hebrew University. See Zvi Lamm, "A Secular Approach to Jewish Education," *Avar ve-Atid* (Jerusalem: Joint Authority for Jewish-Zionist Education of the World Zionist Organization) 1:2 (1995): 39–49.

[4] This is clearly the most diversified of the three groups, and for most of modern Jewish history, relations among its various branches were characterized by animosity. The leaders of the early Mizrachi movement distrusted and disliked 'Ahad Ha'Am and his spiritual Zionism, and modern Orthodox Jews have traditionally viewed Conservative and Reform Jews with suspicion and some disdain. Yet, widespread assimilation (in the Diaspora) and polarization between a "de-Judaized" left and a politicized *Haredi* right (in Israel), appear to be creating a universe of discourse that justifies seeing this group as sharing a basic educational-cultural position and that, indeed, is leading them to adopt one.

[5] Michael Rosenak, *Roads to the Palace: Jewish Texts and Teaching* (Providence, R.I. and Oxford: Berghahn Books, 1995).

[6] Ibid., pp. 19–20.

[7] Martin M. Buber, *Israel and the World: Essays in a Time of Crisis* (New York: Schocken Books, 1963), especially "Hebrew Humanism" and "The Jew in the World."

[8] Just as right-wing Orthodoxy may well be more at home in the *Haredi* school of thought, so left-wing spokespersons of liberal Judaism may well be more at home in the secular-naturalist camp than in the religious-cultural one. I suggest that the criterion for the latter be: Are the basic assumptions and beliefs grounded in the social sciences or in irreducibly theological ones?

[9] The prominent spokesman of this position in Israel in its varied educational ramifications is the Hebrew University's Professor Eliezer Schweid. In his numerous books, he has articulated a view of Jewish culture that relates seriously to its religious features, through which it makes normative demands, which the modern Jew will have to confront though not necessarily to accept. See Eliezer Schweid, *The Idea of Judaism as a Culture* (Tel Aviv: Am Oved, 1995) [Hebrew]. In English, see Eliezer Schweid, *Israel at the Crossroads* (Philadelphia: The Jewish Publication Society, 1973).

[10] A recent, already celebrated discussion of this issue in modern Orthodoxy is Hayim Soloveitchik, "Rupture and Reconstruction: The Transformation of Contemporary Orthodoxy," *Tradition* 28:4 (1994): 64–130.

[11] For a recent discussion of the issue within the Conservative movement, see Gerald L. Zelizer, "Conservative Rabbis, their Movement, and American Judaism"; and Responses by Jonathan D. Sarna, Jenna Weissman Joselit, and Henry Feingold, *Judaism* 44:3 (1995): 292–313.

[12] Luzzatto's popular book has been published frequently over the years. A recent edition in English is *The Path of the Just,* trans. by Yaakov Feldman (Northvale, N.J.: Jason Aaronson, 1996).

[13] Jakob Schoeneveld, "New Meaning in Ancient Sources," in *Studies in Jewish Education* V, eds. H. Deitcher and A. J. Tannenbaum (Jerusalem: The Magnes Press, 1990), p. 51.

[14] Reuven Hammer, "Two Approaches to the Problem of Suffering," *Judaism* 35:3 (1986): 300–305.

[15] Rosenak, *Roads,* chap. 6–8.

PART
5

CHANGING GENDER
EXPECTATIONS AND ROLES
IN
JEWISH COMMUNAL LIFE

14

CHANGING GENDER EXPECTATIONS:
AN INTRODUCTION AND *CRI DE COEUR*

Rachel Schlesinger

In the past, scholarship and religious observance were valued above all else within Judaism. But while men were encouraged to study, women were not given equal opportunity to learn the sacred texts, and they were excused from performing time-bound *mitzvot* (commandments). The sages linked education with sexuality, and they accepted antique gender myths about the limitations of women. Some of the ancients believed that a man should not teach his daughter Torah because she would trivialize it. The twelfth–thirteenth-century sage, Maimonides, asserted that women may study Torah, but that the Talmud, the oral tradition, should be denied to them. Women were told they could not study the same texts as men or study with males, lest their sexuality distract the men.

In recent times, the position of women in the secular, and even in the religious, sphere has changed dramatically. Feminists have struggled in the last two centuries to transform the role of women in Western society, and Jewish women have been in the forefront of many of these battles. Women today benefit from those earlier conflicts. They can get an education, work for wages, vote in elections, and make choices about their position in a family unit.

In this twentieth century, long after the start of the *Haskalah* (Jewish Enlightenment) movement, Jewish women straddle the inner Jewish world of family, religion, and community and the outer world of non-Jewish society. Indeed, women often provide the bridge between these two worlds. The authors of the two chapters in this section explore the role of Jewish feminism in redefining how women can live productively in both worlds. Norma Joseph highlights women's desire to obtain a Jewish education. She argues that educational opportunities, prayer, and ritual all lead to new ways of connecting to Judaism. Indeed, with an education, women's participation in the community may also change. Recent evidence indicates that the higher the level of Jewish education, the more people volunteer in the community.[1] Paula Hyman insists that the experiences of women and men together comprise Jewish history and culture. The question now is how to incorporate women in Jewish communal affairs with a sense of equality. Why did it take so long for women to seek education? Why are the roles of women still not valued within the power structures of the organized community? Hyman and Joseph help frame the questions and provide tentative answers which can serve to strengthen future Jewish communal life.

The impact of feminism on Jewish communal life has already been significant. Jewish women have come to recognize their unique contributions to the whole community and the need to carve out a sense of self and identity apart from the constructed definitions others provide for them. In the future, the strength of the community will depend on the support of all its members. If one hopes to create a viable Jewish future, new inclusive paradigms must be developed.

Kol isha—the voice of a woman—is a warning cry; it will not be sexually provocative, but a call to be heard within the Jewish sphere. Unless the many voices of women are heard, the future of the Jewish community is endangered. Each woman has her own story, yet each woman lives within her own silence. No less than men, women need to find their voices in each generation. The voices of women can speak to us from the past, but women now also need to speak to each other and to the children of the future. Often women's expectations have been constructed for them. But these norms can be challenged. Emancipation and modernity opened many windows. Now may be the time to fling open the doors. To do so, new language and terminology are needed. Women are "half the kingdom." They are engaged in a discussion of how to claim their half, not in terms of diversity, but in terms of inclusivity. In speaking of gender roles the goal is not greater divisions, but bringing the parts together to strengthen the community. *Kol isha* . . . The voices will vary; the messages differ, but for the strength of the Jewish community, women's voices will be heard.

Notes

[1] Sylvia Barack Fishman, *A Breath of Life: Feminism in the American Jewish Community* (Hannover: Brandeis University Press, 1993), p. 265.

15
WHERE DO WE GO FROM HERE?
FEMINISM AND CHANGING GENDER
EXPECTATIONS AND ROLES
IN JEWISH COMMUNAL LIFE
Paula E. Hyman

The impact of feminism on Jewish communal life in North America in the past generation has been substantial. Challenging all varieties of American Judaism, feminism has been a powerful force for popular Jewish religious revival.[1] Even such a conservative critic of many aspects of feminist ideology as Jack Wertheimer has noted as much in his thoughtful survey of the state of Judaism in America in the last half of the twentieth century.[2] Feminism has enabled women of talent to contribute to the Jewish community in a wider variety of ways than was possible only a generation ago. It has done so by blurring the boundaries of gender roles, increasing options for men as well as women, but at the same time causing a loss of the sense of security that accompanies knowing exactly how one is expected to behave. Moreover, to those who accept the necessity of a hierarchy of authority between husband and wife, feminism has subverted the so-called "natural" order of family life by fostering female empowerment and by pointing to the costs of a romanticized traditional family life that depends upon assigning housework and child care to women as *their* primary responsibility. Feminism has indeed challenged the traditional division of family roles, broadening the definition of family and calling for a sharing of household tasks. It has proclaimed that women, like men, can legitimately subordinate commitment to family to personal fulfillment through other means, a message that social conservatives find pernicious. Because of the perceived importance of women as transmitters of Jewish identity within the family, over the course of the last century and a half, Jewish communal leaders have criticized social and ideological changes that they see as weakening that female role, and feminism has been no exception.[3]

As I have begun to suggest, feminism and its consequences have both enriched North American Jewry and exacerbated tensions within its ranks. In fact, the acceptance of feminist definitions of gender equality by the majority of American Jews and their leaders complicates relations among different sectors of the Jewish community—Orthodox and non-Orthodox, cultural traditionalists and cultural radicals and moderates. The politicized strength of Israeli ultra-Orthodoxy and the state-endorsed lack of religious pluralism in Israel also cause gender to loom large among the issues that divide Israeli from North American Jews, an important subject that I will not explore in this chapter. Most significantly, feminism problematizes the very concept of "Jewish unity" that drives much of Jewish communal activity. Feminists have championed diversity and inclusivity in Jewish life, questioning traditional definitions of family structure and religious authority at a time when some segments of the Jewish community are turning inward and using rigid gender distinctions as a marker of their fidelity to tradition. After evaluating the impact of the changes that feminism and accompanying social forces have introduced into North American Jewish life, I will briefly suggest strategies, within a context of commitment to gender equality, to forge alliances in order to achieve common goals.

As far as the Jewish community and its public rituals are concerned, the most striking and visible achievements of feminism have occurred in the religious sphere. Let me provide a thumbnail sketch of those aspects of Jewish religious life that have been profoundly transformed by feminism. Of North America's four Jewish denominations—Conservative, Orthodox, Reconstructionist, and Reform—all but the Orthodox have accepted women as rabbis and cantors. The first woman rabbi was ordained in 1972. Today, some twenty-five years later, there are about 400 women rabbis in North America and over 180 cantors.[4] Although they have encountered some obstacles in the advancements of their careers, their presence in pulpits, Hillel programs, and hospital chaplaincies has changed the image of religious leadership. Female rabbis and cantors demonstrate simply through carrying out their professional responsibilities that women can be public religious figures, interpreters of the tradition, and spiritual guides. Along with their male peers, they serve egalitarian religious communities, where women are called to the Torah and chant the Torah portion. To a generation of young Jews such egalitarian congregations seem routine. Although gender egalitarianism does not exist within the Orthodox synagogue, Orthodox feminists, seeking greater access to the Torah and the possibility of experiencing equality in prayer, have established women's *tefilla* (prayer) groups, despite the opposition of much of the Orthodox establishment.[5] Female congregational interns now serve two New York Orthodox synagogues in pararabbinic roles, and two "Orthodoxy and Feminism" conferences, held in New York City in 1997 and 1998, attracted 1,400 and 2,000 participants respectively. The creation of new opportunities for women to expand their participation in Jewish religious life and the flourishing of varieties of egalitarian Judaism have enabled Jewish women to deepen their religious experience, and, as I can testify personally, have been crucial in enabling some feminists to remain practicing and deeply passionate Jews.

Feminists have also introduced new ritual and liturgy into North American Jewish life. In contrast to the past, girls are now welcomed into the Jewish community with impressive ceremonies that celebrate their birth. Feminists stimulated the creation of special rituals for newborn girls and also inspired Orthodox communities to disseminate the traditional Sephardi "Zeved Habat," a feast in honor of infant girls.[6] The Jewish women's movement has reclaimed *Rosh Hodesh*, the beginning of the new month, as a woman's holiday, celebrated by some groups with ritual and some form of study. Although most *Rosh Hodesh* celebrations are small and informal, others are connected with institutions. Ma'ayan, a Jewish women's center based in New York City, sponsors *Rosh Hodesh* events that combine ritual and study, while the Department of Jewish Education of the New Haven Jewish Federation holds regular study sessions for women to mark the beginning of each month.[7] Some Jewish women have added a feminist dimension to the Passover *seder* by holding a third *seder* that integrates women's experience, told with the aid of feminist *haggadot*, within the traditional Jewish framework of oppression and liberation.[8] Public feminist *sedarim* have attracted several hundred participants in such centers of Jewish life as New York City and Los Angeles and have been popular on college campuses in the United States. Feminism has also enabled women to offer their own interpretations of classical texts and has persuaded publishers that there is a market for women's responses to the Torah.

Feminism has spurred serious exploration of our language and concepts of prayer. Scholar-activists such as Judith Plaskow and Ellen Umansky have challenged the male-dominated concepts of Jewish theology and God-language that draw primarily upon masculine imagery. They have suggested that the language of Jewish prayer should reflect how contemporary Jews think about God. The poet and Hebrew scholar, Marcia Falk, has created blessings that supplant traditional liturgy with innovative forms that introduce feminist concepts: a subversion of hierarchy and naturalistic images of God gendered in Hebrew in the female.[9] The issue of God-language raised by feminists has, to one extent or another, influenced prayerbooks and other liturgical texts, particularly in the Reform and Reconstructionist movements. In 1975 the Reform movement introduced some gender-inclusive language in English sections of its new prayerbook, *Gates of Prayer*, and published fully gender-sensitive versions for the Sabbath and weekdays in 1992. The Reconstructionists have also created a gender-sensitive *siddur*, *Kol Haneshamah*, with both a Sabbath and a weekday edition. Although the Conservative movement has been reluctant to introduce feminist-inspired changes in liturgy, the preliminary version of its revised *Sim Shalom* prayerbook offers the option of including the names of the matriarchs along with those of the patriarchs in the *amidah*, a central section of the prayers.[10]

Most importantly, partly under the impact of feminism, girls are being educated Jewishly at higher rates than in the past. In a 1992 report based on the 1990 National Jewish Population Study, almost 42 percent of Jewish women aged 18–24 who identified themselves with the Conservative movement and more than 14 percent of those identifying with Reform were categorized as having a "substantial" Jewish education as compared with about 26 percent and 10 percent respectively of the cohort aged 25–44. (Young women have not achieved parity with their brothers, however; about 49 percent of young Jewish men identified with Conservatism and 29 percent identified with Reform have a "substantial" Jewish education). Although many Orthodox Jews claim to have been untouched by feminism, a significant Orthodox response to feminist challenges has been the intensification of Jewish education for girls and women. The 1992 report found that while almost 54 percent of Orthodox women aged 65 and older had minimal Jewish education or none at all, such was the case for only 37 percent of those aged 25 to 44. There are no statistics on those 18 to 24, but those familiar with the current state of Jewish education would testify that the figure has fallen further.[11] Girls in Orthodox schools may be educated separately and have less access to the study of Talmud than their brothers, but their education in Jewish subjects is taken seriously. Shoshana Pantel Zolty, an Orthodox educator who makes clear her rejection of contemporary feminism, speaks for an important group of Orthodox women when she asserts that "Jewish women, and indeed Orthodox Judaism as a whole, could only gain by having this soul [the study of the Oral Tradition] as part of themselves."[12] In fact, Orthodox women have participated in establishing educational institutions, like New York's Drisha, that seek to provide women with rigorous instruction in rabbinics. Jewish women of all denominations also flock to adult education courses, in search of spiritual and intellectual nourishment often denied them in their childhood.

Many young Jewish women, and some young men as well, have encountered feminist scholarship in the field of Jewish Studies at their colleges and universities and in adult education classes. Feminist scholarship has begun to recover the previously ignored experience of Jewish women and has offered new perspectives for the interpretation of classical Jewish texts and the analysis of central issues of Jewish history. Daniel Boyarin's *Carnal Israel*, for example, demonstrates how a feminist reading of Talmudic *sugyot* (topical discussions) elucidates the tensions in traditional Judaism between asceticism and sexuality.[13] Looking at a very different Jewish culture, that of late nineteenth-century German Jews, Marion Kaplan's *The Making of the Jewish Middle Class* shows that women and the family domain were critical to the processes of modernization of Jewry.[14] These books and many others indicate that we cannot understand Judaism without exploring issues of power relations encoded in gender and investigating how Jewish men and women experienced and expressed Judaism in their lives. Nor can we understand how we came to be who we are at the end of the twentieth century simply by studying the activity of men alone in the public spheres of politics, work, and synagogue; or by reading only texts composed by a learned male elite.[15] Women's roles in the family as well as in philanthropy, neighborhood activism, and education have been crucial in shaping Jewish identity and culture. Besides introducing the names of some women into Jewish historical consciousness, feminist scholarship has expanded our very definitions of Jewish religious experience and community and has suggested new criteria for the evaluation of such central historical issues as assimilation. Most importantly, it has demonstrated that any consideration of Jewish history and culture that ignores women's experience is incomplete and therefore flawed.

Although women have begun to assume leadership roles, particularly in smaller and mid-size communities, men still predominate in positions of power within the organized Jewish community. A recent report of the Council of Jewish Federations reported that the percentage of female officers and board members of federations had risen from 17 percent about twenty years ago to 32 percent in the early 1990s. A subsequent federation study found, however, that in the largest Jewish communities it was extremely difficult for women to enter into the top leadership of communal institutions. The glass ceiling for women remains a phenomenon of American Jewish communal life. In the nineteen largest federations the percentage of female presidents dropped from 10.5 percent to only 7 percent in the years since 1986, and no federation of a major city has a woman as executive director.[16] Shoshana Cardin's selection as chair of the Conference of Presidents of Major American Jewish Organizations may have marked a breakthrough in the opportunities available to women in the Jewish communal world, though it is only when the choice of a woman for a significant leadership post occasions no comment that one can speak with some confidence of gender equality. Ultimately more important than the singular careers of token women is the impact of more anonymous women as professionals and lay leaders in the infrastructure of the Jewish community and in the North American university. The presence of feminist Jews in communal institutions, for example, ensures that issues of gender equality are discussed rather than suppressed. It is now legitimate to question the absence of women when they are not included in decision-making roles or public activity. The Council of Jewish Federations regularly investigates the participation of women in leadership roles, both lay and professional. A book such as this exploring the Jewish community, had it been published a generation ago, would not have included issues of gender. Most importantly, the equality of women and men as a value and the blurring of gender distinctions in the public sphere of contemporary Jewish communal life in North America are increasingly taken for granted, as is the case in the larger society. Studies based on focus group interviews reveal, however, that many Jewish women still perceive the organized Jewish community as less than supportive of women when they attempt to combine marriage, childbearing, and careers and also as failing to reach out to women as participants in communal life.[17]

Many critics of feminism have attributed to its ideology the increase in women's employment outside the home, and particularly the employment of mothers of young children. Jewish women's participation in the labor force has indeed changed dramatically in the past generation. In 1957, 30 percent of Jewish women aged 25–44 were employed; in 1990 that figure had risen to 75 percent.[18] A study of Jewish families in twelve geographically dispersed United States cities conducted in the late 1980s found that between 50 and 66 percent of the mothers of children under the age of six participated in the labor force. In half of those locales, more of the mothers worked full time than part time.[19] Although some younger women, and many Orthodox women of all ages, shy away from the label "feminist," they organize their working and family lives under the impact of a combination of feminism and economic forces.

It is always risky for a historian to attempt to predict the future, even in the most general of terms. Yet, there is every reason to assume that the sociocultural and economic forces that have promoted feminism and changing gender roles and expectations among North American Jews will continue into the next century. Women are likely to continue to work in large numbers outside the home throughout their lives, for example, partly because of the structure of North American economies and partly because of the consequences of Jewish values, in particular the Jewish commitment to education.

The economies of North America necessitate that in most households two adults have to work for wages in order to maintain the prerequisites of middle-class family life. The participation of adult women in the labor force has therefore grown steadily since the 1960s, independent of ideological factors. Feminism alone has not pushed women out of the home to seek employment; rather, it has helped working mothers not to feel guilty about their choice. Feminist organizations have also led the fight for equal pay for equal work.

Jewish women are particularly likely to be employed because North American Jews have long endorsed the value of secular education, including higher education, as an end in itself and not merely for pragmatic reasons. The Jewish investment in education is reflected in the achievements of women as well as men; in fact, in a 1990 ranking of American white women with higher education by religious affiliation, Jewish women led the list. Eighty-four percent of Jewish women aged 25 to 44 had some higher education as compared with 50 percent of the entire sample.[20] Women with higher education tend to marry later and have fewer children than those whose education ends with high school; with more adult years free of the care of young children, they have fewer obstacles to work outside the home. Even when they have children at home, highly educated women are more likely to participate in the labor force.[21] The attainment of higher education also correlates among women with acceptance of the equality of women and men, and the desire to realize that equality personally within their households. The combination of high levels of post-secondary education and of labor force participation among Jewish women today suggests, then, that the role changes of the past generation and a half with regard to family and work will continue into the twenty-first century.

Feminism is thus only one component of complex social and economic forces that together have resulted in pervasive change in gender roles. The contemporary socioeconomic climate in North America has led to diverse family patterns even among those who vilify feminism and consider themselves social conservatives. It is worth noting, for example, that quite a few conservative United States politicians assiduously promoting traditional family values are not themselves living in traditional nuclear families; many have working wives; many have been divorced, and some who have fathered children have not been custodial parents.

Jews resemble their middle-class neighbors in their family patterns and therefore differ in some demographic characteristics from the general population that is more heterogeneous in its class composition. In contrast with the situation a generation ago, Jews in the United States are marrying later, having smaller families, and divorcing more frequently. Jews are single for a greater part of their lives than has ever previously been the case. There are also more single parents within the Jewish community than ever before as well as households without children.[22] The increasing acceptance in the United States of the claim of homosexuals to protection from discrimination, if not to full equality, has affected the Jewish community as well. Gay individuals and the families they form are part of the American Jewish community, despite powerful opposition particularly to male homosexuality within Jewish law. Jewish families in the twenty-first century are likely to be as diverse as they are now. Insofar as the organized Jewish community is perceived to be unfriendly to or uninterested in singles and in families that diverge from 1950s norms, it will fail to attract the participation of large segments of the North American Jewish population.

Changing gender roles and expectations that have accelerated since the 1960s have contributed greatly to the social, cultural, and denominational diversity of contemporary North American Jewish life. The changes that I have described in Jewish religious and communal institutions and in family structures have been tarred with the brush of feminism, a pejorative term for conservative Jewish as well as Christian social critics. Feminism has become a convenient target for traditionalists seeking to mobilize Jews to counter the corrosive effects of assimilation. Few concerned with the survival of the Jewish community in North America would dispute the bleak findings of the 1990 Jewish Population study, which found that about one-half of all Jews marrying today are marrying non-Jews. There are, however, legitimate differences in strategies proposed to strengthen Jewish identity and to deepen commitment to Jewish living and to the Jewish education of the younger generation. These range from outreach to the unaffiliated and the uninterested and to families of mixed religious backgrounds, on one end of the spectrum, to the building of strong walls against secular Western culture in all its forms, on the other. Recognizing the shrinking size of the American Jewish community along with the diminution of communal financial resources, the leadership of the organized Jewish community has sought to unify its disparate constituency in a common struggle for "Jewish continuity."

Unity, however, presupposes either shared values or, at the very least, a common recognition of the value of diversity. Yet, in the area of gender roles and expectations, there are profound differences in values, not just behavior, among Jews. Most North American Jews see the expansion of women's roles in the synagogue and the public domain and the fluidity of gender roles in general as an ethical good; others see these changes as corrosive of family and social stability and, for some, as a violation of God's will or of biological dictates.

At the heart of these two different readings of the consequences of changed gender roles is a disparity in their understanding of the meaning of equality, (for I presume that virtually all Jews reject the notion of female inferiority and most Jews endorse the Enlightenment vision of equality which has brought them full citizenship). Gender equality for those in favor of recent trends requires equal access to all positions that are not dependent on one's biology as well as the erasure of social hierarchies between the sexes; individual predispositions matter more than group attributes. For those opposed to the changes of the past generation, gender equality necessitates recognition of the different needs and social purposes of men and women; each sex, according to this view, is valued equally and thrives best in its own separate sphere. It is tempting to attribute these two positions to feminists and anti-feminists, but there is a sector of radical feminists, often called "essentialists," who support separate spheres and argue that all women share essential traits that differentiate them from men. Where "essentialists" part company with the conservative critics of feminism lies in their insistence on women defining their own nature and controlling their own sphere.[23]

There is a specifically Jewish component to the opposition to liberal feminist changes in the gender roles of men and women. The Orthodox interpretation of *halakhah* (Jewish law) presents radically different roles for men and women, particularly within the realm of prayer and ritual. According to Jewish tradition, women are exempt from positive time-bound commandments, including public prayer. Because they are not obligated to pray publicly, they may not be counted in a *minyan* (the quorum of ten necessary for public prayer), and they may not serve as a *shlihat zibbur* (the representative of the community who leads the prayer).[24] Jewish tradition considered a public ritual role for women unseemly, drawing on the Talmudic statement that *kol b'isha ervah*, the voice of a woman is sexually provocative.[25] More generally, those who oppose the blurring of gender roles see such a process as a fundamental assault on the basic world view of Judaism. Judaism rests on the drawing of distinctions—between kosher and non-kosher food, between holy time (the Sabbath) and secular time (weekdays)—and gender distinctions, according to this view, are therefore a God-given essential component of Judaism.

Opponents of changed gender roles also assert that the traditional nuclear family with its clearly divided responsibilities has been essential for the survival of Judaism and the Jewish people. As I have shown elsewhere, the patterns of Jewish family life have varied over time in accordance with the socioeconomic status of the Jews and the nature of the societies in which they have dwelled.[26] But the issue is not who is right and who is wrong.

Different views on gender roles are deeply held, and no ideology is likely to bridge the differences between two sets of fundamental convictions.

What this means for Jewish communities in North America is that dreams of unity cannot be realized on a wide range of issues. As a Jewish historian, I would add that unity has been a rare commodity indeed throughout Jewish history. In the modern period whatever structural support had previously existed for Jewish unity was eroded. Emancipation, to all intents and purposes, eliminated the autonomous corporate Jewish community, which had some power to constrain its members and thereby enforce a semblance of unity. Contact with modern secular thought ripped the sacred canopy of traditional Judaism, which had offered Jews a generally agreed upon symbol system to confer meaning on their existence.[27] During the past two hundred years, Orthodox and Reform, Zionists and anti-Zionists, Bundists and non-socialist Jews—to name but three pairs of antagonists—vigorously contended with each other over the meaning of Jewish identity and the strategies necessary to sustain Jewish life and culture. Given their vastly different interpretations of the Jewish past and present as well as of the ties binding Jews together, it is no surprise that they were unable and unwilling to reach a consensus. Nor is there any evidence that achieving unity would have provided protection against the forces that endangered Jewish survival.

Among Jews in North America today who are at all concerned with the Jewish future there are more points of agreement than in mid-nineteenth-century central Europe or in turn-of-the-century Poland or America. Commitment to the survival of the State of Israel and to strengthening Jewish education in order to sustain Jewish life in the Diaspora, for example, characterizes almost all of the diverse groups that comprise North American Jewry. These basic commitments, however, do not translate into consensus about how to promote survival of either of the two large centers of Jewish life.

If they seek to represent and recruit all Jews, as they confront various visions of the good Jewish society, the umbrella institutions within the organized Jewish community must support divergent approaches toward Jewish family life and toward gender roles in the synagogue and Jewish communal institutions. There are many paths that lead to the goal of stronger Jewish religious and cultural expression as well as Jewish learning. Even those who would like to return to the traditional family model of the 1950s, for example, must devise policy for Jewish families as they are and not for a romanticized, historic ideal based on gender divisions that some contemporary North American Jews would find far from ideal. Programming sponsored by Jewish institutions will therefore have to be as variegated as the different Jews who populate North America.

Jews with different conceptions of appropriate gender roles may be able to forge alliances on gendered issues of common concern that transcend ideological divisions. The need for good and affordable Jewish day care, the plight of the *agunah* (the chained wife, unable to secure a religious divorce), and the provision of Jewish education to girls and women are a few issues that come to mind. Jews with different understandings of gender equality can also work together on general issues. There is one prerequisite, however, that a diverse Jewish community must meet, if it seeks to mobilize all its members in support of such common goals as care of the needy and vulnerable both locally and internationally, support for Israel, investment in Jewish education, and defense against antisemitism. Because the commitment to gender equality is as fundamental to some Jews as is the commitment to *halakhah*, communal events that bring together Jews of different backgrounds and affiliations must be designed to be inclusive; women cannot be relegated to the background simply because their presence in the public arena may discomfort one sector of the community. Women's voices, moreover, must be sought and heard in the debate about how the community allocates its resources to meet its various needs. Those who speak in the name of "the Jews" must take care that they have drawn on the resources and insights of all Jews who seek to be spoken for. The challenge of the twenty-first century is to find a way to strengthen the Jewish community by transforming diversity—a simple fact—into pluralism, a value that celebrates diversity.

Notes

[1] On the impact of feminism, see Sylvia Barack Fishman, *A Breath of Life: Feminism in the American Jewish Community* (New York: The Free Press, 1993), and idem, "The Impact of Feminism on American Jewish Life" *American Jewish Year Book* 89 (1989): 3–62; and Norma Baumel Joseph, "The Feminist Challenge to Judaism: Critique and Transformation," in *Gender, Genre and Religion: Feminist Reflections*, eds. Morny Joy and Eva K. Neumaier-Dargyay (Waterloo, Ontario, Canada: Wilfred Laurier University Press, 1995), pp. 47–70.

[2] Jack Wertheimer, *A People Divided: Judaism in Contemporary America* (New York: Basic Books, 1993), pp. 21–22, 72–75.

[3] See my "The Modern Jewish Family: Image and Reality," in *The Jewish Family: Metaphor and Memory*, ed. David Kraemer (New York: Oxford University Press, 1989), pp. 179–93.

4   Conversations with representatives of the Conservative, Reconstructionist, and Reform movements in 1996 yielded figures of 78 females in the Conservative Rabbinical Assembly, 73 female graduates of the Reconstructionist Rabbinical College, and between 250 and 300 female Reform rabbis. The Central Conference pf American Rabbis (Reform) claims not to take note of gender distinctions. There is likely to be an overlap among rabbis since graduates of the RRC may join either the CCAR or the Rabbinical Assembly. The Cantors' Assembly (Conservative) has 39 female members and the American Conference of Cantors informed me that 40 percent of its 350 members were women.

5   Rivka Haut, "Women's Prayer Groups and the Orthodox Synagogue," in *Daughters of the King: Women and the Synagogue*, ed. Susan Grossman and Rivka Haut (Philadelphia and New York: Jewish Publication Society, 1992), pp. 135-57.

6   For an early collection of naming ceremonies for baby girls, see the pamphlet, "Blessing the Birth of a Daughter: Jewish Naming Ceremonies for Girls," ed. Toby Fishbein Reifman with Ezrat Nashim, 1977.

7   Arlene Agus, "This Month is for You: Observing Rosh Hodesh as a Woman's Holiday," in *The Jewish Woman: New Perspectives,* ed. Elizabeth Koltun (New York: Schocken Books, 1976), pp. 84-93; Penina Adelman, *Miriam's Well: Rituals for Jewish Women Around the Year*, 2nd edition (New York: Biblio Press, 1990); Ma'ayan brochure, 1996. For a bilingual Jewish feminist liturgy that includes the celebration of the New Moon, see Marcia Falk, *The Book of Blessings* (San Francisco: Harper SanFrancisco, 1996), especially pp. 327-99.

8   For a description of a veteran feminist seder, see Letty Cottin Pogrebin, *Deborah, Golda, and Me: Being Female and Jewish in America* (New York: Crown Publishers, 1991), pp. 111-27.

9   For two comprehensive Jewish feminist theologies, see Judith Plaskow, *Standing Again at Sinai: Judaism from a Feminist Perspective* (New York: Harper Collins, 1990); and Rachel Adler, *Engendering Judaism: An Inclusive Theology and Ethics* (Philadelphia: The Jewish Publication Society, 1998); see also, Ellen Umansky, "(Re)Imaging the Divine," *Response* 13:1-2 (Fall–Winter 1982): 110-19; and idem, "Creating a Jewish Feminist Theology: Possibility and Problems," in *Weaving the Visions,* eds. Judith Plaskow and Carol Christ (New York: Harper and Row, 1989), pp. 187-98; and Falk, *The Book of Blessings.*

10   See *Gates of Prayer: the New Union Prayerbook* (New York: Central Conference of American Rabbis, 1975); *Gates of Prayer for Shabbat* and *Gates of Prayer for Weekdays and at a House of Mourning,* ed. Chaim Stern (New York: Central Conference of American Rabbis, 1992); *Kol Haneshamah: The Reconstructionist Prayerbook,* ed. David Teutsch (Wyncote, Pa.: Reconstructionist Press, 1993); *Siddur Sim Shalom: Shabbat and Festivals*, Preliminary Edition (New York: Rabbinical Assembly and United Synagogue of Conservative Judaism, 1994).

11   Data were not provided for those aged 18–24, doubtless because there were not

enough Orthodox women in the sample. Table 10, drawn from Sylvia Barack Fishman and Alice Goldstein, *When They Are Older They Will Not Depart: Jewish Education and Jewish Behavior of American Adults*, as cited in Sylvia Fishman, *A Breath of Life: Feminism in the American Jewish Community* (New York: The Free Press, 1993), p. 264. Precisely what constitutes "substantial" Jewish education is unclear.

12 Shoshana Zolty, *"And All Your Children Shall be Learned"* (Northvale, N.J.: Jason Aronson Inc., 1993), p. xv.

13 Daniel Boyarin, *Carnal Israel: Reading Sex in Talmudic Culture* (Berkeley and Los Angeles: University of California Press, 1993).

14 Marion Kaplan, *The Making of the Jewish Middle Class: Women, Family, and Identity in Imperial Germany* (New York: Oxford University Press, 1991).

15 See my *Gender and Assimilation in Modern Jewish History: The Roles and Representation of Women* (Seattle: University of Washington Press, 1995).

16 CJF, *The survey on the status of women in the leadership and professional positions of Fedarations: Summary Report* (1993), as cited in Amy L. Sales, "Surveying the Landscape: Current Research on American Jewish Women," in *Voices for Change: Future Directions for American Jewish Women* (Waltham, Ma.: National Commission on American Jewish Women, 1995), p. 32; and CJF, *The status of women in lay and professional leadership positions of federations* (1994), as cited by Brenda Brown Lipitz, "Life in the Stalled Lane: Women in Jewish Communal Organizations," in *Voices for Change*, p. 94.

17 Rela G. Monson, "Implications of Changing Roles of Men and Women for the Delivery of Services," *Journal of Jewish Communal Service* 63 (1987): 302–10, as cited in Sales, "Surveying the Landscape," p. 30.

18 "The Jewish Family of the Future," undated *Newsletter of the William Petschek National Jewish Family Center*, American Jewish Committee 9:1, p. 3.

19 Table 6, based on a report of Gabriel Berger and Lawrence Sternberg, *Jewish Child-Care: A Challenge and an Opportunity*, as cited in Fishman, *A Breath of Life*, p. 260. See also the information presented in Moshe Hartman and Harriet Hartman, *Gender Equality and American Jews* (Albany: State University of New York Press, 1996), pp. 61–114, especially the table on p. 79. This book is the most comprehensive gender-sensitive analysis of the 1990 National Jewish Population Study. Breakdowns by gender are not included in Barry Kosmin, et al., *Highlights of the CJF 1990 National Jewish Population Survey* (New York: Council of Jewish Federations, 1991).

20 Ariela Kaysar and Barry A. Kosmin, "The Impact of Religious Identification on Differences in Educational Attainment among American Women in 1990," *Journal for the Scientific Study of Religion* 34:1 (March 1995): 54–55.

21 See Hartman and Hartman, *Gender Equality*, pp. 23–59.

22 "The Jewish Family of the Future," *Petschek Centre Newsletter*, p. 1.

[23] Debra Kaufman has drawn the analogy between radical feminists and ultra-orthodox Jews, though without the emphasis on their different views of female autonomy. See her *Rachel's Daughters: Newly Orthodox Jewish Women* (New Brunswick and London: Rutgers University Press, 1991), pp. 131–54.

[24] The Talmudic source for the exemption of women from certain commandments may be found in *Mishnah Kiddushin* 1, 7. For a discussion of the *halakhic* implications of this exemption, see Rachel Biale, *Women and Jewish Law: An Exploration of Women's Issues in Halakhic Sources* (New York: Schocken Books, 1984), pp. 10–43.

[25] BT *Berakhot* 24a.

[26] Paula E. Hyman, "The Jewish Family: Looking for a Usable Past," in *On Being a Jewish Feminist,* ed. Susannah Heschel (New York: Schocken Books, 1983), pp. 19–26; Steven M. Cohen and Paula E. Hyman, eds., *The Jewish Family: Myths and Reality* (New York: Holmes and Meier, 1986), pp. 3–13, 230–35; and Hyman, "The Modern Jewish Family."

[27] I have borrowed this metaphor from Peter Berger's *The Sacred Canopy: Elements of a Sociological Theory of Religion* (Garden City, N.Y.: Doubleday and Co., Inc., 1967).

16

ANTICIPATING THE FUTURE: A JEWISH FEMINIST SCENARIO

Norma Baumel Joseph

The rosh yeshiva enters the room—actually appearing on computer screens from somewhere in cyberspace—but the students accustomed to this format feel themselves to be in the same "room." Tension fills the air in each and every study space. It is a particularly difficult passage. Who will go first? Who will fail those insightful and demanding eyes? She calls on the first one, and they are immediately plunged into the thick of it.

While I trust you are not shocked by this scenario, I hope you are concerned, as I am, by the pervasive androcentrism of our conventions. The title, *rosh yeshiva*, is routinely reserved for males. In the future, however, a female head of a talmudic academy is conceivable, possibly even desirable.

In fact a female *rosh yeshiva* is known to us. Asenath Bat Shmuel Barazani, known as "Rebbetzin Mizrahi," lived in seventeenth-century Kurdistan, where she was the head of a yeshiva founded by her father.[1] Her marital contract contained a clause releasing her from household duties so that she would have time to study.[2] If the past is prologue, it has taken us a long time even to consider building upon this hundreds-of-years-old foundation.[3]

The maleness of our perspective is the impediment, however, not ignorance of this admittedly obscure historical personage. Many of us surely know of prominent contemporary examples that fit the above scenario. We just gloss over all the new approved schools where women are the teachers and directors—the *roshei yeshiva*—because the students are "just" girls. Our prejudices embrace both the *rosh yeshiva* and her *talmidot* (students), encompassing the arenas of leadership and popular practice.

Determining the significance of an event or scenario depends largely on our understanding of the way it fits into our communal pattern of life. How

199

does the scene with which I began relate to the current obsession with communal continuity? Does it in any way reflect the present values of the community? I feel strongly that it is appropriate at this point in time to attempt to develop models that re/present an agenda of communal continuity "with women." We need to reexamine the past and rethink the terms we have used to understand it. This is critical, not just for the purpose of understanding the past and present, but to chart a future. Models of and for continuity that are not gender adjusted will produce an unstable future.[4]

Increasingly, women are taking an active part in the corporate community of Jews. Any future-oriented plan must take cognizance of that fact and of our continued communal mis-measure and disregard of women Jews, as well. The feminist movement has influenced and infiltrated the Jewish world, bringing with it both a great deal of hostility and of creativity. Women have been made aware of their absence in the central definition of Jewish community. Many have walked away; others have decided to work at transforming themselves and their communities.[5]

Two aspects of the modern moment have greatly affected women's standard for their participation in the community. In the past, women may have felt themselves to be firmly rooted in the collective. They appear less frequently than males in biblical narratives, but the holy places and sacrificial system were available to them. After the destruction of the Temple, Jews had fewer personalized rituals, but membership in the community was self-evident. Modernity, however, brought with it both the end of a corporate sense and a powerful new emphasis on the individual and on public display. Thus, feminists have sought greater inclusion in just those arenas from which women had been absent. The issue is not necessarily assessing the shortcomings of the past. The current challenge is to find the right fit in today's circumstances, and that includes both public and individual participation in communal membership and leadership.

In *The Death and Birth of Judaism*, Jacob Neusner presents new models of envisioning Jewishness. He speaks of the Judaism of Holocaust and Redemption as reversionary, as going from a mode of self-evidence to one of self-consciousness. He argues that,

> people sold on the centrality of "being Jewish" in their lives require modes of expression that affect. . . . their lives more deeply, and in more ways, than the rather limited way of life offered by American Judaism. . . . [They look] not for activity but for community, not for an occasional emotional binge but for an enduring place and partnership: a covenant.[6]

Substitute "women" for "people." Women who are feminist Jews want membership in that community in ways not previously available, perhaps not even necessary. They expect to enter the shared covenantal community as full members and as directors and supervisors. They envision a partnership of equals in which autonomy is associated with incorporation into the whole, expecting "to find ways to accommodate the individuation of women within our commitment to the unity of the Jewish people, the community and the family."[7] Thus, we have a re/vision/reversion model, too. But it is not yet decisively articulated; it certainly is nothing like self-evident.

The subject is not just one of equity or access, although even equal remuneration and respect have not yet been achieved. Some Jewish denominations have developed gender inclusive platforms, some of which are more than a hundred years old, but none yet offers comprehensive equality. Though access to greater ritual participation and public leadership is increasing, it by no means addresses or solves all of the major issues.

The dilemma facing our communities cannot be addressed in a piecemeal fashion, item by item, ritual by ritual, organization by organization. The central problem is contemporary women's commitment to being contributing and decisive members of the community. Feminists call this the quest for agency. That does not mean that women wish to be identical to men, nor do feminists invariably reject characteristically female roles or modes of action. Rather, agency addresses the prerogative of being present and representing, of supporting and being supported by, of determining and influencing the course of modern Jewish history.

Although there are signs indicating a backlash and the disintegration of equity achievements, the movement to correct the invisibility and inequalities that mark our society will hopefully continue. People will work toward the integration of gender roles emphasizing human rights and equal citizenship, maximizing human resources. We might even be able to imagine a gender-blind pattern of communal participation and leadership. Conceivably the rabbinate will become more female friendly, as will our liturgical language and religious imagery.

Another path already trodden, albeit lightly, builds on the notion of separate spheres, accentuating female distinctiveness and influence. Some female-centered texts and rituals will be affirmed and amplified. At this juncture we can foresee a world wherein "women's work" or "women's ways of knowing" are valued and respected. It is interesting to note that a separatist agenda of "meaningful distinctiveness"[8] appeals both to radical feminists and to Orthodox feminists. It is even possible to advocate both integrated and separate spheres, as Jews maintained in their early encounters with emancipation. Writing about assimilation in the modern period, Paula Hyman describes "the coexistence of the desire for full civic integration with the retention of what we might today call ethnic particularism."[9] The parallels between the Jewish quest for recognition and feminist concerns for equality with distinctiveness are suggestive.[10]

In the near future, issues of access and agency will most probably continue to be contentious, shaping strategy and consequence. Some activists will operate within the ritual sphere, while others will attack the standards of secular Jewish institutions. Many will plan and act; others will agonize and theorize. Some will seek private, intimate space, while others will demand public place and position. These options are not mutually exclusive. All can be challenging, transformative, and Jewish.

Rather than trying to foresee the shape of the future—a difficult, if not impossible task—I prefer to focus on suitable paradigms for understanding the past and present. I propose to search history for an appropriate context in which to situate the changes. Change is inherent in the human condition; it comes whether we like it or not. Our task is to understand what has happened and cope with it. Continuity is not about stasis or sameness; it is about the power and confidence of communal life to prevail.[11] It is about our ability to weave together old and new stories about ourselves, our ancestors, and our children, carrying forward our sense of ourselves as firmly rooted in an eternal heritage. The world may seem particularly hostile to Jewish survival at this point, but Jewish communities have faced similar challenges before.[12] A historical perspective can lend depth to our discussions and help create self-confidence in the community's ability to weather the winds of change.

Twentieth-century Judaism is radically different from that of previous generations in a number of ways. One of them is its stance on female education.[13] The new attitude developed in a number of different contexts, two of which offer us re/vision strategies. One approach was enunciated at the beginning of the twentieth century by Rabbi Yisrael Meir HaKohen of Lithuania, known, as the *Hafetz Hayim*. He urged educating women even though doing so involved a radical break with tradition. The other approach was suggested by Rabbi Samson Raphael Hirsch of Frankfurt/Main toward the end of the nineteenth century. He claimed that Jewish history had bequeathed a continuous legacy of educating females upon which the community can build.[14]

Feminist Judaism now stands at a crucial point in its transformative power. Which of these strategies can or should it develop and depend upon? What approach can best aid in situating and legitimating the feminist challenge?

In citing these two sources, I do not intend to prescribe a debate wholly within the realm of halakhic discourse or traditional religious practice. But I submit that we can profitably probe these approaches to change in order to direct better our responses to, and our understanding of, the future. I admit to having another objective in using these examples. We are planning for a future during a period of factionalism and of reactionary resistance to change. Yet, these models of transformation come from within the traditional community committed to Jewish law. They offer us an understanding of the ways our observant predecessors struggled for continuity as they responded to a gendered quest.

Until the modern period, education was the preserve of the elite, primarily the male elite. This pattern was not unique to Jews, but its rupture in the modern period is significant for us. Certainly there were educated women in our history. Individuals such as Beruriah, Dulcie of Worms, Bat Halevi, Asenath Barazani, Deborah Ascarelli, Rachel Morpurgo, Sarah Coppia Sullam, Rebecca Tiktiner, Glückl of Hameln, Penina Moïse, and Grace Aguilar were known for their learning and scholarship,[15] although they were exceptions to the rule that frequently and deliberately excluded women.

In the Western world, beginning in the eighteenth century a transformation took place. Education was democratized. It was called upon to solve social ills and to provide economic security. In Europe and especially in North America, public education for the masses became the norm. This revolution affected the Jewish world as well.

The hunger of Jews for knowledge is legendary. Its origins go back to the experience of a scattered, exiled people trying to maintain its distinctiveness, allegiance, and unity through the study of sacred texts—an experience astonishingly analogous to ours today. But that learning, although an ideal, was available only to a few males. In the modern world a large number of Jews gained access to secular study. To a degree, they transferred the passion for knowledge of Jewish texts to secular sources. Jews also recognized that secular education was the ticket of admission to advancement in the open society. In such an environment Jewish women, no less than Jewish men, desired to be educated and to educate.

Examples illustrate the changes that have taken place but also the persistence of some old arguments and positions. When one young girl told her parents that she wanted to go to high school, they refused permission. Their reason: Girls who go to high school become teachers, and all teachers remain spinsters. That girl was Golda Myerson (Meir).[16] Another woman, Annie Nathan Meyer, was prevented from continuing her education, because her father believed that men hated "intelligent wives." She went on to help found Barnard College for Women in 1889.[17] Novelist Anzia Yezierska wrote marvelous semi-fictional accounts of the battle waged by young immigrant women who tried to go to school to better themselves or simply because they loved to learn.[18]   These are the stories we must not forget, stories that we must weave into our self-re/presentation.

These women did not just pioneer for themselves. They created new institutions that benefited the Jewish community and Western civilization with innovative pedagogic techniques and structures. Using the American Protestant Sunday school system as her guide, Rebecca Gratz started a Sunday school in Philadelphia in 1838 for Jewish children that blossomed into a very successful movement. Independently, she created an environment in which women became the primary formal religious educators.[19]   In the twentieth century, Rebecca Bettelheim Kohut ran the short-lived Kohut School for Girls in New York, a precursor of the recent development of preparatory academies for Jewish girls.[20]   Henrietta Szold searched for a way to teach working adults the language of their new country.[21]   There are many more examples of women whose devotion to education became a way of building a community with a brighter future. Many, like Gratz, Kohut and Szold, embraced Jewish education in addition to secular study. And in 1893, the National Council of Jewish Women proposed to "organize and encourage the study of . . . Judaism" by Jewish women so that they would be able to strengthen Jewish life.[22]

The above examples anticipated and participated in a paradigm shift, but they did not legitimate or complete it. They offer an argument for the increased presence of women in education on the basis of women's traditional role, namely that they are responsible for the children. According to this cult of domesticity, women are seen as the prime educators because of their maternal role.[23]

The breakthrough came in Europe. At the beginning of the twentieth century, Sarah Schnirer sought to teach women about Judaism, and her innovative vision and accomplishments are part of the saga of Jewish women's history.[24] From the Hafetz Hayim, she received endorsement for her plans. With his "radical" vision of change in Jewish life,[25] he claimed that the talmudic prohibition concerning "him who teaches his daughter Torah" no longer applied. He saw his generation as beset by the "sins" of emancipation and modernity, and the values of the Jewish community being eroded by the social climate. Girls could no longer learn about the tradition by emulating their parents. It was necessary, the Hafetz Hayim declared, to break with convention and teach daughters formally. In fact, he ruled, teaching women was now not an issue of permission but of duty, of *mitzvah*.[26] His plan, of course, did not extend to Talmud and other esoteric subjects still reserved for men; he did not envision an egalitarian study hall.

That in order to sanction change the Hafetz Hayim presented it as necessary and not just permissible, may offer a lesson worth contemplating. In preparing for a justly gendered future, perhaps we should formulate an agenda in terms of necessity, obligation, and responsibility in combination with, or even omitting, claims of privilege and rights. Certainly, Jewish legal arguments are constructed in terms of obligations, not rights.

The decisions of the Hafetz Hayim (and of Rabbi Hirsch) are stated in the language of obligation. For the former, educating women is a matter of necessity because of the changed circumstances of Jewish life. The fear that women would "leave the path completely and abrogate the principles of the faith, God forbid" motivated drastic but justifiable measures to ensure the greater good during a crisis—שעת הדחק.[27] According to this view, a female *rosh yeshivah* might represent a radical change from past practice that is necessitated by a need to strengthen women's identity. At the same time, however, that the Hafetz Hayim justified women's study and even welcomed this particular innovation, he was certainly not eagerly embracing change. He was practicing brinkmanship. Only the threat to Jewish survival enabled him to propose educating Jewish women.

Rabbi Hirsch legitimated female education while denying any need for change. Astonishingly, he claimed that women had in principle always been obligated to study Torah.[28] By highlighting the universality and eternal truth of Judaism, Hirsch could underscore continuity. Thus, he saw no change. Women, he claimed, always had at least limited access to study; now, as always, he said, women were obligated to study. There are, of course, many traditionalists who see the issue differently. Some Orthodox communities to this day oppose all forms of sacred study for women. Most Jews, however, have rejected this approach.

Hirsch allowed for the legitimate integration of women in Judaism as well as the redemption of Judaism for women. According to his model, the inclusion of women does not threaten Judaism; women's inclusion is part of the mission of Israel. His model presupposes an evolutionary process in which everything is validated through the myth of continuity or through precedent. His ideal, however, reifies a map of divided gender roles. Women are created different and therefore require separate legal and ritual attention. As Hirsch saw it, women do not need all the *mitzvot* or rituals, because they are constructed differently; their mothering roles enable them to develop a relationship to commandments that does not necessitate the performance of rituals according to the schedules prescribed for men.[29] Despite this problematic contention, his strategy for the incorporation of new trends may be a usable model for feminist Judaism. All that is required is a reexamination of the past to find the right precedent or interpretation.

The Hafetz Hayim openly, and perhaps more honestly, proclaimed that

Judaism needs change and can handle innovation. He said that because of our many sins—according to feminists they include misogyny and androcentrism—we must change. His approach to social reality and the historical process of *halakhah* seems more helpful than Hirsch's to the feminist cause. His model, however, denies women's role in the history of our community. It also denies women the right to study justified in terms of their own experience as Jews. In this model, moreover, no critique of the past exclusion of women from study is possible. Although study remains a normative and central Jewish experience, the ideal remains no study for women. If we could go backwards in time, the Hafetz Hayim would not be permissive. His argument is never about women's need to study for themselves. It is only about extenuating circumstances and women's ability to influence or educate their families in such times.

Unquestionably, neither rabbi envisioned female rabbinic scholars, although both approaches open the door for such an eventuality. The question that interests me at this stage, as I noted earlier, is which paradigm to appropriate. Both approaches deny the validity of the feminist critique; both offer interesting possibilities for meeting it. In all probability, if we look at the contemporary academies of advanced Judaic Studies for adult women, we will see their philosophical connection to Hirsch and their halakhic reliance on the Hafetz Hayim. Significantly, however, in those schools that follow Hirsch's philosophy, girls are taught more classical text and in greater depth than in the Beth Jacob schools that were founded by Schnirer.[30]

Other views on change and innovation are variations on the above themes. In *Jewish Women in Time and Torah*, Eliezer Berkovits argues that some aspects of our tradition were tolerated but not taught.[31] Thus, according to him, that women did not study Torah was not divinely ordained but, rather, a historical fact that needs to be overcome. For him, historical changes are part of a divine plan for repair (תיקון) and are consonant with the basic principles of the faith.

Rabbi Moshe Feinstein in his *Iggrot Moshe* subtly combines the approaches of Hirsch and the Hafetz Hayim while advancing a new standard. It is self-evident to him that girls must get a good Jewish education. Nothing can interfere with that basic principle. In his judgments, he fashions a radically new legal and theoretical position. Like the Hafetz Hayim, he takes account of altered sociocultural conditions.[32] But he does not bemoan the contemporary trend of educating females. For him, it is obligatory for a father to pay for his daughter's education, a radical shift from talmudic antecedents,[33] although he maintains a Hirschean view of a continuous pattern of education.[34] In one responsum, Feinstein claims that although a change occurred over time on this issue, it was an unremarkable change; in another, he asserts that the issue of educating females is simple. It is significant to note the way in which he justifies a new practice that contravenes the law or displaces a past convention.[35]

By embracing change and proclaiming continuity while denying change, the education of female Jews became normative. These approaches established as a given for all segments of the Jewish world that girls must be formally educated. And if the content of their education was to be different from that of boys,[36] schools were nonetheless to be built, and money was to be spent on their education. And that was new! Significantly, the new was proclaimed in such a way that it was immediately accepted as part of Judaism, not perceived as a threat, even by the traditionalists.

Judaism and the Jewish community of the twenty-first century will not look like today's community of New York, Montreal or Jerusalem. I do not think we can visualize this future. But just as Jewish schools for girls have not devastated Judaism—on the contrary, in my opinion they have redeemed it—so, too, increased women's participation will not signal the end of a recognizable Judaism. Our future achievements presuppose the necessity of understanding and accepting the motives of the proponents of change and of having confidence in our tradition's endurance. They also require careful attention to our customs and the preservation of our heritage. The two rabbinic reactions to change discussed here pave the way for our future engagement with transformation and tradition.

All of the models for change are "useful." But which approach meets the needs of the moment? Which would be the best approach for my Jewish feminism? Have these things always been there for our discovery, or is feminist Judaism totally lacking any connection to my ancestry? In truth, I would wish to claim a more obviously hallowed prototype. In the book of Numbers (27:1–11), when Moses is detailing the laws of inheritance, a group of women, the daughters of Tslofhad, point out a flaw in the law. Since he has no son, their father has no direct heir; his land and name will disappear. They wish to inherit him in order to preserve family continuity. Given their social status, they wisely do not ask for land in their own names; they merely express a desire to maintain their father's birthright.[37] Moses does not know what to do and presents their case to God. God tells him to give the women a portion (נתן תתן להם אחזת נחלה).

A future-oriented leadership, I propose, will respond likewise to women's legitimate claims for increased participatory action. Whether seeking common or distinctive paths, women's investment in communal representation and presentation must be embraced. The continuity concerns of today's community cannot and should not avoid this opportunity. The historical record presents us with a prototype for response and should inspire confidence in its success.

Notes

[1]   *Encyclopaedia Judaica*, 1st ed. (Jerusalem: Keter publishing), s.v. "Barazani." The entry reads as follows: "Barazani, Asenath bat (daughter) of Samuel (1590?–1670), Kurdish head of yeshiva and poet . . . she headed the Mosul yeshiva."

[2]   Sondra Henry and Emily Taitz, *Written Out of History* (New York: Biblio Press, 1983), p. 109.

[3]   There are many other women who were known as scholars and who functioned in various rabbinic-like capacities. For example: Dulcie of Worms, Miriam Shapira Luria, Bat HaLevi, Eva Bachrach, Rebecca Tiktiner, Hannah Rachel Webermacher, and others. See Shoshana Pantel Zolty, *"And All Your Children Shall Be Learned": Women and the Study of Torah in Jewish Law and History* (Northvale, N.J.: Jason Aronson, 1993); see also various chapters and references in Judith Baskin, ed., *Jewish Women in Historical Perspectives* (Detroit: Wayne State, 1991). A surprising list is compiled by H. Rabinowicz, "Lady Rabbis and Rabbinic Daughters," in *The World of Hasidism* (Hartford: Hartmore House, 1970), pp. 202–10.

[4]   Recently, in a collection of essays on the future of the American Jewish community, two authors used female role models to explore prospective possibilities for the entire community. Judith Kates looked at the story in Talmud Bavli *Berachot* 10a about Beruriah, and Gail Twersky Reimer identified Bertha Pappenheim, in "The Legacy of Beruriah" and "Tell the Truth, But Tell It Whole" respectively, both in *At The Crossroads: Shaping our Jewish Future* (Boston: Combined Jewish Philanthropies and Wilstein Institute of Jewish Policy Studies, 1995), 42–45, 71–73.

[5]   See my "The Feminist Challenge to Judaism: Critique and Transformation," in *Gender, Genre and Religion: Feminist Reflections*, eds. Morny Joy and Eva K. Neumaier-Dargyay (Waterloo: Wilfred Laurier University Press, 1995), pp. 41–70.

[6]   Jacob Neusner, *The Death and Birth of Judaism* (New York: Basic Books, 1987), pp. 304–305.

[7]   Leah Shakdiel, personal communciation, Montreal, Canada, 21 February 1990.

[8]   Sylvia Barack Fishman, in *At The Crossroads*, p. 24.

[9]   *Gender and Assimilation in Modern Jewish History* (Seattle: Washington University Press, 1995), p. 11.

[10] I often find it theoretically illuminating to explore the parallel between Women's Studies and Jewish Studies.

[11] Michael Oppenheim, personal commumciation, Montreal, Canada, 21 July 1988.

[12] For an excellent example see Jonathan Sarna, *A Great Awakening* (New York: Council for Initiatives in Jewish Education Essay Series, 26 April 1995).

[13] I situate this claim in "Jewish Education for Women: Rabbi Moshe Feinstein's Map of America," *American Jewish History* 83 (1995): 205–22.

[14] The contrast between these two positions was first brought to my attention by my teacher, Rabbi Getsel Ellinson, author of the three volume publication, *HaIsha Ve-HaMitsvot* [Hebrew] (Jerusalem: Jewish Agency, 1977). He specifically differentiates their perspectives in volume one, page 159, note 77.

[15] For some sources, see note 3.

[16] Irving Howe and Kenneth Libo, *How We Lived: A Documentary History of Immigrant Jews in America, 1880–1930* (New York: Richard Marek, 1979), p. 129.

[17] Charlotte Baum, Paula Hyman, and Sonia Michel, *The Jewish Woman in America* (New York: Dial Press, 1976), p. 47.

[18] Anzia Yezierska, *Hungry Hearts and Other Stories* (New York: Persea Books, 1985), reissue.

[19] Sondra Henry and Emily Taitz, *Written Out of History: Our Jewish Foremothers*, 2nd ed. (New York: Bibilo Press, 1983), p. 219.

[20] Jacob Rader Marcus, *The American Jewish Woman: A Documentary History* (New York: Ktav, 1981), 480–84.

[21] Susan Dworkin, "Henrietta Szold-Liberated Woman," in *The Jewish Woman: New Perspectives*, ed. E. Koltun (New York: Schocken Books, 1976), p. 166.

[22] Sarna, *Great Awakening*, p. 25.

[23] Paula Hyman points out the irony of this assimilationist value. Historically, a child's (son's) education was the responsibility of the father or the community, never the mother. In America, education and religion became mama's job. Hyman, *Gender and Assimilation*, p. 48.

[24] Schnirer had already received permission from the Belzer and Gerer Rebbes, but sanction from the Hafetz Hayim was the most important. It was published in the *Bais Ya'acov* magazine of 1933. See D. Weissmann, "Bais Ya'acov," M.A. Dissertation, Hebrew University, 1975, p. 52. The event is also referred to in Deborah Weissman, "Bais Yaakov," in *The Jewish Woman: New Perspectives*, ed. E. Koltun (New York: Schocken, 1976), pp. 139–48.

[25] *Likutei Halakhot, Sotah* 21.

[26] Ibid.

[27] This principle of Jewish law is cited in rabbinic responsa issued in varied crisis situations.

[28] Rabbi Samson Raphael Hirsch, *Horeb: A Philosophy of Jewish Life and Commentaries*, trans. Dr. I. Grunfeld (London: Soncino Press, 1962), vol. 2, chapter 75, section 494, p. 371. See also Ellinson, *HaIsha Ve-Hamitsvot*, v. 1, pp. 158–59.

[29] This philosophical perspective is clear in other sections of the *Horeb*, especially in the commentary on Genesis 1–3.

[30] Naomi G. Cohen, "Women and the Study of Talmud," *Tradition* 24 (1988): 28–37. See also Ellinson, *HaIsha Ve-HaMitsvot*, v. 1, p. 159, note 77.

[31] Eliezer Berkovits, *Jewish Women in Time and Torah* (Hoboken: Ktav Publishing House, Inc., 1990).

[32] Rabbi Moshe Feinstein, *Iggrot Moshe, Yoreh Deah* (New York: Rabbi M. Feinstein, 1981), 3: 87, 3:73.

[33] Feinstein, *Yoreh Deah*, 2:113.

[34] Feinstein, *Yoreh Deah*, 2:102, 3:80, 3:87b.

[35] For a detailed analysis, see Norma Joseph, "Jewish Education for Women," *American Jewish History* 83 (1995): 205–22.

[36] Rabbi Joseph B. Soloveitchik went even further in teaching Talmud to the women at Stern College. However, he did not justify it in any formal document.

[37] The Talmud relates that these women were wise and knew how to argue a point of law. TB *Bava Batra* 119b.

PART
6

DEMOGRAPHY
AND ECONOMICS:
THE
INSTITUTIONAL RESPONSE

17

DEMOGRAPHY AND ECONOMICS: AN INTRODUCTION

Sydney Eisen

What distinguishes our age is not the assimilation of Jews—Jews have always assimilated in greater or smaller numbers—but the appearance of an impressive body of literature devoted to documenting the process. While demographers may be better at projecting than predicting (as Morton Weinfeld notes in his chapter here), they have not been reluctant to sound an alarm nor to proffer remedies to deal with the large-scale defections of our own day. Barry Kosmin and Morton Weinfeld have written complementary papers on the present state and future prospects of Jewish life in North America. While Kosmin devotes more space to population data and Weinfeld to interpretation, both insist that a profound transformation is called for in Jewish attitudes and in the structure and mission of Jewish institutions if communities are to respond effectively to the dramatic changes taking place in the position of Jews in mainstream society, in family life, and in other areas. Both are convinced that in any program of renewal, difficult choices will have to be made between quality and quantity (Weinfeld's emphasis). Should the limited resources of the community be spread thinly to pursue the great body of unaffiliated Jews (over 50% according to Kosmin), or should they be concentrated in order to strengthen the committed core? Both scholars lean in the direction of quality, and both, in different ways, are cautiously optimistic about the Jewish future.

Clearly, funds will be essential in effecting any transformation, but we know that funds in themselves will not make for stronger commitment. Appealing to traditional Jewish guilt or to *dos pintele yid* (that small core of Jewishness that was thought to reside permanently in all Jewish hearts) will not likely bring forth an enthusiastic response in the present context. The kind of commitment being sought usually grows out of strong feelings, whether religious, historical, national, geographic, or linguistic. How, then, can the wellsprings of emotion that will nurture the love of being Jewish be tapped?

More than ever, Jewish thinkers and leaders now put their faith in education, particularly the education of the young. There are various legitimate forms of formal and informal Jewish education, but strong evidence exists that an intensive, prolonged period of Jewish learning, involving the study of classical texts in Hebrew, along with an examination of historical and contemporary issues, when experienced within a warm stimulating milieu, provides the most effective means of assuring that the next generation will live a full Jewish existence and that Jews will survive as a people in a free society. The Hebrew day schools, which have expanded enormously in these decades of crisis, offer the greatest hope. But can the schools alone bear the responsibility, as they are sometimes asked to do, for the future of Jewish existence?

Traditionally, of course, the family has been the partner of the school in the task of rearing future generations. Some schools, especially those whose clientele includes parents with little knowledge of Judaism, have instituted programs designed to make the family a more active participant in the education of children. This task is made difficult by the fact that the family itself is in a state of flux. The "standard" Jewish household—two Jewish parents, with children—is a shrinking phenomenon and its decline has significant consequences for Jewish institutions, particularly schools.

More delicate as a social issue, but of fundamental importance in "creating the Jewish future," is the rearing of children in households where both parents are fully employed outside the home. The much maligned/revered institution of "the Jewish mother" as the model of devotion and the guardian of family values, though by no means defunct, is, in our day, often relegated to folklore. I do not advocate a return to the past, but rather for the need to address this issue in any serious consideration of the role of the family in shaping a new generation.

Jewish worldly success, whether financial, political, or cultural, never goes unnoticed in any discussion of the Jewish community. It is a source of pride as well as envy. No one should underestimate the importance of a strong material foundation in sustaining Jewish institutions (their actual humble beginnings are seldom remembered). An overemphasis on material success, however, creates problems of its own: It may become absorbing to the exclusion of other values; it may alienate young people who reject their elders' notion of achievement; and it may discourage students from choosing less lucrative, though essential, professions and occupations, such as teaching. The issue of personal finances is all the more serious, because a full

Jewish life, including choice of neighborhood, education, philanthropy, and memberships, is so expensive. Even moderately well-off families stagger under the weight of day-school fees.

As we move from mapping life style and population shifts and look at individual people and places, we are faced with a basic question: What are Jews, confronted with a weakening of the community in the short run, and population decline (except for the more orthodox elements) and massive assimilation in the long run, willing to do? Certainly, there is an increasing awareness of the need for a variety of social and educational programs for young and old—in the community, the university, and in Israel. More specifically, to what extent would concerned Jews be prepared to modify their high standard of living in order to provide all children and young people with the opportunity to get the best Jewish education available? This ideal, to which some communities subscribed in the past, is now deemed to be less attainable because of a shortage of funds. But if the most affluent and the freest communities in the history of the Jewish people cannot adequately fund education, how seriously can anyone take the *cri de coeur* for heroic measures to reverse the tide of assimilation? The sacrifice of some comfort in the name of Jewish values (already practiced by many education-minded parents) would be a salutory example for young people and perhaps an inspiration for those who remain on the margins of the community.

It is painful and ironic, especially in the wake of the losses suffered by Jews in the Second World War, to see the voluntary exodus of Jews from the ranks of their people. At the same time, it is heartening to witness the passion of Jewish communities in the process of gearing up to reverse these trends. There is no guarantee that large numbers can be wooed back. In all likelihood, however, the programs for renewal, if wisely directed, will not go unrewarded. At the same time, it is virtually certain that lasting benefits can come from sustaining and strengthening the commitment of those who have chosen to remain solidly within the fold, yet have difficulty coping with the attendant burdens.

The two chapters that follow will do much to stimulate readers to respond to these economic, demographic, and institutional questions.

18

THE DEMOGRAPHICS AND ECONOMICS OF THE JEWISH MARKET IN NORTH AMERICA

Barry A. Kosmin

The confusion of our Jewish communities and organizations over what they are or should be doing for whom and why is natural and understandable. In large measure, it is an outgrowth of the fast changing and bewildering environment we inhabit. Yet a lack of understanding or knowledge of the current Jewish condition is unacceptable if institutions are to survive and flourish in the future.

The title of this chapter suggests that there is a distinct and identifiable Jewish market in North America. It presumes that there is a bounded population of North American Jews rather than divergent and separate populations of Canadian Jews, California Jews, Reform Jews, Sephardic Jews, married Jews, and so on. In reality, of course, there are both a unified and a discrete market. It depends on the purpose we have in mind. Are we engaged in elite or mass activities? Do we want to distribute readily available products as widely as possible, or do we want to ration scarce goods for a clearly targeted market segment?

We live in a paradoxical world—the world of the Internet, of enlarged trading blocs, such as the European Union and NAFTA, and the world of increasing tribalism and emphasis on identity politics. At one level, our personal lives are becoming homogenized under the influence of globalization in the economy, technology and communications. As we might expect given an increasingly interconnected world economic order, the living standards and consumption patterns of Jews in New York, Toronto, Mexico City, London, Paris, and Rome, as well as their socioeconomic profiles, have probably never been closer. The social and structural issues and challenges that face these Jewish populations are also very similar. Yet, it appears that our various communities are diverging, some might say polarizing, in the

Jewish cultural and organizational spheres. Our response modes and prospects at the local and national levels are quite heterogeneous. This is probably because, though we have a world economic order, our societies reflect the diversity of cultural and historical responses to the challenge of modernity. In other words, our personal lives and life styles are divergent and our Jewish collectivities reflect that divergence. In this chapter I shall discuss the apparent paradox and highlight the difficulties and challenges it poses for the organized Jewish community.

The Similarities of U.S. and Canadian Jewry

Identity Constructs

My first task is to correct the notion that there is a wide gulf between Canadian and American Jews and that they are set on different trajectories in terms of their development. By the accepted standards of social scientific analysis of international comparisons, the populations are virtually indistinguishable. Canada and the United States are, of course, two separate societies with distinct histories and different political systems. The two nations have differing ethnic and religious population compositions, as well as differing government policies and legal provisions regarding ethnic and religious matters. Yet, in terms of technology, economy, and lifestyle, there are many points of similarity. This is particularly true for the Jewish population of the two countries, which is concentrated in the major metropolitan centers, has a very high level of education, and, as a result, is mostly engaged in professional and managerial occupations.

The Jewish immigration histories of the two countries do differ. Generally, the roots of the Canadian Jewish community are not as deep as those of American Jews. In the early 1990s, American Jews were as likely to be U.S.-born as the U.S. population as a whole (90.6% vs. 92.1%), but Canadian Jews were considerably less likely to be native-born than the average Canadian (70.6% vs. 86.3%). Thus, it is commonly suggested that Canadian Jews are one generation behind American Jews in the process of acculturation and assimilation into the North American environment.

What hard data do we have with which to make comparisons? On the U.S. side, we have the CJF 1990 National Jewish Population Survey (NJPS). This private, Jewish community-sponsored, voluntary, telephone sample survey required respondents to self-identify as Jews, and inquired whether respondents considered themselves Jews by religion or Jews of no or another religion. On the Canadian side, our data source is the official Government of

Canada Census of 1991 managed by Statistics Canada, a compulsory mail census of the entire national population which asked respondents to self-identify as Jews in answers to questions on both their religion and ethnic origin.[1] Though not a perfect match, these systems of categorization allow comparisons to be made between the internal patterns of Jewish identification of the two national Jewish populations.

The table on the following page provides details of how the two populations compare according to a set of Jewish identity constructs created by the researchers in each community.[2] Once allowance is made for the substantial difference in the size of the two populations, the patterns of Jewish self-identification are surprisingly similar. Among the "core" populations, the proportion of people who identify as Jewish, both by ethnic origin and by religion, is almost identical (79% and 76%) in Canada and the U.S.

The proportion of Jews by choice (gentile ancestry) in the U.S. population appears to be smaller than in Canada. It is very likely, however, that this categorization system exaggerates their number in Canada. Even though one may report more than one origin, some Jews prefer to identify ethnically with the original homeland of their ancestors (e.g., Hungary, England, Morocco) rather than as Jews. The controversy over the Canadian preference which surrounded the 1991 census (the public campaign to have "Canadian" included as an ethnicity option over the opposition of Statistics Canada) may also have affected these numbers. The comparison between the "not religious" or secular ethnic identity constructs is probably more accurate. It suggests that Canada has proportionally fewer secular Jews than the U.S.

The lower portion of the table brings into the statistics the peripheral population of Jews who self-identify as Jewish in terms of ethnic origin or ancestry but presently follow another religion such as Buddhism or Christianity. This varied population consists of apostates who have recently left Judaism, as well as those never raised in Judaism who have had little personal contact with the Jewish community in any form, but who are children and grandchildren of Jews. As one might expect given the greater proportion of third, fourth, or more generation Jews in the United States, this fringe population is relatively larger there. The difference, however, is not vast.

In conclusion, this statistical data suggests that the societal processes affecting Jews in both nations are similar and that the resulting Jewish identity constructs run along similar lines. Canadian Jewry is indeed more traditionally Jewish at present, but the gap is not as wide as some expected.

U.S. and Canadian Jewish Populations by Identity Constructs

Population Group (Definition*)	U.S. 1990 NJPS N	%	Canada 1991 Census N	%
JEWS BY RELIGION				
Jewish Ethnic Origin				
BJR (US)	4,210,000	76		
JRJE (Canada)			281,680	79
Other Ethnic Origin				
JBC (US)	185,000	3		
JROE (Canada)			36,390	10
Total	4,395,000	80	318,070	89
JEWISH BY ETHNIC ORIGIN				
No Religion				
JNR (US)	1,120,000	20		
NRJE (Canada)			38,245	11
Total CJP (US)	5,515,000	100		
JSD (Canada)			356,315	100
JEWISH ETHNIC AND RELIGIOUS PREFERENCE POPULATION				
Jewish Ethnic Origin/ with Other Religion				
JCO/JOR/JCOR (US)	1,325,000	19		
ORJE (Canada)			49,640	12
Core/Standard Jewish Population				
CJP (US)	5,515,000	81		
JSD (Canada)			356,315	88
Total	6,840,000	100	405,955	100

*Abbreviations, in the order in which they appear, are as follows:

BJR: Born Jewish;
JRJE: Jewish by religion and Jewish by ethnic origin;
JBC: Jewish by choice;
JROE: Jewish by religion and other than Jewish ethnic origin;
JBR: Jewish by Religion;
JNR: Secular Jews, no religion;
NRJE: No religion, Jewish by ethnicity only;
CJP: Core Jewish Population;
JSD: (Canada) Jewish by religion, or Jewish by religion and Jewish by ethnic origin, or no religion and Jewish by ethnic origin;
JCO: Adult born/raised in Judaism, converted to another religion;
JOR: Adult of Jewish ancestry, born/raised and currently of another religion;
JCOR: Child under 18 being raised in another religion;
ORJE: Other religion and Jewish by ethnic origin (see note 1).

Age Structure

There is a myth abroad that the North American Jewish population is fast vanishing. In reality, at this moment in time, this is not true, although the demographic prospects in the long term, as we shall later see, are negative. Both Jewries saw an increase in the number and proportion of children during the 1980s. The age structures of both communities are remarkably similar and closely resemble the profiles of the national Canadian and U.S. white populations. For example, 46 percent of Canadian Jews and 47 percent of American Jews are under 35 years old. Canada has a slightly larger child population with 21 percent under age 15 compared with 19 percent in the U.S. At the other end of the spectrum, the over-65 populations are of almost the same proportions: 17.3 percent of Canadian Jews and 17.2 percent of American Jews. As a result of Jewish longevity, both Jewish populations have a higher median age than the respective national populations; only 11 percent of Canadians and 13 percent of U.S. whites are elderly.[4]

The age makeup of the Jewish population is characterized by a large proportion of "baby boomers" born between the end of World War II and the mid-1960s now well into their childbearing years. As a result, by the beginning of the next century, the number of Jewish teenagers will expand, and an increase in the size of the Jewish college and university population will follow. Over the next decade, the elderly Jewish population will remain stable, but the proportion over age 75 will grow bringing increased service needs.

The size of the core Jewish population will probably grow very slowly until about the year 2000, but it will begin to show a perceptible decline by the year 2010. The population decline after the year 2000 will start as the number of Jewish women in their child-bearing years decreases. Some stabilizing effects will be felt from a "baby-boomlet" born in the late 1980s and early 1990s. Immigration from the former Soviet Union and other countries has kept the North American Jewish population stable so far, but the future of immigration is uncertain. On the local level, some communities will grow while others will shrink, mainly as a result of migration, rather than through natural growth or decline.

From the policy perspective, the demographic picture that emerged from the 1990 survey and the 1991 census suggests some medium-term structural problems for communal philanthropy. Half of adult American Jews are "baby boomers," while compared with the total American population, there is an over representation of the elderly, particularly those over 75. Finally, there is a "missing generation," the so-called "empty nesters" aged 50 to 64, as a result of low Jewish birth-rates during the Depression and World War II. There are two "thirty-something" Jews for every "fifty-something" Jew. Because people in the latter age group are usually at the height of their earning power and traditionally have formed the foundation for both volunteer and leadership groups, its size means high dependency ratios in terms of the philanthropic economy of a volunteer community.

The economic implications, or rather the planning and service challenges posed to Jewish communities by demographics, can be illustrated by an examination of the elderly population. While the number of Jewish elderly over 65 is stable, the percentage is growing slowly as the total Jewish population remains static. The age 75-and-over segment of the Jewish elderly population (currently 44%) is growing and will likely soon reach just under 50 percent. The over 85 years segment is growing even faster. These trends are general, although individual communities may vary. For example, the 65-and-over segment of the Jewish population in some parts of Florida is already in excess of 25 percent of the total, whereas the elderly group in other areas of the sunbelt constitutes less than 12 percent of the total.[5]

Larger numbers of elderly, particularly in their 60s and 70s, remain active and in good health. Since Jewish males will continue to live longer than males in the general population, the percentage of married Jews over 75 will continue to be higher than in the general population, although the imbalance of females to males will grow as the community ages. As a result, Jews in long-term care institutions (mostly women) will continue to be about 5 percent to 7 percent of all elderly Jews.

The older population can be an important resource, as well as a potential burden for the community. The young elderly comprise a large pool with the time and expertise to devote to volunteering. This potential is enhanced because the younger, North American-born Jewish elderly tend to be more educated and affluent than other elderly in the Jewish or general population.

But the Jewish elderly tend also to be financially polarized. Many are at the extremes of income distribution. While an expanding Jewish elderly middle class is financially secure and moderately well off, others remain poor. For example, the Jewish elderly now aged over 85 are more likely to be immigrants and to participate more in Jewish rituals and practices than are the younger elderly. Many, including Holocaust survivors, Soviet Jews, the poor, Alzheimer's victims, and those with marginal incomes, have special needs. We can predict that in the future, the elderly will enter long-term care institutions at an older age, frailer, and with more disabilities.

This analysis of the elderly market suggests that, increasingly, local communities across the continent will be facing the following sorts of challenging questions:

- What should be done to redefine the system of Jewish elderly services to make them more effective, efficient, and responsive to need?

- As the costs of long-term care continue to rise, what are the options and alternatives for payment and service delivery?

- Should the Jewish community fund only services and programs that are uniquely Jewish?

- Should the marketing of services be directed to those who can afford to pay?

Fertility and Family Formation

In contrast to the exaggerated emphasis on misunderstood changes in population size and age structure, the very significant changes in family and household types have been overlooked by many communal observers. Fertility patterns and family formation are the processes which effect change in household structure. The number of Jewish households or the address list in most communities has increased in recent years as average household size has diminished, meaning that the Jewish population is dispersed over many more homes than ever before.

In recent decades, the average number of children born to Jewish mothers has fallen. Very few three- and four-child families now exist outside the Orthodox community, and even in this segment of the population, fertility patterns tend to be exaggerated. Non-marriage, late marriage, and serial marriage, however, probably contribute as significantly as declining marital fertility in creating the current pattern of zero-population growth among Jews in North America.

Of the 4.2 million core Jewish adults between 18 and 80 years of age in the U.S. in 1990, 2.6 million are presently married; 970,000 have never been married; 350,000 are either divorced or separated; and 290,000 are widowed. By the age of 45, an overwhelming majority of Jews will have been married at least once, although the percentage has dropped to 89 percent from 96 percent in earlier generations. Nevertheless, the family will increasingly be redefined, as diversification of family types continues with larger numbers of single-parent, intermarried, and two-wage-earner families.

The family norm of the future may not be the nuclear family of two born-Jews in their first marriage: Intermarried couples with children are the fastest growing household types. Already core Jewish couples living by themselves outnumber nuclear core Jewish couples with children. Only 17 percent of households containing a core Jew are nuclear Jewish (both parents) families. The number of "step-families" with children from previous marriages of spouses is becoming increasingly common: Over 300,000 children in Jewish households now have a step-parent and over 250,000 remarried parents have children from a previous marriage in the U.S. Some 50,000 children in American Jewish homes (nearly 3%) are adopted, and a significant number come from Korea and from Peru and other Latin American countries. About 13 percent of married couples wanting to have children over the next three years are considering adoption. At present, some 4 percent of all households with a core Jew are made up of a single parent with children. Homosexual households are also becoming visible in some Jewish communities.

A quarter of all Jewish homes now contain only one person; that is and will likely continue to be the most common Jewish household type. Being single will have to receive greater acceptance as an alternative, if only because singles' financial support is required by the community. How never-married singles can be fully accepted as adult members of the Jewish community continues to be a real issue for Jewish continuity on the practical level.

Federations, organizations and agencies, and synagogues should be encouraged to ensure that programs and services are accepting and welcoming to young singles. Communities can increase opportunities for Jewish singles to congregate and interact, even to encourage relationships that may lead to marriage. Above all, the system can create meaningful roles for younger singles who have limited time and limited resources. Singles programming can also direct more attention to older and divorced adults. Undoubtedly, current trends suggest the organized Jewish community ought to encourage and support endogamous marriage and the production of Jewish children. Programming must be developed for dating and to prepare for marriage and parenting. However, the same demographic realities suggest that an overemphasis on young families with children could alienate the majority of North American Jews who are beyond, or uninterested in, parenting.

These demographic trends are unlikely to reverse in the coming decade. Feminism and a growing emphasis on women's careers and education will continue to contribute to later marriage. More singles including a growing number of widowed aged, will mean an increase in the number of Jewish households (with a smaller average household size) even if there are fewer Jews in the population.

All these trends pose challenges for service providers. Educators face children in the classroom with changing home backgrounds. With delays in marriage and child bearing, demand for adoption and surrogate parent services is likely to increase. Emerging parenting alternatives will require new services; services also will be needed to replace extended families and family support systems. Programs directed to nuclear families, single-parent families, intermarried couples with and without children, and to joint-custody situations and "step-families" will all be required. Communities may increasingly be asked to support programs that provide places and activities where divorced Jews can meet.

Certainly, we may anticipate a greater variety of service needs: programming for the newly emerging family, day and after-school care, transportation to youth services, special care for children of divorced adults, car-pools, and elder care. Mobility and the disappearance of multi-generational linkages in the community, the growing responsibilities of the "sandwich generation" to care both for aging parents and dependent children, and the increased occurrence of two working parents will put increased stress on the Jewish family and require community intervention.

Regional Variation—Migration

The tremendous regional and local residential change that has affected our communities has also not been fully appreciated by many communal leaders. Our communities and institutions are still largely organized on a neighborhood basis, often in the form of local franchises. They face an enormous challenge, when, as in the U.S., about half the Jewish population changes address and nearly a third of the mobile population moves to a different state at least every six years. The overall trend is that Jews are spanning the continent and gradually acquiring about the same geographic distribution nationally as other North Americans. For the first time, more Jews are living outside the Northeast than in it. The Jewish population will continue to concentrate on the coastal areas away from the center of the continent, although some large centrally located cities, such as Chicago and Toronto, will continue to be exceptions.

Yet, present patterns of Jewish population distribution and community type preference will persist. The movement to sunbelt communities will continue with some return of elderly Jews to their former communities. Significantly, each of the three generations of a family is likely to live in different states or provinces. Modest but increasing percentages of Jews live in small cities and rural areas, even while other small cities, particularly in the Northeast and Midwest, lose their Jewish population. Small Jewish communities lose young Jews who go off to college and university and do not return. Jewish singles concentrate in the largest east and west coast urban centers and in the new "boom towns."

The recently published book, *Jews on the Move*, showed definitively that increased geographic dispersion means a weakened Jewish identity and a lessened sense of community.[6] In part, this is because new Jewish communities may not have adequate communal infrastructure, and rootedness and community spirit may be lacking. Bringing new residents into the communal structure will increasingly be a priority for the Jewish community.

As noted earlier, it is not possible to predict the extent of Jewish immigration from abroad. Possible sources of influx are the republics of the former Soviet Union, as well as Israel, South Africa and South America. In the next ten years, the continental Jewish community should expect to receive at least 200,000 people, the majority coming from the former Soviet Union. How to serve and acculturate these populations Jewishly will be a top agenda item, especially for Canadian communities, which are proportionately more affected by international migration.

Even within metropolitan areas, Jewish migration remains a significant factor. In general, despite the instances of "gentrification" and inner-city regeneration, the overall trend is outwards and, therefore, towards greater dispersal. The movement of Jews to suburban fringes of cities will likely continue. Many Jews will continue to congregate residentially but different cities will exhibit differing patterns of suburban Jewish population distribution with concentrations variously in the near or far suburbs. We can predict that mobility and the dispersion of the Jewish population will create an ongoing need for proactive outreach, for recruitment and retention policies, and for the building of new facilities in changing and developing neighborhoods and communities.

Education and Occupation

The area where Jews differ most from the rest of the inhabitants of North America is in the area of socioeconomic variables. Jewish parents have often made a much larger investment than others in the human capital of their children, especially their daughters. This is reflected all the way up the educational ladder, from much higher than average SAT scores, to proportionally greater enrollment in higher education, to greater college graduation rates and entry into postgraduate education. At every stage, the gap widens so that compared with other U.S. whites, Jewish men are three times more likely, and Jewish women four times more likely, to hold a postgraduate degree. In fact, Jewish women have far higher educational attainment and occupational prestige scores than white males in general.[7] This means the overwhelming majority of Jews under age 50 have attended college or university, and a majority have graduated. Jews are students for longer periods than others, with a proportionately much larger student population.

The occupational returns on education in a meritocratic society are clear. The Jewish educational investment translates directly into higher status professional and managerial occupations. Jewish men remain unequally represented in sales and in professions such as law, medicine, and academia, and continue to make inroads into the corporate world. Jewish women will continue in increasing numbers to enter and advance in the professions of law, medicine, engineering, and science, as well as in executive positions. Generally, fields such as teaching and social work are losing their appeal for young Jewish women as well as men. In large metropolitan areas, especially on either coast, Jewish women still tend to move into fields offering larger salaries.

It has been claimed that Jewish identification with certain professions, such as law and medicine, has apparently substituted for Jewish identity.[8] What the Jewish identity pattern will be for Jews in various management levels of the corporate world and in science and academia, remains to be seen. Yet, working-class Jews, who do not attend college or university have the highest rates of intermarriage and are those most likely to be lost to assimilation.[9]

Increasing numbers of two-income families in the Jewish work force will have a significant impact on communal life beyond the impact felt in terms of delayed childbirth and a lowered birth rate. There exists the need for child-care services under Jewish auspices, for different patterns of family decision making (regarding charitable contributions, for example), and for changing patterns of voluntarism. The move to treat women as equals in power sharing and decision making and to encourage their involvement in communal activities results directly from their improved socioeconomic position.

Income

Jewish household incomes in both Canada and the U.S. are the highest of any ethnic or religious group, and are expected to remain so for the foreseeable future.[10] Consequently Jews comprise an attractive market for diverse products and services, and Jewish organizations face fierce competition for the time, attention, and resources of the Jewish public. By nature of their demanding education and incomes, Jews have become sophisticated and demanding consumers. Therefore special efforts in marketing may be required to reach the middle- and upper-income segments of the Jewish community that have latitude to chose from many options.

Growth in numbers of Jewish professionals results in a Jewish community with more widely distributed wealth, whose affiliations and self-identification may not be exclusively or even predominantly Jewish. Such changes in occupation and income patterns have an impact on giving and *tzedakah*. With consumers demanding the highest quality services in health care, housing, and schools, cost issues will be critical. Jewish institutions will need to seek opportunities for creative funding, fundraising, and communal planning. A solution may require increased sophistication in the marketing of programs and services by federations and agencies.

At the bottom end of the income pyramid, there are also serious problems. There is poverty, particularly among the elderly, divorced women with children, and unemployed Jews in depressed industries and professions. Marginal Jews who are not highly educated feel disfranchised. Government spending cuts in services to individuals through the lowering of eligibility levels will hurt the Jewish community most severely, because poor Jews are disproportionately on the upper end of low income levels.

Communal institutions will have to face the fact that for many people, membership and participation in Jewish life are difficult to attain, because of financial pressures. For a significant percentage of North American Jewish families, the cost of living Jewishly can be prohibitive. The expense of synagogue membership, Jewish education, Jewish community center membership, and contributions to Jewish causes may compete increasingly with other family demands, such as food, clothing, shelter and the cost of higher education.

Religious Composition

Religious composition is probably the area where the differences between American and Canadian Jews are the most measurable. American Jews are much less religious than their gentile compatriots and even than Canadian Jews. Canadian Jews are more traditional, while Canadians as a whole, are behaviorally and attitudinally less religious than Americans. The result is that, in terms of religiosity, Canadian Jews are much closer to the national average than American Jews. This pattern is reflected in the denominational sphere. In terms of preference, American Jews are roughly 42 percent Reform, 38 percent Conservative and 7 percent Orthodox. In Canada, no precise figures are available, but it appears that there are about equal numbers of Orthodox and Conservative Jews and that only 20 percent are Reform.

Recently released data from the Conservative movement reinforces the picture of a Canadian preference for traditional forms of Judaism.[11] Canadian synagogues were notably less egalitarian in their religious outlook than

American Conservative congregations. And they were much less inclined to adopt recent innovations in Conservative *halakhah*.

To some extent, these findings bear out a well known sociological rule in terms of Jews. After controlling for other factors, the longer an individual's family has resided in North America, the less likely that individual is to be traditionally Jewish. On average, Canadian Jews are one or more generations closer to the Old World than American Jews. The identity construct data suggests, however, that at the individual level behavior and beliefs are similar in Canada and the U.S. It may be simply that Canadians are institutionally less innovative and flexible than Americans.

The underlying communal trajectory in the two countries is similar. Synagogue membership remains the most frequent point of Jewish attachment in every local community, but the overall rate of affiliation is in decline. Again, demographic factors are influential. The fall in the proportion of people in nuclear families, the traditional market for synagogues because of the life-cycle nature of many of their activities, has weakened affiliation. On the other hand, the full impact of this defection has been somewhat blunted by the recent baby boomlet.

The seriousness for all communal activities of the problem of religious disaffection is revealed by the U.S. figures. Only one-third of households containing a core Jew currently hold synagogue membership. About half of these 860,000 synagogue households are also affiliated with another Jewish organization, such as a community center or Hadassah. About 12 percent of households are members of some Jewish organization but not religiously affiliated. In other words, a majority, 55 percent of households, are unconnected with the organized Jewish community. Above all, this figure demonstrates the nature of the Jewish continuity challenge. To comprehend fully the impact and causes of these numbers, we must factor in the socioeconomic variables analyzed in the previous section. Clearly we face a major challenge. Most Jews are not motivated to participate in Jewish life on a continuing basis. At best, they are episodically involved. Judaism is not attractive to many of them in any of its forms. Moreover, our survey data suggests that there are few convinced believers.

IMPLICATIONS OF THE DEMOGRAPHIC AND ECONOMIC PROFILE FOR ORGANIZATIONAL AFFILIATION AND PARTICIPATION IN THE EMERGING SOCIETY

The survey and census data we have examined confirms that North American Jewry has achieved socioeconomic success and social integration. We found a more "American" and less "Jewish" population, a geographically mobile and increasingly unaffiliated population. Both individually and collectively, North American Jews find more acceptance in society today than ever before. General levels of antisemitism have diminished, and exclusionary practices in the economic sphere, restrictive regulations in housing, and quotas in Ivy League colleges, all in force in the 1950s, have now vanished. [12] At the same time, extended families and concentrated ethnic neighborhoods have also largely vanished. Traditional forms of Judaism have lost adherents, and the general level of people of religious practice and behavior has declined. And since "people give to people," these trends have proved detrimental to the social networks that promote both community involvement and philanthropy. [13]

The social implications of the socioeconomic patterns of North American Jews are paradoxical. A relatively affluent elite group tends to prefer boutiques to department stores. These sophisticated consumers seek unique and individualized products. Moreover, the fact that they operate within tolerant, accepting, open, and free societies means that they are far less constrained by external forces than previous generations of Jews. In fact, the challenge for contemporary North American Jews is one of the most profound that any Jewish community has faced in history: to flourish and evolve in freedom. Individual Jews and families do not regard this as a challenge, since their social standing and success demonstrate their ability to adapt to the opportunities available to them. The problem lies in the collective sphere. It is Jews as an organized social entity, not the Jewish population *per se*, who have a problem.

One aspect of our newly won normality is a much more normal distribution of opinions in religious and political matters. We now have more "extremists" of all types; people feel free to indulge their spiritual proclivities fully and in a range of styles. Growing diversity and pluralism have led to polarization and make a unified community much more difficult to sustain. This lack of common interest and purpose in turn leads to problems of viability. Recruitment is difficult among a variegated population containing large numbers of subgroups, each of which requires an undifferentiated product or service. The last problem is exacerbated by the contemporary consumerist tendency, which undermines the common citizenship that a voluntary community such as ours requires. In practical terms, it means that progressive young Jews are becoming reluctant to support kosher facilities for the observant elderly, and that empty-nester couples and single persons often feel no compelling obligation to subsidize the Jewish education of other people's children.

The key question for our umbrella organizations, such as federations, is how to develop effective policies and strategies that fully recognize the diversity of the Jewish population, while maintaining some semblance of unity and common purpose. To maintain numbers, recruitment needs to be a priority, meaning that federations will have to develop diversified outreach programs in religious, cultural and secular Judaism that are directed to core Jews, to the almost 1.3 million non-core individuals of Jewish descent, and to 1.35 million gentiles living with Jews. Such outreach might include ways for making Judaism more appealing and relevant for all. It might involve families in various Jewish identity-building experiences and might promote efforts to gain more converts. An alternative policy would be to accept current trends and manage communal decline by deciding to serve and support strongly affiliated groups and mainline Jewish institutions, rather than allocate resources for the unaffiliated and intermarried.

Federations will need to weigh and chose between the alternatives: whether to concentrate on increasing the intensity of involvement of affiliated Jews or to reach more of the unaffiliated; whether or not to create incentives and support systems for families to practice Judaism; and how to create a balance between programs that focus on domestic Jewish life and overseas Jewish concerns. Our leadership will increasingly be asked to what extent multiple entry points should accommodate the acceptance of people "as they are" in order to reduce the "compatibility barrier" that many feel?

Of course different communities will be differentially affected by negative and positive trends. Jewish institutions in areas of declining Jewish population might limit investment in capital structures and focus on services and programs in alternative settings. Growing and declining communities could develop regionalized services together or programs without walls, although wide dispersion creates havoc for the delivery of services. Most local communities will have to accommodate intra-city dispersion creating new problems of facility location and accessibility. Competing interests will vie for attention. For example, resettlement of Jews from the former Soviet Union will have to take its place alongside other services in the competition for funds. The outgrowth of high mobility and geographic redistribution may be to require Jewish acculturation of entire communities, not just new immigrants. Some will ask if special efforts to integrate newcomers into the local community justify the costs. Not to make those efforts increases the likelihood of decline in numbers and eventually in communal resources, which in turn will impact negatively upon morale. The reality of a successful elite is that it does not want to become associated with failure. The elite are not losers, and they will not support a losing team.

The recent emphasis on "marketing" appears to suggest that the leadership of federations may wish to pursue a pro-active policy of active engagement and take their product to the marketplace. They will, however, have to learn how to hold their own in a competitive and crowded market. They will have to learn from the Christian evangelists how to mobilize an active sales force which views retention to be as crucial as recruitment. Our organizations will have to look after Jews as their lives progress: teenagers, students, singles, newly-weds, young parents, empty-nesters, retirees, and the dependent elderly. This will require more attention to operational issues and systems. Jewish organizations will have to learn that intake systems require attention. Since first impressions are critical, who answers the telephone and how inquiries are dealt with colors the unaffiliated Jew's opinion of organized Jewish life.

Outreach to all newcomers will require more creative strategies. Increasing mobility makes affiliation an even greater federation priority than at present. Some outreach might be coordinated on a national level, and federations may have to be more interconnected in campaigns and in service delivery. Established communities might assist, consult with, and share their expertise with newer ones.

Jewish organizations might develop linked services across the continent from community to community with networking service providers. Federations could share information about people leaving their communities, and population tracking could be implemented continentally. Information and referral services for Jews on the move can be advertised and made easy to access. A computerized national finder/locator system may be desirable. Cooperation with other federations in the state or regional area may be especially important for small communities. We could even become so pro-active that small Jewish communities would consider recruiting young families by offering job incentives.

In the light of the changes and trends outlined in this chapter and elsewhere, the North American Jewish leadership appears to agree that the emphasis for Jews today should turn toward resisting assimilation and securing long-term viability. Raising children as Jews is a necessary prerequisite to raising dollars for Jewish causes. There is, moreover, a general consensus that fundraising and giving are tools for Jewish involvement and betterment, not ends in themselves. The new buzzword is "Jewish continuity," which means an investment in Jewish identity-building processes, particularly Jewish education and trips to Israel for young people. The success of such a cultural renewal will take at least a generation to evaluate. But the emphasis on inner, rather than outer, directions seems in keeping with the *zeitgeist*. We shall soon learn whether one can inspire people to raise large amounts of funds in order to erase cultural and spiritual deprivation, as was done to fight social deprivation and antisemitism.

Availability of the necessary resources does not alone guarantee success. All these plans for social engineering imply important questions: Do we have compelling ideas? Can the product, that is, Judaism, be improved and made significant to large numbers of currently unaffiliated and uninvolved Jews? Above all, do we have the inspired and inspirational lay and professional leadership our people demand? Only if we can assure positive answers to these questions can we create responsible Jewish citizens out of what are presently, at best, only episodically involved consumers.

Notes

[1] The following definitions have been developed for the purposes of analysis. They are derived from the combined *Ethnic Origin* and *Religion Census* variables.

According to Census Canada, respondents to the question on *Ethnic Origin* were asked, "To which ethnic or cultural group(s) did this person's ancestors belong?"

For the *Religion* question, respondents were asked to indicate "To which religion or denomination does this person belong":

JR	Jewish by Religion
JE	Jewish by Ethnic Origin
JRJE	Jewish by Religion *and* Jewish by Ethnic Origin
JROE	Jewish by Religion *and* Other Than Jewish Ethnic Origin
NRJE	No Religion *and* Jewish by Ethnic Origin
ORJE	Other Religion *and* Jewish by Ethnic Origin
NJ	Not Jewish
JSD	"Jewish by Religion," or "Jewish by Religion and Jewish by Ethnic Origin," or "No Religion and Jewish by Ethnic Origin."

The JSD definition serves as the basis for Jewish communal planning. It is the same definition used by the Council of Jewish Federations and the McGill Consortium for Ethnicity and Strategic Social Planning in 1981, thus permitting an analysis of trends and changes during the past decade. The number of Jews who identify themselves in this manner is different from official Census publications where Religion and Ethnic Origin numbers are presented separately.

2 Barry Kosmin, et al., *Highlights of the CJF 1990 National Jewish Population Survey* (New York: Council of Jewish Federations, 1991); Jim L. Torczyner and Shari L. Brotman, "The Jews of Canada: A Profile from the Census," *American Jewish Year Book* 95 (1995): 227–60.

3 The Core Jewish Population (CJP) is an aggregate which reports no non-Judaic religious loyalty. It comprises three identities: those who currently report their adherence to Judaism, both Born Jews and Jews by Choice (BJR, JBC), as well as those Born Jews without a current religion (JNR). This population is the one which most Jewish communal agencies seek as their clientele. This population can be subdivided when necessary into the Judaic population (JBR), i.e., currently of Jewish religion, and the secular Jews with no religion (JNR).

4 Sidney Goldstein, "Profile of American Jewry: Insights from the 1990 National Jewish Population Survey," *American Jewish Year Book* 92 (1992): 77–173.

5 Barry Kosmin and Jeffrey Scheckner, *The Older Jewish Population of North America* (New York: North American Jewish Data Bank, Reprint Series, No. 1, 1987).

6 Sidney Goldstein and Alice Goldstein, *Jews on the Move: Implications for Jewish Identity* (Albany: SUNY Press, 1996).

7 Moshe Hartman and Harriet Hartman, *Gender Equality and American Jews* (Albany: SUNY Press, 1996).

8 Calvin Goldscheider, *Jewish Continuity and Change: Emerging Patterns in America* (Bloomington: Indiana University Press, 1986).

9 Barry Kosmin, Egon Mayer, and Nava Lerer, *Intermarriage, Divorce and Remarriage Among American Jews 1982–1987* (New York: North American Jewish Data Bank, Family Research Series, No. 1, 1989).

10 Barry Kosmin and Seymour Lachman, *One Nation Under God: Religion in Contemporary American Society* (New York: Harmony Books, 1993).

11 Jack Wertheimer, *Conservative Synagogues and Their Members* (New York: Jewish Theological Seminary, 1996).

12 Institute for Jewish Policy Research and American Jewish Committee, *AntiSemitism World Report 1996*, London, 1996.

13 Barry Kosmin and Paul Ritterband, eds., *Contemporary Jewish Philanthropy in America* (Savage, Md.: Rowman and Littlefield, 1991).

19

BETWEEN QUALITY AND QUANTITY: DEMOGRAPHIC TRENDS AND JEWISH CONTINUITY

Morton Weinfeld

Here I shall present some thoughts on ways to interpret the demographic trends described in detail by Barry Kosmin in the previous chapter. My theme will be the tensions between what one can call qualitative and quantitative demographic approaches to group health. The central argument I shall develop is that Jewish demographic behavior—notably patterns of marriage, intermarriage, and fertility—cannot be evaluated without consideration of the cultural and sociopolitical features of Jewish life. And the behavior cannot be changed without also changing Jewish life itself. I will then describe the case for qualitative strategies as an important element of an equilibrated set of Jewish public policies, particularly in the light of technological innovations.

Differences in demographic patterns and their corresponding cultural contexts have polarized feelings among many Jews. The following angry letter to *The Jerusalem Report* of October 31, 1996, illustrates this theme:

> Why is it that the defenders of the ultra-Orthodox life style invariably quote their higher birth rate as being one of the major achievements? (Letters, Oct. 3)
>
> Humankind as a whole derives little, if any, benefit from yet more *yeshivah* students whose undoubted intellectual energy might better be applied to seeking solutions for some of the world's problems.
>
> Perhaps the ultra-Orthodox should ponder the suggestion that, in human terms, one Jonas Salk has done more good and brought more "light to the nations" than all the rabbis in their *yeshivot*.[1]

Apart from the evidence of the religious-secular rift, the letter assumes there can be no possible link between Jonas Salk and the ultra-Orthodox rabbis. To the writer, the religious and secular dimensions of Jewish life exist in a clear zero-sum relation. It is this assumption which we shall explore. But first it is best to recall both the strengths and limitations of demography.

PROJECTION AND PREDICTION

The basic strength of demography is the ability to describe a current population, make some assumptions about fertility, mortality, and net migration, and then project population size and composition into the future. Apart from the assumptions, we expect that demographers know what they are counting. While this is true for national population counts, or subgroups clearly defined by gender or age, it is much less clear when dealing with ethnic, racial, or religious groups. Different ways of defining Jews—or Blacks, Hispanics, Chinese, or Italians—will yield different counts.

In fact, most demographers make several sets of assumptions, which yield a range of projections of future populations, some higher and some lower. This is actually a straightforward exercise, particularly important for projecting future population size and age-specific events. We know now who has already been born and therefore we can anticipate, leaving aside immigration, exactly how many Jewish children will turn thirteen in given years and thus roughly how many bar mitzvahs there may be, or how many seniors we can expect. That is the strength of demography, the ability to make projections.

Prediction is a different story, and represents the major limitation of demography. Many unforeseen or unknowable exogenous factors may intervene to upset any set of assumptions. It is difficult to predict future changes in human behavior. Projections presuppose that all variables outside their assumptions remain constant. But they never do. Demographers, and indeed all social scientists, have a uniquely dismal record in predicting major changes in social and political life and new cultural trends. Demographers did not predict the baby boom of the post-World War II period, nor the baby bust movement towards zero population growth which has typified the past two decades in North America and western Europe. In the recent past, they did not predict the dramatic changes and demographic consequences brought on by the women's movement, the sexual revolution, the increased use of birth control, the rise in divorce rates, or other related developments.

Because of this poor track record, I was pleased to see that the title of this volume was neither "Projecting the Jewish Future" nor "Predicting the Jewish Future," but rather "Creating the Jewish Future." Jewish communal leaders must not be prisoners of gloomy predictions. The ultimate task of a volume such as this is to leave the confines of projection and prediction and speak about the ability to create, or the need to create, a vision, a new sense of civic purpose to animate Jewish life. Even as we wrestle with demographic patterns, we have to have an underlying vision about what we are going to do with this information and why we need it: survival for what?

In 1964, *Look* magazine featured a cover story on "The Vanishing American Jew." Three decades later American Jewry is here, but *Look* magazine has vanished. One of the first articles that I wrote on Jewish life was published in *Midstream* in the late 1970s.[2] It was a response to a projection made by a demographer who looked at some data from the first NJPS (National Jewish Population Study) and predicted that in one hundred years, all or most of American Jews would disappear. He may yet be right; we still haven't reached that point. I offered then an optimistic interpretation of the trends, including those on intermarriage and was taken to task by at least one critic for seeming to advocate intermarriage.[3] My optimism is somewhat tempered now in view of the increasing rates of intermarriage of the past twenty years, but the despair to which I responded still seems a bit premature. Jews have not disappeared in North America. As the 1990 NJPS has shown, intermarriage rates have been increasing, and more Jews than ever before find themselves in homes which also have Christmas trees. Still, some analysts take a positive view;[4] I believe that the short-term trend for the North American Jewish population is likely to be stability, rather than decline.

DEMOGRAPHY AND GROUP SURVIVAL

Groups concerned about survival and continuity can develop various demographic strategies or approaches to achieve those goals.[5] There is a debate in the community of social scientists who study North American Jewry between optimists and pessimists. My overall assessment tells me that despite the demographic challenges, there are grounds for optimism. This is because minority groups can adopt both quantitative and qualitative strategies for survival.

What is a quantitative strategy? The more, the better. Think of the Hutterites, the Amish, or Hasidim. Demographers are often fascinated with the Hutterites because of their demographic uniqueness and their geographic isolation on agricultural colonies.[6] Groups like the Hasidim have almost no intermarriage and extremely high rates of fertility, even if the average is not the twelve children per family found in some cases. This is a quantitative survivalist demographic strategy. There is, moreover, no partial or plural or varied mode of Hutterite identity. One is either a 100 percent Hutterite, living on a Hutterite colony, faithful to basic Hutterite values and way of life, or one ceases being a Hutterite. There are no urban Hutterites, no Reform Hutterites, no Hutterite physicians or philosophers.

But the pattern of Jewish demographic behavior reveals a paradox. Jews are considered a survivalist group par excellence, a model for other minorities. Yet Jewish intermarriage rates have been increasing, and Jewish fertility rates have fallen below zero population growth. That Jews have lower rates of fertility than other groups is not new. In the modern period in the United States, Jews were the first group to attain zero population growth. Jewish family size among the early waves of immigrant East European Jews to North America was, of course, much larger than at present. But it was still not as large as that of other (mainly Catholic) European groups. And it may be that the relatively small size of Jewish families enabled them to achieve a high level of education despite their low incomes.

Given the different demographic patterns, could we therefore say that the Hutterites are committed to survival and the Jews are not? Of course not, because there is also a qualitative dimension, a qualitative route to group survival. Let us be clear that both quantitative and qualitative approaches are legitimate means of meeting the communal objective of survival. In fact, it may not be possible for an entire group to maximize both the qualitative and the quantitative. (Within the Jewish group, different subgroups display identifiably different demographic patterns.) The blend of strategies will be linked indelibly to the culture and, indeed, to the collective agenda of any group.

For Jews, the twin demographic demons are low fertility and mixed marriage. But—and it must be said—it is possible to recognize that patterns of this type found among some sub-groups of Jews may yield benefits for the larger collectivity. Anthropologists have long argued that exogamy can serve to meet strategic needs of groups by forging alliances between communities as a sign of friendship and acceptance. Clearly, rates of outmarriage which are too high can threaten the group. The large numbers of marginal Jews who are intermarried or the children of intermarrieds (without conversion to Judaism) are far less committed than are the "core" Jews, to use the NJPS term.

An equilibrium must be found. There is no doubt that at the micro or individual level intermarriage is identified as both cause and effect of assimilation. But the relationship is more nuanced at the macro or group level.

There, demographic patterns can be understood as shaping and reflecting the general cultural characteristics of Jews. Increasing rates of Jewish intermarriage must be understood as more than simply a flight from the heritage. They also confirm the greater degree of acceptance by non-Jews and a decline in social antisemitism. Jews who engage with the non-Jewish world, particularly at the level of social relations and close friendships, take risks. As long as Jews wish to win Nobel Prizes, or have non-Jewish friends, or send effective lobbyists to defend Jewish interests before government, there will be a risk of intermarriage. (Actually, many "who is a Jew" hardliners tend to soften when compiling lists of Jewish Nobel Prize winners.)

Consider again the demographic behavior of a group like the Hutterites. One can only make sense of that behavior within the context of an entire culture and its corresponding agenda. Hutterites emphasize the minimizing of contact with the outside world. There is no political agenda relating to a homeland that requires political lobbying or effective interlocutors. No Hutterites have won or wish to win a Nobel Prize. As a result, the Hutterite pattern of no intermarriage, of maintaining the traditional status of women within the family, and of having a large number of children, makes a great deal of sense.

But the same argument could be made for the Jews. Jewish demographic behavior has reflected the cultural and political agenda of the Jewish community and of individual Jews. Smaller family size can be seen as a strategic choice that has had a positive impact on longterm qualitative characteristics of the Jewish community. As noted earlier, it is linked to greater educational attainment, to greater nurturance for each child, and later to occupational success. Smaller family size provides more opportunities for Jewish women to contribute to Jewish communal life and to the general society. They can fulfil their own career aspirations without relinquishing all parental roles. Intermarriage, especially where there is no conversion, is often seen as a tragedy for individual, committed Jewish families. In a demographic sense, it is a clear loss for Jews as a whole. But the points of contact which may ensue may be used to help secure the strategic or tactical alliances needed to foster other Jewish political objectives.

It is important to recognize that the use of the term "qualitative" is not meant to denote any inferiority—or lack of quality—among those Jews who demonstrate high levels of fertility. It is descriptive and simply denotes a socio-demographic situation in which fewer children lead to the possibility of greater familial and communal investment per child. This may lead to greater contributions from each family member toward attaining group objectives and to successful competition with the non-Jewish world in common domains of endeavor. The training, strategy, and tactics of the Israel Defence Forces over the past fifty years have emphasized qualitative approaches—out of necessity—and have been rather successful.

To illustrate again the link between demographic patterns, collective group survival, and cultural characteristics, consider the case of the Québécois. After World War II there was a dramatic drop in the fertility rates of this group. Would we therefore conclude that the French in Quebec had given up on "la survivance" and that they were less able to meet the challenges of survival? Certainly some Québécois leaders bemoan the quantitative threat posed by the drop in fertility, sounding much like Jewish leaders condemning intermarriage. Much to the consternation of feminist critics, the Quebec government has periodically tried to encourage Quebeckers (basically women) to increase their fertility through baby bonus programs. But the Quebec drop in family size did not indicate a rush to collective suicide. Along with the change in fertility came the transformation of certain cultural patterns. The political context changed, as Quebec society modernized rapidly, invested in education, and abandoned the high degree of church control over social institutions. The flight from rural life, which had begun before the War, continued. The commitment to survival remained the same, but now it was pursued with a qualitative, rather than quantitative, approach. Demographic change occurred at the same time, and there was therefore a new correspondence between demographic behavior and the social, political, and cultural agenda of the Québécois. And the same logic applies to Jews as well.

A final example. If all Jews were Satmar Hasidim and behaved with the social demographic characteristics of Satmar Hasidim, the Jewish population would, of course, grow. The quantitative future would be secured. And each Jew would have in-depth knowledge of Torah. At the same time, the nature of Jewish life as we know it would be dramatically different. There would be no books like this one. There would be no Jews like me or like many of the other contributors to this volume. There would be no intermarriage; there would be very large families, but no Jewish cultural life as we understand it, and no Centre for Jewish Studies at York University. The capacity to organize effective lobbying or public relations efforts would be highly constrained. That is one extreme.

Now suppose the entire Jewish population were secularist. They would still identify as Jews. They could be interested in Jewish literature, Jewish philosophy, the security of Israel, Jewish communal institutions, and Jewish culture. They could speak Hebrew and perhaps Yiddish. (In fact, the NJPS evidence suggests they would score less favorably on all these sorts of measures than religious Jews.[7]) They could speak the language of government bureaucrats. But assume they never darkened the door of a synagogue, never fulfilled a single *mitzvah* of any kind. They would be likely to intermarry in droves. In those conditions, I think there would be no more Jews left in two or three generations. The community would suffer the decline experienced by Jewish secularists in this century. That is the other stark extreme.

What Jews have developed more than any other comparable group is that (at times unstable) equilibrium that tries to harmonize both extremes. Some Jews have larger families, do not intermarry, and live very traditional Jewish lives. Others lie at the other end of the spectrum. And still others fall in the middle. They all contribute directly and through their interactions to the organic whole that we call modern Jewish life.

Jewish Pluralism

And what is the result? We have a highly pluralistic Jewish community. As the buzzword, "continuity," yields to the newer one, "unity," many are dismayed, viewing pluralism as leading to disunity—which it often does. But in the modern period, Jews have rarely been united. There have been great divergences in beliefs and values. In the post-emancipation era, sharp ideological and ascriptive differences have marked Jewish life: Orthodox, Conservative, and Reform; Hasidim and Mitnagdim; Germans and Russians; Zionists and non-Zionists; religious and secular; left-wing or right-wing Zionists; uptown and downtown Jews; workers and capitalists; Israelis and Diaspora Jews; old-timers and "greeners"; Litvaks and Galitzianers; Ashkenazim and Sephardim; doves and hawks. Disunity has been the rule, and pluralism has sometimes been fractious. A remarkable exception may have been the short period between the Holocaust and the early years of the State of Israel, when Jews fashioned a communal consensus. But that period seems to be over. Jews remain a stubborn people. With apologies to both Daniel Bell and Francis Fukuyama, neither the end of ideology nor the end of history has arrived for the Jews, if it has for anyone.[8]

In the wake of the murder of Yitzhak Rabin, there have been understandable calls for Jewish unity. But we ought not confuse unity with tolerance of diversity. A respectful pluralism—I think of the positions outlined by Hillel Halkin and Avi Ravitsky in this volume—is much preferable to an inflexible, suffocating homogeneity. And difference is not to be confused with treason. Some claim that especially now Jews cannot afford too much difference, too much disunity. Perhaps not. But let us recall that in the ghettos and even in the concentration camps, Jewish differences persisted. Difference, dissent, and debate may be essential ingredients of Jewish contemporary identity.

But there is more. Fractious pluralism is not simply a burden which Jews must bear. It can be a source of Jewish strength. It is not a problem that we have to solve, the solution being the creation of a unified mode of Jewish life, with a single demographic pattern and a single dominant cultural orientation. In fact, the various poles of Jewish life complement each other rather well. The subgroups within the Jewish world perform different strategic and collective functions, which together help achieve the diverse goals of the communal agenda. Jewish survival owes much to a blend of quantitative and qualitative strategies. When other minority groups seek to emulate Jews, it is precisely this successful balance which they admire: a commitment to group and cultural survival combined with full participation in the mainstream society.

IMPLICATIONS FOR JEWISH PUBLIC POLICY

Just as quantitative and qualitative perspectives can describe Jewish sociodemography, they can also guide Jewish policy. Quantitative policies would maximize numbers; qualitative policies would focus on maximizing each individual's potential contribution. What are some of the consequences of the two approaches? A quantitative approach would emphasize outreach. A large number of Jews is totally unaffiliated or only marginally affiliated. If the community could only bring them into the fold, it would increase its numbers dramatically and defeat the danger of assimilation. So Jewish communal agencies seek out those who belong to no synagogue or Jewish organization, who have intermarried, or who have children needing a Jewish education. Often it is assumed that these Jews are ignorant of what Judaism and Jewish community are all about and await only the appropriate information to opt in. And no doubt, for a certain percentage this is so.

But a qualitative approach focuses on inreach. Inreach seeks to take those Jews who are already committed and work to raise the level of their involvement. It relies on the old sales maxim: "The best customer is the one already in the store." Outreach and inreach represent two investment strategies for the Jewish community.

Outreach seeks to maximize "value added." The potential for a net increment to Jewish life is great. The idealized metaphor for outreach is the *"baal teshuvah,"* one who has returned to traditional faith and an observant life style. Such Jews start at zero. If we can strike it rich with them, the assumption is, we've really maximized the return on our investment. That's a legitimate investment strategy: Buy many penny stocks and hope for windfall profits.

Inreach strategy suggests that we "build on strength." It is a blue chip investment approach. One buys quality stocks and hopes for incremental gain. Such a strategy focuses on investment in the already affiliated to prevent loss. Alas, I am not a successful investor, so perhaps my advice ought to be discounted. I do know that there is no set of rigorous program evaluations which can let us generalize about the comparative efficacy of inreach versus outreach programs over the long haul. This may be the single most important question on the Jewish research agenda. But in the absence of knowledge, we can only say: We need both—a balanced portfolio.

Still, precisely because of concerns over outmarriage and declining numbers, I suggest a bit of a tilt towards inreach. Not too long ago I had occasion to actually do some fieldwork related to this issue. I studied an experimental inreach project in a Conservative synagogue in the midwestern United States.[9] I observed how this synagogue, which actually had a relatively high level of Shabbat observance, was able to raise the level of religious commitment among its members. Even though they were already quite observant, there was a demonstrable increase in the level and intensity of members' Shabbat experience as a result of specific initiatives. Using survey responses, as well as participant observation techniques, I was able to demonstrate that after attending workshops on how to organize a Friday night meal or a family Shabbat retreat, participants enriched their Sabbath celebration by singing *zmirot*, attending Shabbat services, and even reading from the Torah. This is an example of a qualitative approach of inreach.

Quantitative strategies focus on finding or creating new members. I remember attending a meeting where a community leader advocated a kind of Jewish family allowance plan. He argued that federations should pay families to have more children, dedicating 30, 40, or 50 percent of their budgets to the task. This, he claimed would lead to a rise in the fertility rate. A similar natalist policy in Quebec has had only limited success, and is being phased out. It is even less likely to succeed among Jews, given the socioeconomic and education level of Jewish women.

Let us look at the field of Jewish education in terms of this quantitative/qualitative dichotomy. Research has confirmed a link between increasing levels of Jewish education and subsequent higher levels of Jewish identity.[10] How strong that link is, how autonomous it is, is the subject of debate, but it is there. Now a quantitative strategy would provide more hours of schooling for more children. A qualitative approach would try to add another dimension. It might seek to ask what it is about Jewish education that produces desirable outcomes? What is the essential element in Jewish education? Is it the curriculum? Is it the study of Torah itself? Is it the teachers, and if so, which teacher characteristics? Is it the peer group, just the phenomenon of having other Jewish children around? Or is it the experiential, non-cognitive domain?

Years ago I was a student at a Jewish high school, and I asked my Hebrew teacher the following question. I said, "Supposing, hypothetically, there was one vacancy in *Olam Haba*, in heaven, and two people showed up at the same time, Rabbi 'Akiba and Theodor Herzl. One did a great deal for the Jewish people but was thoroughly unreligious; the other, of course, was a great rabbi. How would God decide whom to admit?" My Hebrew teacher's response was to shout, "Weinfeld get out!" One presumes—one hopes—that few teachers today would respond in that manner.

We should reject the "vaccination approach" to Jewish education, that Jewish education is the vaccine and intermarriage the "disease." Instead of relying on fear campaigns, Jewish education has to be sold on its merits, *leshma*, because of the intellectual and spiritual sustenance it offers every Jewish child and adult. Some analysts might say that if a child with a good Jewish education intermarries, the education has been a waste. A different perspective might argue that given the increasing prevalence of intermarriage, a Jewish education may make possible a return to Jewish life before or following such a marriage. It is a foundation on which one can build at any time. It may lie unused at first, but it is not wasted.

There is no doubt that important challenges face the educational community as it turns to creating the Jewish future. People of vision, talent, and imagination are needed in leadership positions. It is time to recognize a broad definition of qualitative outcomes for our Jewish educational enterprise. Future generations of Jews cannot simply be Jews in a nominal sense. We need children imbued not only with Judaic knowledge but with a sense of *ahavat Yisrael* and *klal Yisrael*, with love of their people and a sense of community.

In addition, Jews of tomorrow must be equipped to compete successfully in the wider educational and occupational arena for their benefit and for that of the community. The alumni of our schools must be psychologically well adjusted and animated by a sense of decency, of *menschlichkeit*, which will permeate Jewish homes and institutions. It is not clear how much of the educational success of children from Jewish schools is due to the school and how much to other home characteristics. No scientific research can allow us to conclude that children in Jewish schools display particularly high levels of decent, considerate behavior. Frankly, we do not yet know what "best practices" would produce such results. But we do know that the future must lay a foundation for a new ethical vision of Jewish citizenship that will offer meaning to a wide variety of Jews. If we are successful in creating a high quality Jewish community with self-knowledge and self assurance, then problems of outreach will become moot. Non-affiliated Jews will seek us out, eager for what we have to offer.

GEOGRAPHIC DISPERSION AND TECHNOLOGY

Demography is interested in far more than natural increase and marriage patterns. One of the more neglected aspects of recent Jewish demographic research, lost in the concern for continuity, is migration and the distribution of Jews throughout the world. The old concept of Diaspora pioneered involuntarily by Jews has acquired new vigor and new pertinence in the era of globalization and a shrinking, interdependent planet. As the centrality of states and state boundaries is challenged by the growth of both multinational regions and sub-national localities, other forms of social organization increase in importance. The Jews and Israel are becoming part (and actually have always been part, but only now are we beginning to recognize it) of the world population system. Historically, Jewish migration has impacted not only on Jewish life, but on the host societies. And in recent years, in an ironic twist, for the first time we see large numbers of non-Jews from Asia, Africa, and Europe migrating to Israel legally and illegally, seeking work, and wishing to settle.

While Jews have pioneered as a diaspora group with transnational linkages and at times multiple—but usually non-conflicting—loyalties, many other groups are directly or indirectly seeking to emulate the Jewish model. For groups such as the Chinese, South Asians, or Africans, the term "Diaspora" has become reality. For these groups and for Jews, the term means more today than ties to a homeland by a group of dispersed exiles. It refers to the linkages among members of the group, including the homeland tie. These horizontal contacts are facilitated by migration and technological changes. In some cases, the homeland is imagined, not real.

Jews are on the move. Within the North American continent, they are moving from cities to suburbs to exurbs, from the Northeast in the U.S. and Canada to the West and South.[11] Jews are also on the move internationally, more so than in the recent past. The great mass migrations of Jews at the turn of the century have not and will not be replicated. But large numbers of Jews from Eastern Europe, Israel, Ethiopia, Latin America and South Africa are on the move to Israel and North America.

Today's movement does not necessarily add to an actual, felt dispersion of Jews. The transportation and communications revolutions of our time are changing the finality and the binding nature of geography. Migration is less limiting than in the past. Even as Jews move about, the ongoing contacts, from frequent return travel to telephone, e-mail, and the information highway, break down boundaries and facilitate transnational and interdependent linkages. Jews can now be linked to one another within countries, between countries, and to Israel in ways heretofore impossible. In keeping with the theme of this chapter, all these innovations are qualitative changes. They do not increase the numbers of Jews. But they have the potential for increasing the impact of each individual Jew on the totality of Jewish life.

Their full implication for enhancing prospects of Jewish survival and creating a new and vibrant future has not yet been realized. To be blunt, the Jewish community is still looking for the on-ramp to the information superhighway. We have not fully assimilated the potential transformations that are under way. One does not have to be excessively McLuhanesque to speculate about some of these impacts. Consider the structure of Jewish communal institutions. Just as local federations have emerged as dominant, their power is being challenged by numerous factors. Money is one issue; another is the shifting of the balance of Jewish authority from the local to the national and international Jewish polity. Mobility within North America may force local communities to adapt to national commitments and patterns. In other words, the changing regional demography of North American Jewish life requires more coordinated centralized structures. Certain regions see increases in student-age populations, others in seniors, others in young families, and still others in new Jewish immigrants.

In a more fundamental sense, the new communications technology can be used to promote global Jewish awareness. There is no reason why there cannot be a high quality Jewish CNN linking the entire Jewish Diaspora. An international Jewish television network could offer Jews a variety of local, national, and international programming, including linkages with Israel or other centers as news stories warrant.[12] Why not copy from the Lubavtichers who used the powers of closed circuit cable television to broadcast the late Rebbe's "farbrengens" to five continents? The community has yet to exploit the talents of Jews in the telecommunications industry and the high tech area to move Jewish life online. This is unfortunate, since we may be at the dawn of a new age that can be as transformative of Jewish life as printing was four hundred years ago.

My point is simple. In the long-run, the potential of such technological changes and the qualitative potential they will unleash may counterbalance the negative quantitative trends related to intermarriage and low fertility. How will all these developments affect the Jewish future? As I suggested earlier, it is difficult to predict. Let us return to the notion of equilibrium between qualitative and quantitative strategies and the issue of Jewish pluralism. I have suggested the potential of the new information technology to act as a force for unity, for linking and reinvigorating Jewish life. But this kind of globalization empowers individuals as well as larger political units. To be honest, there is potential for anarchy, for fragmentation, and for hyper-pluralism if you will. The old saying used to be, "Every Jew makes his or her own Shabbat." The new saying may be, "Every Jew will have his or her own web page." We may see new waves of multiple challenges to Jewish authority. My own sense is that, as has often been the case in the Jewish past, a form of equilibrium will emerge between the centrifugal and centripetal forces unleashed by the new technology. The balance will likely be favorable to enhancing the sense of global Jewish community. Jews must now begin to think creatively about how to harness these technologies. Success in that objective is also a way of pursuing a qualitative strategy for creating a secure Jewish future.

CONCLUSION

General Jewish demographic behavior is an aggregation of different patterns found in subgroups, a minority in which intermarriage is low and fertility high, as well as a majority population with reverse trends. These different patterns reflect the reality of Jewish pluralism, which is a strength and not a weakness. The fear that Jews are willfully or carelessly committing collective suicide is misplaced. Jewish survival has entailed an equilibrium of qualitative and quantitative demographic strategies, which reflect the evolving sociocultural agenda. In the current period, a tilt toward inreach and qualitative strategies will help maximize the potential contribution of every Jew, particularly if this includes harnessing the potential of new technologies toward communal goals.

So Jews should take a collective moment to pause and think positively. We should try not to misread conflict and tension, which flow from our contentious pluralism, as signs of weakness and doom. Conflicts must, of course, be managed with civility, and herein lies a challenge for Jewish educators and communal leaders. But those tensions, those conflicts, can be a source of strength and dynamism. It is precisely from such tensions that we can recreate a new equilibrium and a bright future.

Notes

1 *The Jerusalem Report* (31 October 1996).

2 Samuel Lieberman and Morton Weinfeld, "Demographic Trends and Jewish Survival," *Midstream* 23 (November 1978): 9–19.

3 David Singer, "Living with Intermarriage," in *American Jews: A Reader,* ed. Marshall Sklare (New York: Behrman House, 1983), pp. 395–412.

4 Steven Cohen, "Why Intermarriage May Not Threaten Jewish Continuity," *Moment* (December 1994): 54.

5 Milton Himmelfarb and Victor Baras, *Zero Population Growth for Whom: Differential Fertility and Minority Group Survival* (New York: Greenwood Press, 1978).

6 John Hostetler and Gertrude Huntington, *The Hutterites in North America* (New York: Holt Rhinehart and Winston, 1980).

7 Sidney Goldstein, "Profile of American Jewry: Insights from the 1990 National Jewish Population Survey," *North American Jewish Data Bank* (New York: Council of Jewish Federation, 1993). Reprinted from *American Jewish YearBook* 92 (1992).

8 Daniel Bell, *The End of Ideology: On the Exhaustion of Political Ideas in the Fifties* (Glencoe, Il: Free Press, 1960); Francis Fukuyama, *The End of History and the Last Man* (Harmondsworth: Penguin, 1992).

9 Morton Weinfeld, "Judaic Inreach: Enhancing Shabbat Observance in a Suburban Congregation," *Jerusalem Letter* (Jerusalem Center for Public Affairs) 339 (1 August 1996).

10 Steven Cohen, "The Impact of Varieties of Jewish Education on Jewish Identity: An Intergenerational Perspective," *Contemporary Jewry* 16 (1995): 68–96; Seymour Martin Lipset, *The Power of Jewish Education* (Los Angeles: Wilstein Institute, 1994).

11 Goldstein, "Profile of American Jewry."

12 Morton Weinfeld, "Jewish Television for the Next Century," *Jerusalem Letter* (Jerusalem Center for Public Affairs), 313 (16 April 1995).

AFTERWORD

From Theory to Practice:
An Afterword
Irving Abella

"Creating the Jewish Future" was a conference with a difference. As noted in the introduction to this volume, the organizers were very careful in choosing internationally acclaimed scholars to speak. That is usual. But, we also wanted to hear the voices of community leaders and activists. It was our hope right from the beginning to act as *shadchanim*, as a link between academics and community representatives, between town and gown. The instrument for that connection was to be a series of workshops to discuss ways of applying the scholars' insights to community realities.

Our plan was to bring together in one room a cross-section of the North American Jewish community. And for the most part we succeeded. The workshop participants included scholars, rabbis, students, and Jewish civil servants, as well as leaders and rank-and-file members of the Jewish community. Each seminar was assigned a facilitator and a resource person, and there were no restrictions on discussions. It was both an opportunity to opine and to vent. And what emerged was precisely what we had envisioned.

Two hundred and forty committed Jews from all walks of life came together to listen, to talk, and to learn. Each felt he or she had a stake in the Jewish future; each felt that he or she had something important to contribute. And what transpired was magic—passionate and inspiring debate, provocative and creative ideas. All realized that there was no more important topic in the Jewish community than continuity.

Yet the irony of the topic was not lost on the seminar participants, especially those living in Canada. Objectively, they wondered what they had to worry about. Things have never been better for Canadian Jews. They are now arguably the most affluent, educated, integrated ethnic community in the country. According to the most recent census data, there are now more

Jews in Canada then ever before. And Canada has one of the fastest growing communities in the Diaspora. A generation ago there were approximately 100,000 more Jews in the United Kingdom than in Canada. Today the figures are reversed; Canada has 100,000 more Jews than the U.K.

And life has never been better for them. The quotas, barriers, and restrictions of earlier periods of Canadian history are all gone. Jews now hold positions in government, business, academe, the judiciary, medicine, indeed in every sector of Canadian society, that were unattainable a generation or two ago. Day schools are full; new synagogues and giant community centers are being built; Jewish homes for the aged are the envy of every other community. Jewish organizations are more politically potent then ever before, and vast funds are raised annually for both Israeli and domestic needs. Canadian Jews give more per capita to charities than almost any other group in the world.

In fact, there is no area of Canadian Jewish life that is not thriving—or so it seems. Book fairs and film festivals, special lectures and educational programs, cultural events, and galas, all clog the Jewish calendar. Several universities house comprehensive Jewish Studies programs. And yet, Canadian and American Jews, like Jews everywhere, are worried, as noted over and over again in this volume.

Our worries, of course, are real. Can the Jewish community continue on into the twenty-first century with the same vigor and vitality which mark the close of the twentieth? Today's community worries more about rates of assimilation than rates of antisemitism. Its greatest concern is for its children and grandchildren. Will they remain Jewish? Are the seeds of destruction implanted in its very success? Can Jewishness in North America survive freedom? Can it survive in an open, tolerant, multicultural society?

Throughout our history, Jews have confronted the most terrible horrors—pogroms, expulsions, even attempted genocides—and yet we have survived. Today, North American Jews are confronting something they have never confronted before—total freedom—and some experts argue that it may be our undoing. As the *Report* of the North American Commission on Jewish Identity and Continuity rightly concluded, North American Jews have discovered that threats to their existence do not come only from without, from antisemites, but from within. As it asserted: "We have learned that the forces of modernization and the attractiveness of a welcoming host society can combine to weaken the fabric of Jewish life, to dissipate the intensity of Jewish identity and to loosen the bonds of Jewish community with even greater effectiveness than our visible enemies."[1]

The Problem Areas

Doubts about the significance of Jewishness for their fellow Jews were expressed by many seminar participants. They pointed out that, while many North American Jews take part in some community events or contribute to some Jewish causes, they get little personal satisfaction out of their Judaism except vicariously through what Israel or other Jews may accomplish. This anecdotal evidence was buttressed by a recent survey of American Jewish college students who were asked about their best and worst Jewish experiences. Many reported that they never had a "best" or "really good" Jewish experience, while most named Hebrew school as their worst.[2] That is not good enough, if we wish to create a future for North American Jewry.

What do young North American Jews care about today? What concerns not only university students but all those in "Generation X," those in their 20s and 30s? They care about things young non-Jews care about—jobs, the environment, feminism, social justice, their spiritual existence. Speak to young Jews about the importance of community, and most of them will likely not disagree. Many of them, however, especially those disengaged from normative Jewish religious beliefs and policies, will assert that they have found their community elsewhere. As they leave home to go to university or jobs across the continent, their link to the community is often severed. Now and again when Israel is threatened, or when the family gathers, there may be some guilt, maybe even a brief return. But a return to what? To a community which provides them with obligations, burdens, and guilt, but with little spiritual sustenance and little Jewish authenticity.

Each workshop in its own way acknowledged that the present situation will not do. It seemed self-evident that the major challenge to our Jewish leadership in the next generation should be building a Jewish community that is not simply concerned with survival, but one that is creative and attractive to our children—a community with substance and content, a community that stresses not only memory but other important values of our traditions—primarily social justice, equity, compassion, and spirituality. We will need a Jewish community in North America whose members will take pride in its activities and achievements. We will have to find ways to convert alienation to action and passivity to pride, the pride of being possessors of a great legacy, a legacy which has meaning for today and beyond.

If we wish our community in the next century to be guided by Jewish principles and values, we should insist that our leaders have some knowledge of them. We should ask of our leaders that they know something about Jewish history, of the precepts of Judaism and its traditions. These should be a prerequisite for leadership. In fact, many federations are now sponsoring learn-ins and other educational programs for their professional and lay leaders. But more will be necessary, if we are to create a dynamic Jewish community in the future. Our Jewish lay and professional leaders have to be role models of organizational excellence and Judaic understanding. Yes, we need organizational wizards more than we ever have, but they must have Jewish souls and understanding.

As we define our future, most seminar participants argued that we will have to confront head-on the fact that what has kept us together over the past generations may no longer be relevant. For our generation, aside from Holocaust remembrance, what has united all Jews has been concern for an embattled Israel and for oppressed Jewish communities throughout the world. These struggles have helped shape our identity. Now, with the collapse of the Soviet empire and the escape of Ethiopian and Syrian Jewry, there are scarcely any oppressed Jewish communities to mobilize our energies. With the possibility of real peace in the Middle East, it may even come to pass that the phrase "embattled Israel" will disappear into the dustbin of historical clichés whose time has passed.

What then? What, aside from religion, will bind us together, when there are no Jewish communities to save and no deep anxieties about the survival of the Jewish state to provide the social adhesive?

As part of the agenda for the future, there will have to be a fundamental reappraisal of Jewish identity. We Diaspora Jews will be forced to look into ourselves and our communities and ask: In addition to our religious heritage, what makes us Jewish? We know that the synagogue and the Torah bind us together as a people, but what about those who are neither religious nor affiliated to the community? How do we attract them?

These were the general questions and themes discussed in the workshops. The debates were passionate and stimulating. It seemed everyone had something to say—everyone had an opinion, and was determined to share it with others. No one seemed cowed by the academics or the experts. The struggle for the Jewish future was too important for anyone to remain silent.

FAITH AND THE SYNAGOGUE

The workshops on faith and religion dealt with some of the most intriguing—and to some the most pressing—questions of Jewish life. Are synagogues a passé institution? Can they be made more meaningful to Jews who today shun them? Will another institution become the real center of Jewish continuity? Will religious affiliation be the Jewish identity of the future?

All the workshop participants recognized that the synagogue and home are the prime centers for faith development, but that many people remain unaffiliated and/or have families where Jewish tradition and religious practice are marginalized. Through animated discussion, the participants began to develop the idea of the synagogue as an institution which mediates between large-scale social structures (government, places of employment, or commerce) and intimate/personal relationships. In order to play this role properly, synagogues must foster small-scale opportunities for study and prayer and develop programs which support or inspire families seeking a Jewish spiritual path. Many took the position that the synagogue must be seen as standing for justice and not just accommodating contemporary conservative social trends. In the best sense, the synagogue is counter-cultural, articulating Jewish values which are distinctive and often at odds with the majority culture.

Orthodox participants felt that their sub-community did not experience a disjunction between daily life and Jewish patterns of observance. Many others, however, contended that insufficient education had produced serious gaps in people's knowledge of Jewish texts and practices. This ignorance, in turn, has created anxiety about participation in synagogue life even for many of those who desire such involvement.

Most people seemed to feel that Jewish faith is personal. There was also consensus that faith is best nurtured in the home, in the framework of a family. The synagogue can aid the process by strengthening the ability of families to provide intense and memorable Jewish experiences. It was recognized that families with two parents in the same household are able to provide the most nurturing and support for Jewish life, and that new family configurations (single parents, blended families) create challenges for faith development. Also, many people now live outside the geographic or cultural framework of the traditional Jewish community, and synagogues need to reach out to them.

New strategies for the "marketing" of Torah study, ritual practice, prayer, and other expressions of religious faith are required. Jewish community centers were seen as vehicles for reaching marginalized Jews. Synagogues should be supported in their efforts to develop creative new programs. They are currently underfunded and understaffed for the important tasks which they are now understood to have. Exciting programs (such as "Turn Friday Night into Shabbos") should be replicated. One person even suggested breaking up larger synagogues into smaller, more intimate ones—where "real spirituality" would be possible.

In one group an extended discussion took place about whether communal resources are best expended in efforts to reach Jews who are on the periphery of the community or whether funds should be expended to strengthen the involvement and intensify the experience of those already associated with communal institutions (schools, synagogues, camps, etc.) A triage approach was advocated distinguishing among (1) the knowledgeable, (2) the marginal/peripheral, and (3) the vast majority or "Jello Jews" (that is, Jews without a solid core of Jewishness). It was agreed that Jewish communal institutions in general, and synagogues in particular, must be more sensitive to marginalized populations and more open to those seeking to find an entryway into Jewish life. And ultimately, since faith is so personal, different avenues of entry must be acknowledged and supported. The role of the community is to support structures that enable varieties of Torah study and Jewish experience to take place.

Some workshop discussions argued that synagogue life in North America was on the decline because of a failure of leadership. As one delegate put it: "We have emasculated our rabbis and teachers. Our spiritual leaders are afraid of leading and challenging us. . . . They are too much in awe and fear of their synagogue boards." All participants agreed that greater spirituality was necessary, especially for those, who, in one participant's memorable phrase, "are comfortable with inertia."

EDUCATION AND COMMUNITY RESOURCES

While spirituality was clearly important to conference participants, the workshops on education brought home the fact that the Jewish future in its various aspects depends upon the Jewish school system. All were aware of the limited resources of the community; yet they felt that spending on Jewish education was the best investment for ensuring a Jewish future. Some discussions decried the inability of the community to provide a free Jewish education for all as a failure of vision. They argued that Jewish education for children seems to correlate highly with Jewish identification later in life. Furthermore, the longer the education continues, the higher the correlation.

The question was raised whether the status of Jewish education could be improved. That must mean an improvement in the quality of education by developing first-rate schools that happen to be Jewish rather than accepting mediocre education because it is Jewish. To do this, educators need to be paid a wage that will attract the best. The situation of women Jewish educators was identified as needing particular redress. Some expressed the concern that we seem to be able to raise money for new buildings but not for new programs.

These discussions, like those about the role of synagogues, identified as fundamental the question of "outreach" versus "inreach." Do we as a community choose to spend money to attract into the fold those who are not at all or only marginally affiliated or to ensure (or enhance) the Jewish identity of those who are already actively affiliated. For example, should we support day schools, supplementary schools, or Jewish identity programs in public schools? Several in the group rejected the bipolar nature of this model ("secular versus Satmar") and suggested that the actual make-up of the community is far more complex. Changes occur throughout life; the educational needs of the young segments of the population are different from those of older people.

The seminar participants concluded that planning was the key to making educational decisions. Community planning in this regard needs to be more long-range rather than immediate and requires expert forecasting. Changes need to be anticipated and tough choices need to be made.

The seminars also discussed the role of schools as catalysts within the community for addressing issues of identity. Participants deliberated over the proper focus of the schools. Should the child or the whole family be the "focus" of the school? Such questions underscored the need to prepare role models in the family to complement the child's school learning. Clearly implied was the importance of consistency between the practices taught in school and those experienced in the home. It was believed that we should not allow parents to turn all the responsibility of providing a Jewish education over to the schools. There was a sense that we need to raise levels of Jewish literacy. Furthermore, we should look at exit outcomes for the families, as well as for the children.

One delegate suggested that we should build a number of model institutions and evaluate their program effectiveness. This would provide us with exemplary models and programs to replicate in order to improve our resources for reaching out and educating. Three types of justifications were identified as being largely ignored in terms of innovative programming: supplementary schools; overnight and day camps run by Jews essentially for Jewish children; and academies (including those for the performing arts) for gifted children.

With regard to the supplementary schools, some initial areas for consideration included more outreach to parents, having families sign contracts with the schools, starting programs at earlier ages, and enhanced teacher preparation. With regard to summer camps, some areas for consideration included special Shabbat and Jewish-content programming, staff preparation, advertising specialty camps throughout the community, outreach to parents through children, and integrating the camp experience with school. With regard to schools for the gifted, it was noted that some of our most talented students are in special programs where they are largely removed from Jewish education. We need to identify these programs and try to implement special interest clubs or activities.

Yet another area of concern was the need to develop educational materials appropriate for the communities of the Diaspora. Materials prepared for use in Israel are often not appropriate for students whose first language is not Hebrew. We need books, audio-visual materials, and computer software that are sensitive to our needs and levels of ability.

Considerable discussion centered on Jews and Jewish Studies in the university. A recent poll indicating that academics in college and university Jewish Studies programs do not consider themselves as role models for their students disturbed many of the workshop participants. They felt that professors may be role models to others whether they wish to be or not. The example was cited of a teenager who returned from the March of the Living and announced that she wanted to become a Jewish community professional. Clearly this decision had been motivated by the fact that at least one of the chaperons on the trip served as a valued role model in her mind. Mention was made of Jewish teachers and professors (not affiliated with a Jewish Studies program) who teach on Rosh Hashanah and Yom Kippur. This led to the question of whether a Jewish Studies program in a secular university can be a vehicle for Jewish continuity? And what about secular universities that don't have a Jewish Studies program? What can be done on those campuses?

Perhaps because the conference was held at a university, or more likely because most seminar participants had confronted the problem in their own extended families, almost everyone expressed the belief that the real crisis of Jewish continuity was in our universities and colleges. There, they felt, were the greatest wastelands of Judaism and Jewishness. It is there that the community was losing its children. Most participants felt that not enough was being done for Jewish university students at a moment when they needed the broadest community support. As well, there was general agreement that Jewish Studies programs were of utmost importance to the Jewish future. If nothing else, they give academic legitimacy to studying Judaism, which many young Jews might otherwise feel belongs only in synagogues. For many in the seminars, strengthening community ties both to universities and to Jewish students was no less important than increased funding for Jewish education at the primary and secondary level.

Discussions recounted pleasant and rewarding experiences of taking courses in Hebrew, Jewish history, Yiddish, the Bible, and archeology at universities.

Others felt that if possible, entry points to Judaism might be made through programs such as Women's Studies. All believed that Jewish Studies programs must be strengthened. With the cutbacks in funding from federations, Jewish students argued that their organizations were being nickel-and-dimed to death. This, most people in the seminars felt, was a disastrous message to be sending to young people. At precisely the moment these organizations need to be invigorated in order to protect our future, they are being gutted.

And what message are we sending our students who are on front lines of the continuity battle and of the vicious, politically correct, anti-Israel onslaughts in the academic world? Are we telling them that they don't count—that we don't care what happens to them once they leave home for the first time and are susceptible to a whole variety of new and seductive influences? This may not be the message the organized community wishes to send, but, according to the student delegates, it is the message that is being received.

At the same time, it was felt that there was a desperate need for dynamic leadership amongst Jewish students and more coherent programming for their organizations. Some complained that Jewish student organizations had a stigma of beinwg "nerdy," clannish, and parochial, and thus "turning off" Jewish students. Others pointed out that the organizations were now undergoing vast changes and that a more "invigorating" climate for Jewish students was being created.

One of the recurring themes of the workshops was the question of economics. Can we afford the cost of remaining Jewish? Has it become too expensive? How many families can comfortably send their children to day schools, especially if they are too proud to ask for financial assistance? Education, trips to Israel, synagogue dues, donations to U.J.A. and other charities, are becoming too costly to permit full participation in the community. On the other hand, almost all in the seminars were prepared to make significant financial sacrifices to ensure a Jewish future for their families.

Much of the workshop discussion centered on prioritizing the use of resources. Education was a major priority. It was noted that Israel was built by the young, and they will be tomorrow's leaders. At the same time, retired people represent a major communal resource. Many have skills, experience, and money that can be utilized in the community. And they have time to work, in some cases harder than during their years of employment.

THE CENTRALITY OF ISRAEL

Defining the relationship between Israel and the Diaspora was one of the major subjects of discussion in the workshops. While no one denied the importance of the Jewish state to Jewish survival, some echoed Hillel Halkin in arguing that most Israelis do not seem to care whether their country serves as a center for world Jewry. The great majority of participants, however, were seeking ways to strengthen the connection to Israel. All agreed that one of the most practical ways of re-enforcing the mutual bonds of Israeli and Diaspora Jews was to encourage tourism and especially study in Israel. There was overwhelming support for the policy of many community federations of subsidizing summer trips to Israel for teenagers, although most felt that such trips were meaningless if they were not part of an ongoing educational program.

GENDER ISSUES

For those who attended the workshops on gender issues, there was little question that more room would have to be made in community leadership circles for women. It was agreed that there is a need for a pluralistic view, to accept women in traditional and non-traditional social and economic roles, to allow and provide for different models and patterns of relationships in community planning. Entrance into the community, it was felt, should be gender blind and class blind.

It was pointed out that professional women in Jewish communal positions are not adequately supported by the lay leadership, and that federations and Jewish organizations should be female friendly. As well, gender issues should be integrated into the mainstream as part of overall community planning. The community should address the issues of the *agunot* (that is women whose estranged husbands will not consent to divorce) and of violence against women. It was recommended that a conference of lay and professional women should be organized to draft an agenda of issues important to women and to prepare strategies for implementation.

Participants agreed that there was a need to look at trends among feminists with respect to levels of affiliation and to consider the status of women in smaller communities. Finally, the seminars recommended that not only should women come together to study, but that changes be made to the educational curriculum so that the contributions of women would be valued. This might be accomplished through a series of "women sensitive" workshops provided for teachers. Everyone agreed that efforts must be made to enhance the appreciation of women as caregivers and mothers.

CULTURE AND PLURALISM

For the most part, the workshops on culture discussed the problems of transmitting Jewish culture. With the decline of Jewish languages (Yiddish, Ladino, and Judaeo-Arabic), Hebrew and English have become the major vehicles of Jewish culture. Yet participants felt that community federations were miserly in underwriting cultural activity even with those two languages. Suggestions were put forward to create institutions where, unlike synagogues, people can meet on neutral ground, and where lectures and literary events can take place. Above all, it was felt that a sustainable adult education program will be essential for maintaining cultural continuity in the twenty-first century.

There was also concern about the divisiveness in the Jewish community. Pluralism, inclusivity, and tolerance were three important recurring themes. "Outsiders" do not feel comfortable with people perceived as "insiders." It is therefore our responsibility to try to be inclusive, tolerant, and pluralistic so that more people can feel a sense of belonging. Several people noted that initially feminists weren't welcomed as insiders. Now the feminist movement in Judaism is viewed by many as having revitalized Judaism. Here, it was suggested, is a good model for how to identify and view those struggling with feelings of being "outsiders." For such groups, the goal is to make sure that their needs for being affiliated are accommodated, that they can become "insiders."

The tensions specifically mentioned were those between the observant and the non-observant, between Israelis and the rest of the community, between the Sephardim and Ashkenazim, and between generations within the family unit. It was noted that many Israelis feel alienated because of the cultural difference in the ways of being Jewish in North America and in Israel. One Israeli stated that he found it difficult to understand or accept the need for affiliation with a synagogue in order to educate his children and feel a part of the community. The Sephardim, it was noted, are trying to make their way within a strong Ashkenazi establishment. Perceiving themselves to be late arrivals, the Sephardim fear their identity may be at risk as they attempt to take root and thrive economically and socially in their new home. Intermarriage, not only between Jew and gentile, but between Sephardim and Ashkenazim, was seen as another aspect of the identity crisis our community faces. Community leaders, it was stressed, must strive to offer more choices for cultural and educational experiences that will facilitate the reintegration and acculturation of those who currently view themselves or are seen by others as marginalized. Those experiences will serve to bridge the implied divide between culture and faith.

It was agreed that community and federation leaders must be directed toward strengthening social institutions in order to effect changes necessary to address the issues of pluralism, education, and acculturation. It was suggested that these leaders actively support the offering of courses that enable dialogue among the diverse groups, promote greater efforts aimed at the acculturation of Israelis and Sephardim, encourage synagogues to provide alternative prayer services, and ensure the accessibility of Jewish education.

Some urged the notion of a soft entry—using recreational and social functions as means for people to meet Jews. Often, it was felt, such a connection propels people to learn more about their Judaism or to be more involved in Jewish activities. We need to appeal to "the heart and not just the head." This raised again the affective component of identification that often seems to be overlooked in our efforts.

CREATING THE JEWISH FUTURE

There was clearly an unstated assumption among all the delegates at the conference that in North America living as a Jew is only one option of many. No external force imposes it upon us; no one forces us to live in ghettos, to wear badges, or to carry identifying labels in our passports. And, when living as a Jew is a choice, we must be able to offer our children more than simply an invitation to survive. We must provide something better and more saleable than the other options. When the brightest of our young ask what it is that out survival will make possible, we must have ready and convincing answers for them. What are Jews about? What dreams do we fulfill by surviving?

The time has come to dream a new dream, one that focuses on North American Jewish life as we would like it look in the twenty-first century. For me, the dream flows directly from the historic mission of North America's Jewish community: to demonstrate that Judaism and Jewishness can succeed and flourish in a free democratic, pluralistic Diaspora environment. Classical Zionism insisted that emancipation was a failure, that assimilation was inevitable, and that only in Israel could Jewish life thrive. North American Jews responded that America was different. In the United States and Canada, they argued, Jews could achieve what they never did elsewhere in the Diaspora: equal treatment, economic prosperity, and at the same time a distinct spiritual and cultural identity.

And that is the central question facing us today. Can Judaism survive in an atmosphere of unprecedented freedom. If it doesn't, then the old-time assimilationists—and Zionists—will be proved right. In the end, America may not be so different. If that's true, then Jewish life will not succeed anywhere outside of Israel. And that suggests the unthinkable: that Judaism cannot hold its own within a competitive, pluralistic religious environment.

The task facing Diaspora Jewry is formidable. But we are a formidable people. Our future is in our own hands.

Notes

1 Commission Report, Draft 2, pp. 8–9.

2 Ibid., p. 18

INDEX